AFRICAN ECONOMIC DEVELOPMENT

AFRICAN ECONOMIC DEVELOPMENT
Cooperation, Ownership, and Leadership

Omotunde Evan George Johnson

With a Foreword by
Afeikhena Theo Jerome

The Edwin Mellen Press
Lewiston•Queenston•Lampeter

Library of Congress Cataloging-in-Publication Data

Johnson, Omotunde E. G.

African economic development : cooperation, ownership, and leadership / Omotunde Evan George Johnson ; with a foreword by Afeikhena Theo Jerome.

p. cm.

Includes bibliographical references and index.

ISBN-13: 978-0-7734-5409-5
ISBN-10: 0-7734-5409-8
1. Africa--Economic policy. 2. Africa--Economic conditions. I. Title.

HC800.J64 2007

338.96--dc22

2007018213

hors série.

A CIP catalog record for this book is available from the British Library.

The Edwin Mellen Press
Box 450
Lewiston, New York
USA 14092-0450

The Edwin Mellen Press
Box 67
Queenston, Ontario
CANADA L0S 1L0

The Edwin Mellen Press, Ltd.
Lampeter, Ceredigion, Wales
UNITED KINGDOM SA48 8LT

Printed in the United States of America

To the memory of my late father (Rev. Evan George Abogay Johnson)
and to my mother (Elizabeth Olatunde Johnson)

Table of Contents

Foreword by Dr. Afeikhena Theo Jerome		i
Acknowledgments		iii
Chapters		
1	Introduction	1
2	Domestic Demand for Good Economic Policy Environment	15
3	The State, Cooperation, and the Development Process	33
4	Country Ownership, Conditionality, and Economic Policymaking	67
5	Ethnicity	101
6	Government Corruption	127
7	Political Leadership	163
8	Facing the Globalization Challenge	185
9	Regional Economic Integration	209
10	Conclusion	235
References		245
Index - Author		265
Index – Subject		271

Foreword

For too long, Africa has had the bizarre and dubious reputation of being the world's leading theatre of conflict, war, poverty, disease, and instability despite advances on several fronts in recent years. Not surprisingly, the study of African development has evoked a lot of attention around the world and this reached a crescendo at the beginning of the new millennium, with several organized efforts to jump-start development in Africa. Yet, there have been few comprehensive texts that interrogates Africa's development trajectory since many of the countries attained independence in the late 1950s and 1960s. This book is a welcome addition. It does precisely that in a clear, rigorous, and elegant fashion.

Dr. Omotunde Johnson, an accomplished theorists and practitioner in development economics, presents in this book a synthesis of his recent and older published works on Economic Development in Africa and in the process raises important questions that will help to set the agenda for future research. A skillful and comprehensive account of economic development in post-Independence Africa, he weaves his experiences from his vantage point of several assignments in various parts of the continent as an IMF official.

A collection of eight essays in ten chapters, Dr. Johnson sums up the trajectory of economic development in Africa over the last five decades and identifies eight problem areas as basic, namely: mobilizing domestic demand for good economic policy environment; strengthening cooperation, including bringing the state back in, to speed up the development process; ensuring country ownership in policymaking; reducing ethnicity; reducing government corruption, especially at the highest levels; improving political leadership; developing coherent strategies to face the globalization challenge; and accelerating progress toward rational regional economic integration.

Dr. Johnson asks questions rarely asked by economist about Africa's development and many of his diagnosis are "painfully honest". His underlying thesis is that, at the dawn of independence, Africans did not establish their institutions using processes that took proper account of the pluralism of the societies, while civil society failed to press for institutions to control the state. A stable equilibrium determination process that could have been used is described in the book. It involves election, to a convention, of delegates with certain specified qualifications; free and open discussion at the convention; and obtaining via a free and open democratic procedure the general consent of the citizens to the institutions proposed by that convention.

This important new collection tackles the failure of neoliberal reform to generate long-term growth and reduce poverty in many African economies. He decries Western "political correctness" in indulging Africa's dysfunctions and calls for a new tough-love approach to foreign aid. Dr. Johnson supports his arguments throughout with examples from around Africa.

Brimming with insights, this comprehensive and timely collection constitutes a critical staging-post in the future of Africa's development. The value of Dr. Johnson's towering work rests not so much in its incisive analysis, or its original insights; it is the sheer readability of the book, combined with a notable lack of sophistry that makes it one of the recent most important works on Africa. There is no doubt that this will be the definitive textbook on Economic Development in Africa for years to come. By demonstrating intriguing connections among a wide variety of issues that are rarely discussed together in the same book, it will prove useful to researchers. And it will be an important resource for policy-makers, who increasingly find themselves dealing with complex issues of globalization, institutions and domestic demand for good policies amongst others.

Dr. Afeikhena Theo Jerome
African Peer Review Mechanism Secretariat
Midrand, South Africa
January 2007

Acknowledgments

This book is the product of more than three decades of close observation of African policymakers, politicians and civil societies; participation in policymaking; and much reflection on the issues involved. Most of the ideas in the book have been explored in papers I previously published in refereed journals, a situation unavoidable since the ideas have been developed over a rather long period of time. Together here, I hope they will be seen more clearly as part of a coherent program.

My intellectual debt, in thinking about the subject matter of the book over the years, has been substantial, as apparent from the references. In the context of the earlier versions in academic journals, the comments of referees and others have also been most helpful. In addition, the issues raised in the chapters have been matters of intense discussion with Africans from many countries and works of life, since the early 1960s. One carries away quite a bit of stimulation from those discussions—with taxi drivers, farmers, tailors, barbers, laborers, market traders, religious groups, journalists, academic colleagues, and ordinary friends—because of their thought-provoking nature.

My interest in the economics of institutions was first aroused when I was a student at the University of California, Los Angeles in the 1960s, particularly by Professor Armen Alchian but also by Professors Jack Hirshleifer and Axel Leijonhufvud. Clearly, in the analysis of governance issues the tools of the economics of institutions (especially the focus on incentives and transaction costs) are invaluable. More recently, I spent the 1996/97 academic year at Oxford University, UK, as a Visiting Research Fellow at the Centre for the Study of African Economies and a Senior Associate Member, St. Antony's College. During that year, I was able especially to catch up on the economics and other literature on cooperation and have maintained my interest since. Over a longer period, namely, 1974-2000, as a staff member of the International Monetary Fund

(IMF), I worked on a wide range of institutional and financial sector issues in many countries. That experience helped me further my understanding of the forces at play for many of the governance issues discussed in this book.

I have dedicated this book to my parents. But I owe a great debt to my wife, Octavia Leonora Olayemi Johnson, for her love and support over more than four decades of marriage. My daughter Olatunde, and sons Omoyemi and Olubayo have also shown the kind of love and understanding that have enabled me to devote adequate time researching and thinking about the kinds of issues discussed in this book, particularly since much of that time was spent outside of my routine work day at the IMF.

I thank the staff at The Edwin Mellen Press, particularly John Rupnow and Patricia Schultz for their patience and diligence. Last, but not least, I thank Ms. Helen Thorington for her assistance in preparing the document for publication.

Still, I am solely responsible for the contents of the book and hence for any errors and omissions.

1

Introduction

African leaders, at the dawn of independence of their countries, in the late 1950s and 1960s, hoped for rapid growth and economic development, diversification of the economies, and a few of the leaders also for economic integration, regionally or even continentally. By 1980 all the independent African countries officially subscribed to these objectives. But a combination of domestic and external factors resulted in African countries being in serious financial crises by the late 1970s and desperate for help. So they turned to the international donor community. Since the early 1980s, the World Bank and the International Monetary Fund, supported by the African Development Bank, the United Nations Development Program, the European Union, and other major bilateral donors, have been orchestrating the economic development strategy in the bulk of the African continent.

Under the so-called structural adjustment programs (SAPs), of the last two decades of the twentieth century, the African state and country lost ownership over economic policymaking, industrialization of the countries was put on hold, and Africa was told to focus on agriculture for the foreseeable future. Of course, where there were minerals like gold, copper or diamonds, or petroleum resources, or widely acknowledged natural tourist attractions like wildlife, their raw exploitation was encouraged as well. Overall, the strategy did not lead to rapid growth in per capita incomes in Africa relative to other continents; in fact, the reverse was the case. There also ensued a general lack of enthusiasm of African states and populations for many of the policies they were asked to implement by their aid donors, which meant that the policies were simply not resolutely implemented.

Under the SAPs, even agriculture did not make much progress in the continent. This was partly due to poor macroeconomic environment. But it was due mainly to structural problems that were not adequately addressed: inadequate property rights; frequent droughts and floods; continued dependence on rain-fed agriculture; declining fertility of land; pests and diseases; very limited access of farmers to credit; ineffective extension services; inadequate market infrastructure; poor physical infrastructure (especially rural access roads); and lack of storage and processing facilities. These macroeconomic and structural problems were compounded in many countries by security problems and by high incidence of HIV/AIDS.

These outcomes led to a loss of confidence by both Africans and foreigners in the capability of African countries for rapid development. At the turn of the century, expectations and aspirations were officially lowered. The aid community and the majority of the African leaders started talking about 'poverty reduction.' Officially, the facility of the IMF is entitled 'Poverty Reduction and Growth Facility,' and the countries are supposed to have greater country ownership in the drawing up of the programs. In practice, the growth objectives are modest and 'country ownership' is greater only as compared with the zero country ownership which existed before. Rapid growth and development, structural diversification and industrialization all continue to be effectively put on the back burner.

I believe that there are two broad fundamental reasons for the failure of the SAPs to move Africa rapidly along the road to sustained development. First, there was inadequate appreciation of the underlying factors accounting for

Africa's slow development, as opposed to mere proximate factors, or even institutional factors, which are somewhat more intermediate causes. The proximate factors include, most notably, the quantity and quality of investment in human and physical capital and policy variables such as currency exchange rates and interest rates. The institutional factors are, essentially, property rights, freedom and enforcement of contracts, and the quality of markets for land, labor, capital and credit. Neglected were underlying factors responsible for all these proximate and institutional factors showing up as they have in the African environment.

The second broad fundamental reason for the failure of the structural adjustment programs is that, at the time of the consensus on the SAP's methodology, there was inadequate understanding, although many would rather say deliberate neglect, of key factors at play in the East Asian Miracle—in particular, the role of the state and the nature of cooperation between the state and business. Thus, the possible implications of those ignored factors for development strategies in the African countries could not be fathomed.

African countries need to create the conditions for rapid economic transformation, growth, and development. For that, they need to make *systemic* changes to address certain problems in their socio-political and economic environment—problems considered basic because of their wide-ranging impact on economic performance, directly and indirectly via their effects on saving, investment, efficiency, and productivity. In this book, I have identified eight problem areas as basic, namely: mobilizing domestic demand for good economic policy environment; strengthening cooperation, including bringing the state back in, to speed up the development process; ensuring country ownership in policymaking; reducing ethnicity; reducing government corruption, especially at the highest levels; improving political leadership; developing coherent strategies to face the globalization challenge; and accelerating progress toward rational regional economic integration. Below is highlighted some of the themes elaborated in these contexts.

The underlying thesis is that, at the dawn of independence, Africans did not establish their institutions using processes that took proper account of the pluralism of the societies, while civil society failed to press for institutions to control the state. A stable equilibrium determination process that could have been used is described in the book. It involves election, to a convention, of delegates with certain specified qualifications; free and open discussion at the convention; and obtaining via a free and open democratic procedure the general consent of the citizens to the institutions proposed by that convention. As regards the delegates to the convention, given the reality of ethnic diversity, it would have been rational to have representation by geographic area at that convention. The populace could have voted for individuals rather than for political parties, and it could have been agreed that the individuals who stood for election as delegates to the convention would become ineligible to run for public office at least for some reasonable period of time (at least for one parliamentary term). The last two requirements for choosing delegates would have been to ensure that individuals with encompassing interests in all future citizens draft the constitution.

The powerful political factions were reluctant to utilize any such process for a number of reasons of which the most important was fear of disintegration of the country at worst or a serious weakening of the state at best. Civil society also failed to organize and insist on an appropriate institutional framework for consultation, transparency, and accountability of the state. The abuse of power and the path to military coups, government corruption, and ethnic conflicts could not be foreseen at the dawn of independence. The benefit of resisting the demise of the autonomy of voluntary associations was also not seen by the civil societies as significant. The concept of social capital had not fully emerged and the line of causation from autonomous voluntary associations to social capital to economic development was not understood. Easily the most important thing that has *not* happened, therefore, in the typical African country is the evolution of substantive parliamentary power vis-à-vis the executive. Over time, the substantial degree of revenue autonomy of the state (due mainly to revenue from minerals, foreign aid, import duties, and state marketing boards) only aggravated the weak bargaining power of civil society vis-à-vis the state and of the typical African parliament vis-à-vis the executive.

Political leaders in the meanwhile have had little self-interest in pursuing good economic policies. With no strong exogenous pressure on them to effect rapid economic growth and transformation of their economies and with weak societal demand for such policies, political leaders have on the whole been able to maximize their utility, without instituting good economic policy environments. The book argues that ways must be found to build agency, on the demand side, for good economic policies, as spontaneous order is likely to be slow in doing so. Such agency would have as its immediate objectives engendering a vibrant *civil society*; a *public* that is literate and well-informed; and a national *Parliament* that is strong and independent of the executive.

Cooperation is important as a factor in the development process and the state can play a critical role in determining the nature and effectiveness of cooperation. The book discusses two forms of order that emerge from cooperation, namely, spontaneous order and authoritarian order. Spontaneous order emerges without central direction by the state. Generalized trust and self-interest facilitate the cooperation, while corruption, free riding, and ethnicity hinder it. Civil society leadership can accelerate cooperation by promoting mutual respect among groups, generalized trust, and self-help organizations, and helping to motivate the state to provide an enabling environment. Authoritarian order occurs when individuals and groups in the society agree to grant authority to a central body or individual to coordinate institutional and organizational activities and to enforce the rules and oversee the organizational structures that flow from such coordination. Under authoritarian order, the emergence of institutions is no longer spontaneous and rules are not necessarily self-enforcing. Instead, the process of change is coercive—rules, regulations, and orders are prescribed and enforced by the state. The book argues that just as Africans can learn from the history of Europe and North America about the importance of an autonomous and vibrant civil society and a strong parliament vis-à-vis the executive for the emergence of cooperation and certain forms of institutional development, so Africans can learn from the recent history of East Asia about forms of cooperation that can speed up the development process. The book discusses the example of the high-performing countries of East Asia as illuminating how cooperation via authoritarian order works and can prove highly efficacious in accelerating economic development. It argues that authoritarian order in successful development efforts is typically founded on collective self-interest and facilitated by focal points, appropriate legitimation processes, and transforming political leadership.

Country ownership of programs will contribute to improving the policy environment in the African countries. The essence of ownership is the acceptance of full responsibility for the consequences of a program. The international community can supplement this with resoluteness in giving non-humanitarian aid only to countries that demonstrate a commitment to good policies. Such selectivity should be forward-looking. For financial support a recipient country must satisfy the donor country or organization as to the reality of ownership, soundness of the program, and adequate implementation capacity. Supporting ownership will help increase demand for good policies within countries, while selectivity will tighten the exogenous constraints on African political leaders and help make them see the pursuance of good policies as being in their self-interest. In such a context, traditional policy-based conditionality is neither necessary nor helpful. That program success is correlated with degree of ownership and that ownership is correlated with implementation, which in turn is correlated with program legitimation, is supported by available evidence.

African leaders have not used processes in constitutional reforms that would help reduce ethnicity (ethnic consciousness and mobilization for effective ethnic group demands on the state). Popular methods used to manage ethnicity have serious costs and weaknesses: central government cabinets get bloated and their bureaucracies politicized; local governments proliferate; power sharing norms are highly unstable, in general; and a culture can develop in the economy with an overwhelming emphasis, in economic relations, on distribution to the detriment of production. Moreover, the current strategies to manage ethnicity do not promote trust across ethnic groups and are likely to cause ethnicity to increase over time, when the objective should be to reduce ethnicity. It is easier to define and maintain standards for good economic governance in a country that seeks to reduce ethnicity than in one satisfied with managing ethnicity at its current level. To achieve this objective, proposed are constitutional reforms via stable equilibrium determination processes. Focal points embedded in the cultures of the groups, relating to political institutions, distributive justice, and societal civility and multiculturalism should facilitate the tasks. Important as enabling factors are leadership activities within civil society to promote mutual respect, generalized trust, and pluralistic solidarity.

Empirical evidence leads us to the conclusion that corruption declines as income per capita increases over time. But the theory is unclear. It is possible that rising income per capita tends to be accompanied by a number of developments—both as cause and effect—that would, on balance, tend to reduce corruption. As income increases, the opportunities for economic agents to accumulate wealth and raise capital for investments tend to multiply, reducing the need to use theft from government as a means to raise capital; democracy increases, and hence eviction from office as a disciplining device becomes more effective; the legal system becomes more efficient in punishing corruption; inter-ethnic cooperation improves, muting the adverse effect of ethnolinguistic diversity on development of institutions that control government behavior; and, after controlling for ethnolinguistic diversity, the quality of government and government efficiency improve, with positive effect on reducing corruption.

There are strong reasons to believe that, in African countries, lack of feeling of ownership of (and hence loyalty to) the state, ethnicity, an absence of generally agreed anti-corruption norms, and low incomes combine to explain the difficulty in controlling government corruption via spontaneous order agency or government self-policing. Africans need education about the economic growth effects of corruption, especially at the highest levels, to induce them to shift their focus beyond the distributional impact which is their current preoccupation. The book elaborates on this theme. As regards, high-level corruption, stressed is that, other things being equal, weak institutions following the failures at the dawn of independence have made available for extraction what can be termed “corruption revenue,” the magnitude over which the political leadership has some control. The attempts of the governing team to capture corruption revenue magnify distortions and misallocation of resources in the economy, with adverse effects on economic efficiency and investment and hence on economic growth. In addition, in Africa, much of the stolen money gets siphoned to foreign countries, with added costs to domestic growth.

Reducing corruption at the highest levels is difficult because the politically powerful thwart attempts to establish and enforce appropriate rules. An indirect approach to reducing such corruption, in the short run to medium run, may be inevitable. Agency that engenders increased societal demand for good policies and makes the government in power accountable for the performance of the economy, should help motivate governments to introduce economic policies of the form that reduce corruption throughout government, even at the highest levels. Such an indirect approach can succeed, as it is far less confrontational vis-à-vis the government than a direct attack on corruption, and popular mobilization for its support is expected to be relatively less difficult. As incomes increase, other channels to reduce high level corruption will begin to emerge. A political leadership which has the incentive to reduce its own corrupt practices to promote economic growth will also have the incentive to introduce and enforce reform measures to reduce corruption throughout the government bureaucracy. As regards control of corruption at the middle and lower levels of government, credibility and legitimacy are the two most important criteria for guiding any program. Such a campaign would be most successful if embedded in a comprehensive economic program stressing economic growth and government efficiency. African countries that succeed in addressing the problem of government corruption, especially at its highest levels, would be ones where the citizens cooperate to (i) bring about a state towards which citizens have a sense of ownership and hence loyalty; (ii) agree on anti-corruption norms; and (iii) to give autonomy (from society) to the state and demand state accountability in return. This may require constitutional reforms utilizing stable equilibrium determination processes.

Following independence, in building political institutions, African societies have focused more on political power sharing than on economic governance. In the absence of broad consultation rights agreed at independence, or obtained since, there has been little cooperation among citizens either to ensure the efficient and effective management of the state or to decide the rules and norms governing the distribution of benefits flowing from the state. The consequence has been free-riding in monitoring the efficiency of the state and an instance of tragedy of the commons ('free pasture for all') in exploiting state benefits. In the latter case, access to political power is important, which is why groups (especially ethnic groups) find it far more rewarding to fight for political power within the state than to struggle for the establishment of institutions and organizational arrangements to control the actions of the government. The book also argues, more generally, that a political leader (or the political leadership in power) must have certain qualities to be able to make a positive contribution to the economic development process. Political leadership can be judged in terms of moral character, societal understanding, persuasive and communicative skills, and innovative ability. Transforming political leadership helps create the conditions or the environment for the efficient organization of society's resources, for investment, and for sustained economic growth. Good (transforming) political leadership (a) reduces the risk of entrepreneurship and (b) erects appropriate signals for efficient allocation of resources, thereby increasing the marginal productivity of all resources available to the economy. Citizens, to be effective in their demand for transforming political leadership in economic governance, would benefit from having shared understandings within civil society and the business community in three areas, namely, the role of the state in economic development; the role of the political leader and his or her team in ensuring that the state perform its assigned role well; and third, the institutional arrangements to ensure that the most appropriate persons contend for leadership, get chosen, and then be held accountable for their performance.

It is sometimes felt that good leadership would emerge with democratization, which in turn is good for economic development and growth. The book argues that the relationship between political leadership and economic development is more straightforward than that between democracy and development. In fact, good political leadership does not necessarily emerge with democratization. The line of causation between economic growth and the political regime is also known to be unclear. It appears that it is legitimate and good political leadership that really matters for economic growth in the end. In the democratization process in Africa, there is a convergence towards a temporary equilibrium before the next leap forward. It includes a strong executive relative to parliament, in economic decisionmaking, and term limits for presidents.

To meet the globalization challenge, African countries would benefit from sound macroeconomic and structural economic policies, tackling corruption, reducing ethnicity, improving political leadership, obtaining country ownership in economic policymaking and achieving regional economic integration. Two responses to globalization still have some adherents in the African countries but are downplayed by the political leaders in discussions of globalization, namely, dependency theory and the proposition that countries that mainly export agricultural commodities and raw materials will face adverse long-run trends in their terms of trade. The book briefly elaborates on the nature of these responses. It then argues that, in meeting the globalization challenge for exports, three approaches have been widely discussed in recent years, namely, participating in commodity agreements; pushing for market access, with or without special preferences; and structuring domestic policies to accelerate diversification of exports. African countries have focused on the first two and made little progress with the third, which the book contends is, in the end, really the best approach. Another globalization challenge, namely, attracting private capital, especially foreign direct investment, is one which the countries are struggling with for reasons having to do with poor policies and hostile socio-political environments. Resolute action, along lines just mentioned, can change this situation. In addition, active support of joint ventures could be made an integral part of a coherent development strategy.

African countries want regional economic integration to augment the effective size of their economies, with positive effects on foreign direct investment, technological innovations, industrialization, and total factor productivity. Traditional problems are of four types: (i) loss of national sovereignty over macro-economic policy; (ii) consumption costs from protection; (iii) unequal distribution of gains and losses; and (iv) reluctance to break up other valued economic relationships. Policies exist that can resolve these problems, given political will. African countries are increasingly implementing economic programs that are expected, inter alia, to lower inflation rates, enhance economic efficiency in government operations and decisionmaking, increase the reliance of central banks on market instruments in the conduct of monetary operations, and promote an institutional framework that fosters market mechanisms in the allocation of resources. These programs, if resolutely implemented, will contribute to convergence of national inflation rates, making possible market-determined exchange rates of all currencies of the countries; they will also enable greater harmony in policy approaches to similar economic problems among the different states. These developments will facilitate the economic integration process. Still, countries need to take steps to obtain domestically the legitimate political authority for integration efforts and agree on use of market mechanisms for location of industries among member states. There is also need for rationalization of regional groupings. Moreover, it is a major mistake to have promotion of intraregional trade as the driving force of economic integration in the continent. Because, for many of the countries, intraregional trade is very small in relation to extraregional trade, and because many of the countries in each of the regions tend to produce similar goods, the urgency for a common market is not sometimes felt. In this context, there is a belief by many that integration would be only formal and not yield substantial benefits, at least for a long time. The book argues that the main motivating force should be integration of small African domestic markets into single regional markets, and that it is along these lines that the most ardent integrationists argued their case for years.

In conclusion, the author believes that fundamentally there is substantial *cooperation deficit* among citizens of the typical African country and that the biggest contributing factor to this predicament is the way the states were instituted at the dawn of independence. To solve Africa's economic problems one must remove this cooperation deficit. For it is via cooperation that Africans, with country ownership over policymaking, will create the institutions that will build loyalty to the state, ensure good political leadership, and put in place economic polices to transform their economies for sustained and rapid economic growth and development.

So how will or should the process for the elimination of the cooperation deficit begin? Throughout, the book stresses the role of agency and of constitutional reform via processes that mimic the stable equilibrium determination process. Ultimately, then, African countries must wait for a critical mass of agents with self-interest and/or altruism to begin the process of eliminating the cooperation deficit. That wait does not need to be long. Still, the emergence of the initial agents will typically have to occur spontaneously, motivated by self-interest or altruism. Those initial agents will do well if they then begin the process of eliminating the cooperation deficit by mobilizing support for constitutional reform via stable equilibrium determination processes, promoting generalized trust in the population, and getting Africans to cease blaming external forces and agents for their problems. In some countries it may be possible for outsiders to "plant" the initial agents. Whether the initial agents emerge spontaneously or via plantation, they would then proceed to mobilize additional local support and sensibly order their program of action as discussed above. Where such agents do not emerge, the African countries would have to wait for an evolutionary process that can hardly be predicted in advance.

Major structural aspects of aid—content and donor-recipient relationship—should change, so that aid donors are not directly trying to impose certain policies but rather to remove domestic obstacles to the emergence of good policies, engage in some capacity building to enable good policies to be effective, and support domestic agents working to raise the domestic demand for good policies and create incentives for governments to introduce good policies.

2

Domestic Demand for Good Economic Policy Environment

The absence of sound national economic policies goes a long way to explaining the economic debacle of the African continent (see, e.g., Sachs and Warner, 1997). The thesis I posit in this book is that the underlying reason for the prevalence of poor economic policy environments in the African continent is that there is weak societal demand (demand outside the state) for good economic policies pursued by the state, in the face of political elites with no external constraints on them to make it their own self-interest to pursue good policies without domestic demand pressures (see Johnson, 2004, where this thesis was first advanced). A good policy is one with positive effect on (economic) growth and poverty. Indeed, a good policy environment enables an economy to achieve growth levels close to its potential. The reverse is true for poor policy environments.

In a good policy environment, the institutional and organizational order empowers mainly decision makers (person, bodies, authorities, etc) with incentives to implement sound economic policies, and contains the means to remove decision makers with poor performance. An implication is that, in most of the African countries, such an order is missing at the current time. Hence, there is a need to take positive action to build demand for good policy environments, by changing the institutional and organizational order, unless other ways could be found, within the current order, to create incentives for those in power to pursue good policies. Three important questions will be addressed in this chapter. First, how did African countries get to this point? Second, what are the chances that strong and effective demand for good policies will emerge spontaneously to exert enough pressure on the authorities to pursue good policies? Third, if such demand does not emerge spontaneously, what can inside or outside agency do to engender it?

The Origin of Poor Economic Policy Environments in Post-Colonial Africa

Regarding the origin of the poor policy environments, the basic proposition is the following: At the dawn of independence, citizens of African countries made mistakes, in their first moves exploiting their freedom to choose political and economic institutions and organizational structures, mistakes which sent them off on noncooperation tracks, where ethnicity, poor political leadership, government corruption, and absence of appropriate rights of citizens to consultation on economic matters have become serious obstacles to the emergence of good (state) policy environments in the continent. The countries made their moves, among other reasons, to avoid certain short-run costs; they did not foresee the long-run adverse effects on cooperation to build economic growth-enhancing institutions. Most fundamentally, the mistakes involved omissions in the early post-independence *processes* employed in holding together the national states and in writing constitutions.

At the dawn of independence there were crucial leadership failures. In the typical African country, leaders (of the state and of civil society) failed to take due account of the significance for future cooperation of the fact that their citizens really were members of several societies[1] without a long history of living together as citizens of one country. Even where the transition to independence had not been too disorderly, the agreements reached (basically, the constitutions signed) were typically the outcome of political maneuvering by the powerful, at worst.[2] At best, the agreements represented short-term opportunistic compromises to achieve the goal of independence.[3]

A stable equilibrium determination process

In principle, in the typical country, just prior to or immediately after independence, an election could have been held to choose delegates to a convention to decide, via open debate and discussion without coercion, on the major institutions of the new community—institutions that would have included a political constitution. Given the reality of ethnic diversity, it would have been rational to have representation by geographic area at that convention. The populace could have voted for individuals rather than for political parties, and it

---

[1] In general, a *country* may not be identical to a *society*. We think of a society as a group of individuals that tend to have shared beliefs (especially about human nature, how the world works, and distributive justice); tend to respond to similar incentives; have important common modes of communication (language, signs, symbols), these having similar meanings to the members of the society; and observe some particular set of rituals, even if with varying degrees of devoutness within the population. These characteristics together give the members of the society an identity sufficiently pronounced to set them apart from members of other societies. We accept that there will be, inevitably, some judgment in the demarcation of many societies.

[2] See Awasom (2002) for the interesting case of Cameroon. Ahidjo exploited a state of emergency declared in the south of Francophone Cameroon to suppress active popular opposition in that area to his approach to constitution-making to lead the country to independence. Then he obtained emergency powers from the Legislative Assembly to rule by decree for six months during which time he would oversee the drafting of a constitution. Ahidjo, of course, had "his protectors among the French administrators and military" [Awasom (2002), p. 10]; the country was still under French trusteeship. As Awasom put it [Awasom (2002) p. 14]: "Thus, Ahidjo assumed executive and legislative powers in a state without institutions and freely dictated how the constitution had to be designed." French technical experts drafted the constitution and, after review by Ahidjo, a Constitutional Consultative Committee dominated by government supporters (reflecting the manner of the selection of its members), also reviewed it and made essentially editorial suggestions. The referendum on the constitution was rigged in favor of the yes vote.

[3] Unfortunately, Liberia and Ethiopia, which never had the colonial experience of the rest of the continent, could not serve as positive examples.

could have been agreed that the individuals who stood for election as delegates to the convention would become ineligible to run for public office at least for some reasonable period of time (at least for one parliamentary term). The last two requirements for choosing delegates would have been to ensure that individuals with encompassing interests in all future citizens draft the constitution [see Mueller (1996, pp. 314-338), and Mueller (2001)].

I designate as a *stable equilibrium determination process* for deriving the major political institutions of the community a process involving election, to a convention, of delegates with qualifications as specified above; free and open discussion at the convention; and obtaining via a free and open democratic procedure the general consent of the citizens to the institutions proposed by that convention. The spirit of a stable equilibrium determination process is in tune with what some have called "polycentric governance" in constitutional design [see, e.g. McGinnis (1999) and Shivakumar (2003)], in the sense that it permits the rules of the various societies to influence the rules of the new collectivity, without weighting these rules in advance or permitting some ideal or abstract model to determine the boundaries of the discussion.

Such a process, I believe, would have conferred upon the new political constitution a legitimacy that would have contributed enormously to the building of a politically stable society. One proof of the suboptimality of the processes of emergence of the new states, as they in fact unfolded, is how quickly the states that emerged effectively collapsed or had to be rescued by coercive methods, and the frequency with which constitutions have been suspended and continue to be drastically rewritten rather frequently since independence.

Leadership failures

Either in deciding the constitutions that would take them to independence or in changing constitutions since independence, it is hard to find an African country that employed a process mimicking the stable equilibrium determination process. The powerful political factions were reluctant to utilize any such process for a number of reasons of which the most important was fear of disintegration of the country at worst or a serious weakening of the state at best. For instance, in Ghana several opposition parties argued for greater autonomy of regions. Nkrumah was opposed. As he put it in his book, *Africa Must Unite*, "the core of dissention between the Government and the opposition" was "the relative power of the centre and the regions." For him, that "involved the whole question of our continuance as a unitary state exercising the democratic principle of majority rule" (Nkrumah, 1970, p. 75)

Apart from trying to prevent disintegration and weakening of the center, a second issue was the legitimacy of the state itself—not simply of the government in power—and the associated problem of ensuring loyalty of citizens to the new state. The social scientist, Immanuel Wallerstein, put the matter aptly, in 1961. "One problem of new African nations is that they are new. People are not used to them. People cannot tell themselves that the ways of the state are hallowed by tradition, justified by experience" (Wallerstein, 1961, p. 89). In relating legitimacy to loyalty, Wallerstein stated: "[t]he legitimation of which we speak, the citizens' sense of loyalty to the nation, is best tested by the willingness of the average person, in the daily events of life, to promote the enforcement of the laws, customs and mores of the state. To some extent it is a question of their thinking of the state as 'we' and not as 'they'"(Wallerstein, 1961, p. 91).

A third reason for the independent leaders' reluctance to use a stable equilibrium determination process was the political reality that the independent leaders might have feared for their own claim to political leadership once the independence struggle was over. After all, in the majority of African pre-colonial societies, political leadership was not open to all. If the constitution of the countries became wide open for fair negotiation, the question of qualification for leadership would have been open as well. In some countries, the democratic choice of national political leaders might have been restricted to only a select group of candidates with "rights" to leadership in pre-colonial societies, plus perhaps some additional educational requirements in light of the realities of the modern state. The fully 'detribalized' and highly Westernized Africans were in a minority—often hopelessly so—in all the African countries.

Civil society and institutions controlling the modern state

Civil society also failed to organize and insist on an appropriate institutional environment for consultation, transparency, and accountability of the state. At the time of independence, many among the African urban elite, who were the leaders of civil society of the modern national state, clearly leaned towards a developmental state,[4] that is, one that takes the leadership in the development process, coordinating, and cooperating with, private entrepreneurs in pursuit of objectives collectively determined by various interest groups in the society. But there was no socially legitimated coherent development strategy in any African country, even though some of the leaders, like Kwame Nkrumah, Sekou Touré, Houphouët-Boigny and Julius Nyerere had worked out their own particular strategies, which they strongly believed would be successful as development strategies. On economic matters, society failed to insist on consultation rights; and the political leadership failed in not voluntarily deciding to consult broadly on the details of their agendas. African urban elites did, of course, clearly insist on certain civil liberties.

An important question becomes why society did not organize and insist on an autonomous role, in setting the economic agenda and in creating an institutional environment that would compel the government to full consultation, transparency, and accountability in its policymaking. I believe that essentially the

---

[4] The kind of sentiment expressed by Mkandawire and Soludo (1999) would have struck a harmonious chord in early independence civil societies where African socialism with its varied meanings was fashionable. They write (p. xiii) in their report on African perspectives: "We stress the role of the state in the development process, which has unfortunately been denigrated by a jaundiced view of the African state, with the result that African states are counseled to be least useful at precisely the moment when their societies need them most."

citizens did not fully appreciate the long-term consequences for economic development of the political leaders' co-optation strategies. There were a number of basic factors at work. One of these was a huge difficulty for ordinary citizens to organize, in the absence of financial incentives or strong ideological motive. Another factor at play was that for those citizens committed to modernization (basically the urban elite) the benefit of the developmental state seemed obvious. In their economic self-interest, they depended heavily on the state, but the cost of not having a clear governance framework was not obvious. The abuse of power and the path to military coups, government corruption, and ethnic conflicts could not be foreseen at the dawn of independence. These disasters were certainly not foreseen by leaders such as Abubakar Tafewa Balewa (Nigeria), Felix Houphouët-Boigny (Côte d'Ivoire), Kenneth Kaunda (Zambia), Modibo Keita (Mali), Jomo Kenyatta (Kenya), Kwame Nkrumah (Ghana), Julius Nyerere (Tanzania), Milton Obote (Uganda), Léopold Senghor (Senegal), and Ahmed Sekou Touré (Guinea).

There were two additional interrelated reasons, I believe, for the behavior of civil society. First, many Africans were concerned mainly with the preservation of their local political and social systems, where these had survived the colonization onslaught; restoring lost land rights under colonialism; or pushing for a return to lost "traditional" ways, if remembered, where these had not survived colonization. Second, among the educated elites, an important attraction of the modern state was connected to its role in distribution. Hence, organizing for political control of that state was more important than organizing to ensure that the state used its resources to improve production and collective welfare. They did not foresee the adverse economic consequences, for all, of the weak institutions governing the state.

The political leaders, in the meanwhile, wherever they could, took resolute steps to consolidate their political power, inherited from the colonial masters, and complete their control over the economic governance agenda. An important step, in that regard, was co-opting voluntary associations into the dominant political parties, which reduced the autonomy of the associations. The benefit of resisting the demise of the autonomy of voluntary associations was not seen by the civil societies as significant. This makes all the more interesting the astute observation of Wallerstein (1964 p. 339): "With, however, the increased social differentiation that accompanies economic development, it is likely that voluntary associations will again turn in the direction of multiplicity, specificity, and autonomy." Even here, the line of causation ran only from economic development to demand for autonomous voluntary associations. The concept of social capital had not fully emerged and the line of causation from voluntary associations to social capital to economic development was not foreseen.

Political leaders and self-interest in good state policies

On the supply side of good state policies, African national (political) leaders did not have at the time of independence a strong exogenous pressure on them to effect rapid economic growth and transformation of their economies. First, with independence, and in the circumstances of the times, Africans had no reason to build a military and industrial capacity to prevent take-over of their states, and they had no particular interest in territorial expansion. The outside world respected their sovereignty, and African states from the early 1960s, in the context of the Charter of the Organization of African Unity (OAU) and OAU resolutions, declared borders at independence sacrosanct. Second, given the natural resources of the African countries, and the normal demands of their populations, the economic survival of the countries was not really threatened. Third, there was no strong fiscal revenue rationale for the government to want stronger economic growth. As sources of tax revenue, the modern state had, among other things, agricultural exports (taxed very effectively via state marketing board pricing policies) and minerals (contributing income taxation, royalties and leases paid by the companies that for a long time were wholly or substantially foreign owned). In brief, political leaders have on the whole been able to maximize their utility, without instituting good economic policy environments.

The African experience vis-à-vis some lessons of history

The earliest of the modern states in Europe evolved via a process that involved much (class) struggle. According to Tilly (1985), power holders' pursuit of war involved them in the extraction of resources for war from the populations they governed and in the promotion of capital accumulation by those who could help them borrow and buy. War making, extraction and capital accumulation interacted to shape European state making. "Power holders did not undertake those three...activities with the intention of creating national states" or foresaw "that national states would emerge from" those three activities [Tilly (1985)]. As national states emerged in Europe so did the rights of the persons who inhabited those states. Tilly (1998) has argued the following: "Citizenship rights came into being because relatively organized members of the general population bargained with state authorities for several centuries, bargained first over the means of war, then over enforceable claims that would serve their interests beyond war. This bargaining enlarged the obligations of states to their citizens, broadening the range of enforceable claims citizens could make on states even more than it expanded the population who held rights of citizenship." Tilly argued that the attempts of states to establish mass standing armies led to direct rule, as opposed to indirect rule; but it raised serious "problems of consent" leading to hot bargaining, "which forged rights and obligations of citizenship." The disputation all came down to finance (taxation), to the opportunity cost of releasing able-bodied workers from households, and to help in recruitment. Tilly (1998) notes the conditions under which the model works, namely: "(1) the claimant and the object of claims each can reward or punish the other in some significant way; (2) the two are in fact bargaining over those rewards and punishments; (3) one or both also bargain(s) with third parties"—for example the rulers of other states—"who have an interest in the claims being made, and will act to enforce future granting of the claims in question; and (4) the three or more parties to the claims thus constituted have durable identities and relations with each other."

Compared with this European history, easily the most important thing that has *not* happened in the typical African country (until recently even in the most democratic of the countries) is the evolution of substantive parliamentary power vis-à-vis the executive. Tilly (1997b) has discussed what he termed *parliamentarization.* He argued that between the 1750s and the 1830s in Great Britain: (1) "Parliament became the object of ordinary people's contention;" (2) "parliamentary action incited ordinary people's claim making, whether directed to Parliament or elsewhere;" (3) "issues currently being considered by Parliament became more central to popular contention;" and (4) "connections with Parliament became more central in a wide range of claim making." He defined claim making, or more precisely collective claim making, as "public joint expression by word and deed of desires that concrete other parties act in certain ways, ways that would affect their interests." One of the most important factors engendering parliamentarization was the role of parliament as a tax authorizer. The rising scale and cost of war increased the political leverage of Parliament as the tax authorizer and enabled Parliament to expand its power over economic and political matters. In the typical African country, one does not observe ordinary persons directing claims against the state to Parliament; they go straight to the President. Parliament's role as a tax authorizer is also either unimportant or simply a rubber stamp. The historical political leverage of Parliament as the tax authorizer to expand its independent power over economic and political matters is still absent in the typical African country.

In Africa, under the stable equilibrium determination process for constituting the state, the power of parliament, as the main body protecting accountability of the state to society, would have been negotiated at the dawn of independence. Adequate safeguards (that is, institutional and organizational arrangements) would have been put in place to ensure that the power of parliament vis-à-vis the executive branch of government would be substantial and sacrosanct. This was almost never effectively done in the continent. Over time, the substantial degree of revenue autonomy of the state (due mainly to revenue from minerals, foreign aid, import duties, and state marketing boards) only aggravated the weak bargaining power of civil society vis-à-vis the state. The revenue factor left the typical African parliament weak vis-à-vis the executive.

Spontaneous Order and the Evolution of Demand for Good Policies

What are the prospects for forces evolving spontaneously in the typical African country to demand and militate for institutionalized power to ensure consistently good economic policy environments? In many of the countries, the prospects do not appear very good. Outside of a few obvious examples (such as South Africa, Botswana, and Mauritius) most of the countries seem stuck in a *poor policy environment equilibrium trap*, to which they tend to return after any temporary deviation in the direction of good policies. One can see only a slow evolutionary process for the typical African country.

The poor and the demand for good policies

The poor in Africa can be divided into two: rural poor and urban poor. Apart from security, the rural poor in most of Africa assess governments mainly using three yardsticks: government response to economic crises (famine, floods, etc,); access to schools; and whether their real incomes are worsening. Otherwise, they are content with spontaneous order and coping behavior[5] and take full responsibility for their own fate. For instance, when Siad Barre's regime fell in Somalia in 1991, and the state finally collapsed in the face of inter-clan fighting,

---

[5] Apart from normal spontaneous order, which is an ongoing process of self-organization among economic agents, African citizens have had to respond spontaneously to crises resulting mainly from poor state economic governance.

spontaneous order had to wrestle not merely with a weak state but effectively with a no-state situation, the duration of which was uncertain but was expected by many to last for several years. Effective spontaneous order took over. Hence, voluntary groups, charities, and self-help organizations that were not there before sprang up and those that existed already were enlivened, to address business security, health, education, provision of electricity and telephone services, and local community law and order. Even formal organizations employed traditional and nonformal devices (use of local chiefs, elders, and religious leaders), for example to collect debts from delinquents. The urban poor are also concerned with the blatancy of corruption; rise in fuel and food prices relative to their incomes; and the rise in transportation costs relative to their incomes. In reality, these are low standards to meet. The only ones that cause headaches for governments are schooling and transportation costs, because of the typically high import content for transportation and the budgetary costs (capital investment and salaries) for education.

The focus of the poor on education should not be surprising. The poor—whether rural or urban—know that education of their children "can take them somewhere." They observe it. Those with education can get good jobs and even survive lack of infrastructure (with generators, four-wheel drives, cell phones, etc.); they can become "big persons" in politics and share in corruption revenue. If they don't like it at home they can go work in foreign countries and help their families back home. Hence, schooling pays and the poor see provision of educational facilities clearly as government's responsibility. When they consider its supply inadequate, the emotional response is much more serious than for health (except for crises situations like the HIV\AIDS epidemic) and sanitation facilities, and certainly than for electricity, running water (except for obviously extreme circumstances), and telecommunications.

The underlying problem for the poor is limited information on what good policies can accomplish. They don't know much about successful governments in far away places and typically none of the neighboring countries are doing much better than their own. Hence, they do not have high standards against which to hold their governments accountable. In addition, the rural poor gets bogged down with local issues—ethnic conflicts, conflicts between farmers and grazers, and local cultural events and activities. They have little time and incentive to investigate government policy potentials and to organize to demand good policies. They only react—rebel—when the failures are gross and clearly hurt them.

The middle class

The middle class has tended to adapt over time. Middle class persons do so partly by exiting the system (including to foreign countries), partly by shielding themselves from the effects of poor policies, and partly by simply exploiting opportunities opened up by the policies. The ability to shield themselves is made easy by a government able to raise revenue from foreign aid, imports, exports, and mineral resources and hence can afford to be lax in taxing middle class citizens (especially the self-employed) who could otherwise be induced to organize and protest. In return, those citizens use the money they earn for self-provision of otherwise publicly provided services, such as electricity, road repairs and maintenance, and security.

Those who do not find it profitable to exit often find ways to benefit from government policies. They do so by exploiting ties with the political leadership (family, ethnic), or by participating in a government-civil service-business coalition that imposes corruption tax on the rest of the citizens of the country (see Johnson, 1975a, and chapter 6 below).

African civil societies have not been strong and autonomous from the state. The typical African civil society has found it difficult to organize and mobilize for direct monitoring of the government. Not surprisingly, "high" organizational costs have played a part, due to ethnicity and the low level of generalized trust among individuals and groups within the countries. Only when the executive branch and its bureaucracy push society to the point of widespread desperation and anger has civil society leadership been willing and able to get African populations vigorously to demand accountability of their governments. This usually means a demand of the population for specific political and economic reforms, as in relations with chiefs in traditional society. This often includes a demand for a change of the political leadership beginning with the president or head of government, but not so much for fundamental institutional reforms.

Strengthening Demand for Good Policies

Ways must be found to build autonomous agency, on the demand side, for good economic policies. This is imperative, given that spontaneous order is likely to be slow in engendering such a demand, and exogenous forces are also unlikely to emerge, in the foreseeable future, to provide the appropriate incentives for the authorities themselves to create such a good policy environment without domestic demand pressure. Such agency would have as its immediate objectives engendering a vibrant *civil society*; a *public* that is literate and well-informed; and a national *Parliament* that is strong and independent of the executive. When the final objective of having an environment with a strong demand for good economic policies is achieved, there will be autonomous and assertive agents for good policies with legitimacy such that the political leadership finds it unavoidable to seek the public's stamp of approval before attempting to implement any major economic program (see, in this regard, Melton, 2001, on the rise of the public in Enlightenment Europe).

Of major importance is the rewriting of the constitutions of many of the African states, utilizing stable equilibrium determination processes. This will provide an opportunity to strengthen parliaments and make them autonomous from the executive branch of government. In doing so, the constitutions must reinforce the role of parliament in economic decisionmaking, including as the tax authorizer. The new constitutions should also widen the public space and give it adequate autonomy to guarantee 'public opinion' a legitimate and powerful weight in influencing government decisions. Moreover, the constitutions should secure for voluntary associations rights recognized in modern democratic societies so that civil society can function with freedom and autonomy from the state.

Several types of mobilization activities will be important as means to build agency on the demand side for good policies. These activities would include: (1) education of other citizens about the nature of good policies and the value of country ownership and appropriate legitimation of economic polices (see chapter 4); (2) promoting voluntary associations as a way to enlarge social capital; and (3) supporting agents focusing on addressing directly the different socio-political obstacles (corruption, ethnicity, poor political leadership) to good economic policies (see chapters 5-7). This means that success in building domestic agency will depend critically on the existence of some initial leadership that emerges spontaneously. If there are stifling domestic political obstacles preventing potential leaders from revealing themselves, then the mobilization process can only begin with the intervention of external (that is, foreign) agency.

There are a number of actions by foreigners and foreign residents that can be helpful in this regard. For example, numerous research efforts and appraisals by economists have concluded that aid and structural adjustment loans cannot buy good policies and that aid has not produced good policy environments [see, e.g., Alessina and Dollar (2000), Burnside and Dollar (2000), Collier et al (1997), Dollar and Svenson (2000), Easterly (2005), Gunning (2001), Killick *et al* (1998), Lancaster (1999), and World Bank (1998)]. I would conjecture that aid directed at civil society and the public with the clear objective of strengthening demand for good policies is one way to change this gloomy outcome. For example, aid money could expand and deepen the enlightened public in many African countries by its financing of public debates, forums and workshops on various socio-political and economic policy issues. Such enlightenment activities could include public lectures on the history and experiences of successful development cases worldwide, and documentary films showing, for example, the kind of infrastructure that promotes development and the inner workings of institutions and organizations of governance in successful developing countries and other late-comers of the last hundred and fifty years or so. In addition, aid money could be used to set up and support research institutes and think tanks in the African countries, especially to ensure that the organizations have highly qualified staff with libraries and other resources to remain up-to-date in their analytical skills.[6] This support could be supplemented by pressure on African governments by aid donors to ensure enhanced participation of the institutes and think tanks in the design and implementation of reform programs. Aid money could also be directed at the development of public libraries and reading rooms that are well stocked with books, journals and magazines designed to raise public awareness and knowledge of governance and selected policy issues both locally and globally. Moreover, bilateral aid donors and multilateral organizations like the United Nations Development Program can target, for enhanced attention, the authorities of countries that stifle mobilization activities of the form mentioned above by civil society and the business community to persuade the authorities to change their ways.

In these and other ways, there is substantial latent agency talent and vigor within the middle class, in the typical African country, which could be nurtured and encouraged to act. A good fraction of this core group is reasonably aware of progress in successful developing countries outside the continent. Such persons must, in addition, be able to identify each other, survive and grow in numbers. For real action, they must also communicate and organize. In most African countries today, this would require much ingenuity. Given that ethnicity (and sometimes sectarianism) is (are) significant at the present time, in the typical African

---

[6] Ohemeng (2005) describes the way Think Tanks in Ghana, financially supported by major governmental and nongovernmental external donors, are exerting substantial influence on public sector policies and management. The Think Tanks improve state governance directly by their impact on the policymakers and indirectly by their education of the larger society about approaches to various policy issues.

country, the leadership within civil society for agency of the sort required to engender good economic policies must be multi-ethnic (and multi-sectarian, as relevant) to have any chance of success. In many African countries such civil society leadership would also find it a rational strategy, in the current socio-political climate, to engage and work with the political leadership, rather than to confront it with an antagonistic posture.

In general, one can envisage the civil society leadership for the required agency coming from any of three types of groups, associations, or organizations: business groups, policy analysis centers/institutes, and civil society governance groups. The leadership will obviously have to be autonomous of the state, national and independent of foreign agents in its decisionmaking and actions. It should also have a national policy focus; it cannot be in operation only to serve the interest of its membership or to serve the interest of some local community.[7] The agency evolutionary process within the typical African country can begin with a small cluster of domestic civil society and business leaders who have a strong desire, for both self-interest and altruistic reasons, to see good economic policy environments and to ensure that economic policies are legitimated via consent without coercion, and are also willing to bear the organizational and other costs of agency. Such a cluster could organize and then enlist others (potential leaders and followers) to bring about the necessary institutional and organizational changes in the economic policymaking environment.

---

[7] Unfortunately, in a country like Nigeria, many civil society groups are militant and violent, "engage in ethnic and sectional skirmishes, and have agenda that are ethnic and sectional." (Ikelegbe, 2001), p. 22]. See, also, Ake (1993).

3

The State, Cooperation, and the Development Process

In the design and implementation of the structural adjustment programs (SAPs), the African state was greatly emasculated in the arena of economic policymaking. I believe that much would be gained by "bringing the African state back in." There is, effectively, cooperation deficit in the typical African country, one consequence of the mistakes made at independence in the processes employed in holding together the national states and in writing constitutions. The state can be an important player, and indeed the leader, in reducing the cooperation deficit. In this chapter, I elaborate on the theme that cooperation is very important in the development process and that the state can help speed up the development process via its contribution to augmenting cooperation. I differentiate two kinds of order that emerge from cooperation, namely spontaneous order and authoritarian order. Both benefit from or depend on leadership—political, civil society and business. Spontaneous order involves leadership from below (civil society and business), and authoritarian order entails leadership from above (political). In both cases, the leadership is most often (but not always) motivated by self-interest, which provides an incentive to promote the appropriate cooperation. Spontaneous order benefits from an enabling role of the state and authoritarian order benefits from an enabling role of civil society and business leadership. In brief, the study of cooperation in the development process is to a great extent a study of government-business-civil society cooperation that promotes economic development.

Just as Africans can learn from the history of Europe about the importance of an autonomous and vibrant civil society and a strong parliament vis-à-vis the executive for the emergence of cooperation and certain forms of institutional development, so I believe Africans can learn from the recent history of East Asia about the forms of cooperation that can speed up the development process. The chapter contains a brief elaboration on the example of the high-performing countries of East Asia as illuminating how cooperation via authoritarian order works and can prove highly efficacious in accelerating economic development.

The Role of the State

Following Tilly (1985), the modern state as a minimum has historically performed four different activities, namely, war making, state making, protection, and extraction. War making eliminates or neutralizes rivals outside the territory, while state making eliminates or neutralizes rivals inside the territory. Protection eliminates or neutralizes enemies of the state's clients. Extraction (otherwise called taxation) involves acquiring the means to carry out the first three activities. Over time, states have expanded their role, again following Tilly, to adjudication, distribution, and production (see, e.g., Tilly, 1990, pp. 96-126). Adjudication is the "authoritative settlement" of disputes among persons; distribution involves state intervention in allocation of goods among persons, while production involves state-owned enterprises producing goods and services, including those for use by the general population. Sometimes this extension of state activity was to help assure success in pursuing the four historical activities as real world circumstances changed, and was often seen as logical extensions of the four basic activities. At other times, the state's extension into adjudication, distribution and production was in response to citizens' demands.

Economists, depending on the context, view citizens as having several objectives when they take collective action to assign a role to the state. Fairly universal among these objectives are: (1) ensuring socially efficient supplies of public or collective goods; (2) enforcing institutional structures that foster internalization of externalities; (3) ensuring low transaction costs to private agents (market participants) of doing business; and (4) lowering investment risks for private agents. Less universal but quite common objectives include: (5) promoting distributional objectives consistent with the values of the society; (6) maintaining the integrity of market processes; (7) promoting private-sector coordination and market development; and (8) supplementing the entrepreneurship of the private sector, made necessary by structural factors in the economy. These less universal objectives are especially influenced by local history, culture, and political and economic ideology. Many of these objectives are also similar to those of Tilly.

In the context of economic development, some social scientists—economists and non-economists—have discussed the role of the state in the economy somewhat differently. For them, the state can engage in direct intervention in production, investment, and saving mobilization; or it can influence production, investment and saving mobilization indirectly by inducing changes in relative prices and profit opportunities (rents) for market participants. In articles in a book edited by Masahiko Aoki, Hyung-Ki Kim, and Masahiro Okuno-Fujiwara (1997), for example, the authors compare three approaches to government and the market. First is a *market-friendly* view, which restricts the government's role to providing a legal infrastructure for markets to work and supplying goods only when there is extreme market failure, such as when markets do not exist—for example, for clean air. Second, is the *developmental-state* view, which sees it as necessary for the government to be active in many areas of the economy because of pervasive market failures (underdeveloped capital markets, oligopolies in currency exchange markets, etc). Third, is the *market-enhancing* view, in which the government is seen as facilitating or complementing private-sector coordination. Seeing the state as fostering cooperation in the economy allows one to take a pragmatic view of the best approach to state governance. In other words, depending on the circumstance, the state should be willing to play any or all of the above roles—market-friendly, developmental state, or market-enhancing—depending on which approach best achieves the objectives of high growth and rapid poverty reduction.

For the state to be effective in fostering cooperation for development, its behavior and structure must meet certain standards. For instance, a corrupt and dictatorial state is unlikely to be successful in fostering the appropriate cooperation. In this regard, Rueschemeyer and Evans (1985) bring out some other considerations. They see the state as expressing several contradictory tendencies. First, the state cannot escape being an instrument of domination. The character of the overall "pact of domination" will be determined by the interrelations between the various parts of the state apparatus and the most powerful classes. Second, the state's role as an instrument of domination inevitably implies a second role as corporate actor. Third, the state typically becomes an arena of social conflict. Fourth, the state typically presents itself as being the guardian of the universal interests of the society over which it has jurisdiction. The authors are interested in looking at the state as a corporate actor. In this role, for effectiveness the state must have at its disposal a well-developed bureaucratic apparatus and a certain degree of autonomy from the dominant class or classes in order to promote economic transformation.

I would think that the developmental state or market-enhancing state would be a corporate actor, and I support Rueschemeyer and Evans on the bureaucratic and autonomy requirements for the effectiveness of such a state. But there are important issues with respect to domination, intervention, and autonomy of the state. An approach that stresses cooperation will include as essential the condition that the nature and scope of all three be legitimated by the populace at large. In addition, intervention must deal with the problem that the state can become an arena of social conflict and attractive for takeover by groups for their own self-interest with little or no benefit to competing groups. In African countries, this means that the institutions agreed via cooperation must be effective in addressing ethnicity and corruption if intervention of the state is going to be encouraged (see Chapters 5 and 6). With respect to autonomy, the obvious questions are: autonomy from whom and to do what? In Africa, I would stress autonomy from society at large, in particular from leaders of ethnic and religious groups pursuing narrow ethnic and religious group objectives. But an approach that stresses cooperation must bring in interest groups that cut across ethnic and religious groups in pursuit of the public interest, in particular economic growth and poverty reduction. Hence, I would not go as far as Skocpol and insist that autonomy itself can relate to the ability of the government "to formulate and pursue goals that are not simply reflective of the demands or interests of social groups, classes, or society" (Skocpol, 1985). Rather, in the context of cooperation, the goals and the instruments could be determined jointly by representatives of civil society, the business community, and the state, even though the state could play a leadership role. The goals and instruments would also be legitimated by the populace at large (see Chapter 4). But, of course, the state would have autonomy in its organization for implementation of the legitimated policies.

Cooperation

The role of institutions in the development process has come to be greatly appreciated over several decades now. Institutions are *rules* governing behavior in human interaction. Typically they are categorized into economic, educational, religious, political, kinship, and legal. Institutions are also classified in forms such as norms, constitutions, and property rights. Institutions coordinate expectations and constrain behavior in interactions of individuals. They also affect the transaction costs (information, negotiation, policing, and enforcement costs) of such interactions, and determine the distribution of the costs and benefits that ensue from the interactions. Hence institutions are at the core of the incentive structure that motivates behavior of the kind that creates wealth. For the economist, property rights are particularly important among the institutions [see, e.g., Alchian (1977), Johnson (1972), and North (1990)]. But institutions are themselves outcomes of cooperation. In other words, they are elements of the order that cooperation brings about. The view in this book, then, is that countries succeed in the development process especially when they are able to cooperate to bring about appropriate political, legal, and social institutions that are favorable to economic development and growth.

Cooperation, in this context, is the willingness to communicate, negotiate, and reach agreement, on the design and maintenance of institutional and organizational arrangements, procedures, and mechanisms, including how to share the ensuing benefits and costs, without fighting, coercion, or total domination by one party. A body of intellectual work has emerged, which seeks to explain how institutions and modes of economic organization in a country or society can emerge and change over time, via cooperation, without central governmental direction. In this discussion, both trust and self-interest play important roles, as do evolutionary processes.

Cooperation and trust

In many kinds of interpersonal relations there is an immeasurable chance of being duped by free riders and dishonest persons, and this uncertainty affects behavior. Individuals and collectivities have reacted to this uncertainty in various ways involving cooperation. One can distinguish four types of mechanisms or arrangements governing cooperation in which self-interest and trust interact [for a discussion of the notion of trust see, e.g., Misztal (1996) and Yamagashi, Cook, and Watabe (1998)]. First there are societies where cooperative relations are based on *kinship* or *commitment*, with persons limiting their cooperation to kin, to persons with whom they have successfully cooperated in the past, or to persons who have built up a favorable reputation for cooperation. Indeed, cooperators often insist on a *coalition time*, namely a time investment that any individual has to make in a prospective partner before either one will agree to collaborate in any exchange of substantial value (see, e.g., Dunbar, 1999). A second characteristic of cooperative relations in many societies is that they are founded on *collectivist norms and conventions*. These typically involve not only informal rules of behavior but also effective systems for monitoring and sanctioning free riders and dishonest persons. A third type of institutional arrangement—namely, cooperation based on *intermediated trust*—is where A trusts B because A trusts C who vouches that B is trustworthy (see the discussion of Coleman, 1990, pp.180-185, of three kinds of intermediaries in trust, namely, advisors, guarantors, and entrepreneurs).The fourth type of institutional mechanism governing cooperation is *generalized trust*. Societies where cooperative arrangements are dominated by those founded on generalized trust are considered high-trust societies [see, for example, Alesina and Ferrara (2002)].

Trust (and most of all generalized trust) reduces transaction costs in relationships. One way it does so is by speeding up agreement as to what to do; all the details of an agreement, including how to handle contingencies, do not have to be worked out (see Macauley, 1963). Trust also permits effective delegation within organizations; supervisory and management costs are thereby lowered, and from a social point of view resources are freed to produce alternative commodities and services. Furthermore, generalized trust is "emancipating," by freeing persons "from the confines of safe but closed relationships" [Yamagashi, Cook, and Watabe (1998)]. Hence, such trust enables people to exploit opportunities from cooperating with a much wider range of persons—the opportunity set in business relationships is enlarged.[1] Trust facilitates specialization, via such emancipation,

---

[1] As Rosenberg and Birdzell (1986) put it, in discussing the earliest forms of large organizations not based on kinship: "the merchant class evolved a moral system suited to life in highly organized enterprises. In no other way could the enterprises that went beyond family and organized such ventures as colonization, foreign trade, and canal building (and, later, railway building) have found the institutional loyalties essential to carrying out their economic

because one feels confident in using the expertise of others; without trust it is hard to see how there could be authority based on expertise. Also, the granting of autonomy would not be possible without trust.

Generalized trust itself tends to be fostered by *social capital.* According to Lin (2001), and consistent with earlier work, especially that of Pierre Bourdieu (1986), investment in social relations produces social ties or, alternatively, embedded resources in social networks, which constitute social capital. The expected returns from social capital, according to Lin, comprise four elements. First, the capital produces useful *information.* Second, it enables one to have *influence* on others with whom one interacts, in organizations. Third, it certifies an individual's *social credentials.* Finally, social capital is a source of *reinforcement* to the individual of his or her identity and recognition, which "not only provides emotional support but also public acknowledgment of one's claim to certain resources" (Lin p.7).

Social capital, thus, can be treated like human capital—individuals invest in it and reap pecuniary and nonpecuniary returns (see Sobel, 2002, for a useful reflection on social capital from an economist's perspective). Of importance in assessing the stock of social capital of a country are the quantity and quality of *voluntary associational life.*[2] The greater the density of networks of voluntary (as opposed to ascriptive) associations—that is, layers of associations inclusive of persons beyond kin and ethnic group—the greater would tend to be social capital, and hence self-organization founded on generalized trust. As suggested for example by Fukuyama (1995), this could have important implications for industrial structure of countries. In other words, the relative role of family

---

functions..." In other words, a shared sense of business morality, which is favorable to the emergence of mutual trust, was always important for the development of large enterprises not based on family or kinship.

[2] In a voluntary association, membership is not foreordained at birth or automatic (see, e.g., Wallerstein, 1964). The impact of associational membership on generalized trust is not necessarily always strong or positive for economic performance; for an interesting empirical exploration, see Knack (2003).

enterprises, of big businesses run by professional managers, and of the state, in successful industrial development, has probably been affected by the social capital stock of countries as they go through the process of industrialization.[3]

Cooperation and self-interest

Economists tend to see all action as driven primarily by self-interest and persons as rational beings. This rational self-interest assumption created a major problem of rigorously explaining why in major real-life situations defection and free riding are replaced by cooperation, even in the absence of a central authority to compel cooperation.[4] The approach that has proved most appealing is that based on commitment, namely, to view cooperation as resulting from repeated interactions of self-interested individuals who come to see such cooperation as in their joint interest and gradually build up a stable and predictable mode of cooperation with each other. It has been shown in the theory of repeated prisoners' dilemma (PD) games, for example, that cooperation can arise if the game is repeated "infinitely" and if outcomes of all previous stages are observed before the current stage begins.[5]

Despite the above conclusion, it has also been shown that even in finitely repeated PD games cooperation is possible if there is a positive probability (due to reputation) that one of the players could play the cooperative strategy [see Kreps,

---

[3] Combining the notion of social capital and spontaneous order, Fukuyama (1995) speaks of spontaneous *sociability*, which is "the ability to come together and cohere in new groups, and to thrive in innovative organizational settings. Spontaneous sociability is likely to be helpful from an economic standpoint only if it is used to build wealth-creating economic organizations. Traditional sociability, on the other hand, can frequently be an obstacle to growth" (p.159)

[4] The articles collected in Mansbridge (1990) are worthwhile reading in this regard.

[5] A known finite number of interactions, however large, will not do the trick (see the exceptions later). It does not pay to cooperate in the final play, because the game has no future. It does not pay to cooperate in the penultimate play because both players anticipate defection in the final play. By use of backward induction, we are led to the conclusion that when the game will be played in a known finite number of moves defection is the dominant strategy for each player.

Milgrom, Roberts, and Wilson (1982)].[6] From this, an equilibrium reputation hypothesis has emerged, namely, individuals will rationally build reputations in finitely repeated PD games. Evidence of such reputation building has been found; most notably, subjects make significant efforts to build reputations for altruism, which increases cooperation. Such altruistic types, by some accounts, appear to form the basis for reputation building.[7]

Various experiments and observations indicate that even in one-off interacting situations or in situations of anonymity, people routinely behave in a cooperative (including altruistic) way. The major conclusion that seems to have emerged is that normally people have a tendency to cooperate until experience shows that those with whom they interact are taking advantage of them. In other words, people seem to conform to some "norm of cooperation" [see, e.g., Frank (1987), Dawes and Thaler (1988), and Elster (1989)]. This particular line also argues that cooperators tend to seek out other cooperators. Another, perhaps obvious, hypothesis that has found support in experiments is that discussion among potential cooperators fosters the evolution of cooperation. A reason advanced for the value of discussion (including public political debates) is that it triggers ethical concerns that yield a utility for doing the "right" thing (see, e.g., Dawes and Thaler, 1988, and Elster, 1986). In Elster's words, "the conceptual impossibility of expressing selfish arguments in a debate about the public good, and the psychological difficulty of expressing other-regarding preferences without ultimately coming to acquire them, jointly bring it about that public discussion tends to promote the common good" (Elster, *ibid*, p.113). Group identity,[8] not

---

[6] On cooperation, rationality, and repeated games, in general, see also Fudenberg (1992) and Pearce (1992).

[7] Andreoni and Miller (1993) make a useful distinction between: (i) pure altruism, (ii) duty, and (iii) reciprocal altruism. Only in the first case does a player care directly about the payoff of the other player.

[8] On the notion of group identity, see Glazer and Moynihan (1975). See Dawes, Van de Kragt, and Orbell (1990) for discussion of the experiments revealing the importance for cooperation of group identity or solidarity, as indicated by universal promising. They conclude from their experiments

surprisingly, also appears to promote cooperation instead of defection and free riding. Finally, experiments indicate that promise making fosters cooperation only when every member of a group promises to cooperate—that is, when there is "universal promising" (Dawes and Thaler, op. cit.). This finding supports the expectation that group identity matters, since such universal promising is often one reflection of such identity.

Due mainly to Axelrod (1981, 1984), a strategy that has aroused much interest is a tit-for-tat strategy; the player who adopts this strategy cooperates on the first move, and then in subsequent moves does whatever the other player did on the previous move. Axelrod found that a strategy of tit-for-tat was very robust in computer tournaments and simulations of PD game situations—it did better on average than other strategies in a wide range of environments.[9] Axelrod calls the tit-for-tat strategy "nice," in that the player adopting such a strategy was always willing to cooperate and would never be the first to defect; but it also could be provoked into retaliation by a defection of the other player, although forgiving after one round of retaliation, and was a clear (easy-to-understand) strategy. In sum, Axelrod argues that the tit-for-tat strategy is evolutionary stable and robust with initial viability to gain a foothold even in an environment which is predominantly noncooperative. It is obvious that this strategy could have empirical relevance in explaining the emergence of cooperation, especially if indeed there exists a norm of cooperation.

In the formulation of Axelrod and others, then, the foundation of cooperation is the *durability of a relationship* not *trust*.[10] This is, essentially, what was termed earlier commitment (to the relationship) as a mechanism

---

that "group solidarity increases cooperation independently of the side payments—either external or internal—often associated with such identity" (p.99).

[9] It has been noted by others, though, that strategies can be devised which successfully invade a community of tit-for tat players [see, e.g., Vronen (1995, p.183) for references].

[10] As noted earlier, the importance of the expectation of continuing relationship for the foundation of cooperation had been widely recognized for a long time; see, for example, Macaulay (1963) and Geertz (1978).

governing cooperation. Of course, the durability of the relationship results in a state of belief or expectation regarding the behavior of another that someone could justifiably regard as "trust."[11] An important point is that an external authority is not necessary for such cooperation to emerge and be sustained. Nor is it necessary to assume rationality, altruism, friendship, or foresight, although the existence of any of these among agents could help speed up the emergence of cooperation. Rather, necessary for cooperation are that: (i) agents can recognize individuals with whom they have dealt in the past; (ii) agents can recall their experiences (especially recent ones) from such interactions; (iii) there is a high probability that the relationship will continue "far" into the future; and (iv) that successful strategies (in terms of payoffs) in interactions do thrive (evidenced by increasing frequency of occurrence in subsequent play of the game in future generations), via the operation of some effective selection mechanism involving learning and imitation, while unsuccessful strategies (even if gradually) become extinct.[12] As in other evolutionary processes, sources of variation in strategies—for instance, experimentation or mistakes—can be good for the evolution of cooperation [see Alchian (1950), Arthur (1988), the papers in England (1994) especially that of Radzicki and Sterman (1994), Hirshleifer (1977, 1982), Hodgson (1993), Nelson (1995), and Vronen (1995)]. But it is important

[11] See, for example, Miller (1992) who regards trust as present if there is a "belief that other members [of a group] are currently cooperating and will do so as long as it appears that everyone else will" (p. 186). Similarly Seabright (1993), in discussing the importance of trust for cooperation, defines trust as "the expectation by members of a group that other members will cooperate" (p. 122). Seabright goes on to suggest why trust can come to be regarded as a kind of capital good embodied in individuals or organizations, influencing the probability of future cooperation independently of the direct payoffs. Also, he argues that institutions can channel trust in the sense that the presence or absence of trust may depend on past institutions.

[12]Fundamental in the economic evolutionary process is the idea that success breeds success—that is, successful strategies will tend to spread and less successful strategies will decline (in the "population" of strategies). In economic environments, this occurs not only through learning, adaptation, and imitation, but also via market or some other form of social selection. Central in the game dynamics involved is the notion of a *replicator equation*, which makes precise the hypothesis that the rate of increase of a strategy i depends on the difference between the average payoff for strategy i and the average payoff for the whole population of strategies; Taylor and Jonker (1978) and Schuster and Sigmund (1983) are excellent references for following up on this subject.

that the process be able to prevent, in Axelrod's terms, "echo effects," whereby each side always responds to the other's last defection with a new defection of its own, since this can set off a long string of recriminations and counter recriminations with both sides' payoffs suffering [Axelrod (1984, pp. 37-38, 186)].[13] Under these conditions, cooperation of the tit-for-tat type can begin with a small cluster of tit-for-tat players and survive and grow over time, even in a world initially dominated by selfish (pure defecting) players.

Spontaneous Order

Friedrich Hayek (1973, Vol. 1, p. 36, italics omitted) considers *order* as "a state of affairs in which a multiplicity of elements of various kinds are so related to each other that we may learn from our acquaintance with some spatial or temporal part of the whole to form correct expectations concerning the rest, or at least expectations which have a good chance of proving correct."

Spontaneous order occurs when economic institutions and governance and organizational structures emerge, via cooperation, without central direction from the body politic. Typically, the process of change is evolutionary. But it could also involve organized and systematic bargaining and negotiation, as well as significant conflict.

---

[13] The assumption that there be no echo effects means that the strict tit-for-tat strategy is most applicable in a world where players do not make mistakes—that is, their hands do not *tremble* in the sense of Selten (1975) and play 'defect' by mistake. For in that case, if players are highly committed to the tit-for-tat strategy, one mistake could send the players to a world of noncooperation until the hand of one of them trembles and plays 'cooperate' by mistake [see also Skyrms (1996, pp. 40-41) on this point]. This is one reason why Sugden (1986, especially pp. 113-121) seems to prefer a variant of the tit-for-tat strategy, which allows mistakes. In such a strategy, players cooperate with other players who are 'in good standing'. To be in good standing a player that defects in one round must pay reparation by cooperating in one or more subsequent rounds (depending on what it takes to return to good standing in the community); during the periods of reparation, the other player(s) of course is (are) playing 'defect' against the first. In general, the point is that the tit-for-tat strategy adopted must be robust against small random deviations.

Conventions and institutions

Conventions (important regularities of behavior), *norms*, and various economic *institutions* (e. g., property rights) are typical elements of spontaneous order. Their emergence, via cooperation, has been widely discussed in various writings stretching over many decades. A defining feature of conventions is that they are self-enforcing; it is in the self-interest of all parties to have than not to have the conventions.[14] They emerge from repeated interactions of agents to deal with problems of pure coordination, property, and reciprocity. Their development is fostered by certain *focal points* and by the recognition of *asymmetries* often embedded in the structure of the game [see Hayek (1973), Schelling (1960), Schotter (1981, 1986), and Sugden (1986, 1989]. Focal points are clues that provide a key to the possible solutions of the game. In general, characteristics of focal points in coordination and/or bargaining situations include prominence, uniqueness, simplicity, and precedence. Asymmetries could relate, for instance, to factors such as power, size, importance, and ownership position.[15] Conventions evolve from payoff experience and the resulting emergence of expectations, in trial and error responses in repeated interactions of agents. Indeed, the payoff experience from experimentation and mistakes play a major part in the

---

[14]David Lewis (1986, p. 58; first published 1969) has defined a convention as follows:

"A regularity R in the behavior of members of a population P when they are agents in a recurrent situation S is a *convention* if and only if it is true that, and it is common knowledge in P that, in any instance of S among members of P,

(1) everyone conforms to R;

(2) everyone expects everyone else to conform to R;

(3) everyone prefers to conform to R on condition that the others do, since S is a coordination problem and uniform conformity to R is a coordination equilibrium in S."

[15]Skyrms (1996) uses the term *broken symmetries* to characterize some of these asymmetries. It appears that he does so in those asymmetrical situations that arise because a person *behaves* differently depending on which side of an otherwise symmetrical situation she finds herself—for example, playing hawk if "owner" and dove if "intruder." In this context, it has been observed that ownership itself changes a person's attitude to, and implicit valuation of, a good [see Kahneman, Knetsch, and Thaler (1991)].

evolutionary process (Young, 1993a, 1993b, 1996). The early popularity of a convention helps it spread quickly in competition with other potential candidates, and so does its versatility (Sugden, 1989, p. 94).

Another outcome of cooperative behavior is the emergence of *norms*—social, political, and economic [Ullmann-Margalit (1977), Axelrod (1986), Ostrom and Gardner (1993), Ostrom, Walker, and Gardner (1992), Elster (1989), Binmore and Samuelson (1994), and Sethi and Somanathan (1996)]. While conventions are regularities of behavior that are self-enforced, one can think of norms as informal rules governing behavior that are enforced by the individuals of the community at large without the assistance of a central authority such as the state.[16] In other words, violation of a norm is expected to invite costly punishment by other members of the community. This also means that, for a single individual, observance of a norm does not necessarily yield the best payoff at a particular time if there is little or no probability that someone in the community would choose to enforce the norm on that occasion.

Norms help economize on transaction costs. An interesting finding by many game theorist—particularly in the context of the so-called ultimatum game[17]—is that experience leads people to use rules of thumb to settle coordination problems that arise in situations, particularly involving bargaining, which embody "fairness" criteria in addition to focal points embedded in the situation or environment. Still, a fundamental problem in the emergence and stability of norms is that they involve a prisoner's dilemma game at two stages: (i) whether or not to cooperate and obey the norm; and (ii) whether or not to

---

[16] Cohen (1994) has argued that society generally chooses between norms and (formal) rules on the basis of cost. In other words, society chooses the most efficient enforcement mechanism. This, of course, is a direct application of the Coase theorem and the economics of transaction costs. On the emergence of institutions, see also the interesting case study and analysis by Greif, Milgrom, and Weingast (1994).

[17] In the ultimatum game, Player I proposes a division of a given sum of money between two players. Player II responds by saying yes or no. If the response is yes, the proposed division is implemented. But if the response is no, both players get nothing [see, e.g., Binmore and Samuelson (1994)].

participate in punishing violators of the norm. The second dilemma arises from the fact of an enforcement cost borne by a person trying to enforce a norm. Using a computer simulation to illustrate his point, and making reasonable assumptions with regard to the cost of punishment, if caught violating, and the punisher's enforcement cost, Axelrod has shown that no one will have any incentive to punish violation of a norm unless there is some mechanism to counteract this disincentive effect of enforcement. Such a mechanism is another norm—a *metanorm*—to punish those who do not enforce the norm by punishing those whom they witness violating the norm. Axelrod discusses other mechanisms, apart from metanorms, which could support and help maintain norms.[18]

Still, Sethi and Somanathan (1996) adopt an explicit evolutionary approach and apply it to the case of common pool resources[19] to show that norms of restraint and punishment can be stable against invasion by narrowly self-interested players. They use a model with defectors (who over-exploit the common pool resource), cooperators who do not over-exploit but do not engage in punishing defectors either, and enforcers who punish defectors and must bear a

[18]In particular, he discusses: (i) *dominance*, that is, having a metanorm requiring one to punish another member of one's own group for failing to observe a norm regulating behavior against persons of another group dominated by the first group; (ii) *internalization* of a norm so that persons who violate the norm will have a bad conscience about it; (iii) *social proof*, meaning that one observes as correct behavior in a given situation whatever one sees others predominantly doing in a similar situation; (iv) *membership* in a group dedicated to pursuing a given end; (v) *law* as a device to give clarity to, and official enforcement of, a norm, thereby spreading the enforcement cost to all taxpayers; and (vi) *reputation*, with obedience to a norm becoming a signal to others in the community of one's type.

[19]A fertile area for testing and observing the evolution of norms has been the governance of common pool resources (CPR). Examples include forests, fishing grounds, grazing fields, and some water and irrigation facilities. The basic issue has been whether norms and credible commitments governing exploitation of CPRs can emerge and be enforced without the intervention of an external agent (government or the state). Empirical evidence and experimental observations tend to support the view that self-governance is indeed possible. Apart from the conclusions of Sethi and Somanathan discussed in the text, among the most important conclusions reached are that for efficient (and indeed stable) norms to emerge and be sustained: (i) the agents must have the opportunity to communicate repeatedly; (ii) essential are sanctioning mechanisms to "punish" defectors; and (iii) that it is preferable for agents to have the right to choose the institutional framework regulating exploitation of and investment in the resource as well as the sanctioning mechanism to punish defectors—that is, the institutional framework should (endogenously) come out of the communication that takes place among the agents exploiting the resource.

cost in so doing. The payoffs to defectors are adversely affected by the punishment they must bear from enforcers. Sethi and Somanathan show, among other things, that, for any given stock of the common resource, the state of affairs consisting of only defectors is, indeed, (asymptotically) stable. More importantly, under the same circumstances, they show that for sufficiently high punishment (of defectors by enforcers) in relation to the benefit of defecting (over-exploiting) there exists a set of stable states consisting of a mix of cooperators and enforcers and no defectors. Endogenizing the resource stock does not change this conclusion but brings out the main beneficial effect (namely, higher resource stock) of the stable cooperators-enforcers equilibria over the defectors equilibrium.

Spontaneous order in economic development

Thus, although it benefits from a sound formal legal system, especially one with clear definition and protection of property rights and low-cost enforcement of contracts, spontaneous order comprises customs, conventions, and norms in place of laws and regulations enforced by the political authorities; rules and arrangements that are self-enforcing in the sense of being in the self-interest of all parties to comply with and hence requiring no enforcement by some governmental authority or even any third party; contractual arrangements that are privately enforced, typically by members of the group cooperating in an activity; and heavy reliance on reputation and past conduct, rather than having legal recourse, to motivate willingness to transact with someone or some organization. Moreover, evolutionary forces—chance, experience from mistakes, repeated interactions, learning by doing, adaptation, path dependence—are very important as factors determining change over time.

Many of the institutional changes responsible for the economic progress of the West occurred historically via spontaneous order. In such contexts, the relationships with the central political authorities have also been noteworthy. For spontaneous order to work, the state or central political authority would provide an enabling environment at best or, at worst, not frustrate spontaneous order activities. In the latter case, sometimes spontaneous order benefited from benign neglect by the political authorities—or simply from lack of knowledge by the political authorities about what the "private" sector was doing. At other times, the private sector was able to organize and resist any attempt of the political authorities to frustrate its self-organization. Institutional changes that benefited greatly from spontaneous order include: the emergence of money and markets, in general, and many property rights arrangements; the evolution of commercial law as the needs of sea-borne traffic necessitated a universal system of law to address mercantile interests and avoid government (including common law) courts and having to deal with diverse local customs (Trakman, 1983, Benson, 1997); the development of agency arrangements in overseas trade to handle asymmetric information problems in long distance trade relations (see, e.g., Greif, 1989); the crafting and evolution of standards, codes, and classification systems in commodity and credit markets (see, e.g., articles in Klein, 1997); the formation of guilds and other organizational arrangements to systematize skill classifications, working rules and standards in labor markets in the absence of centralized certification and licensing systems (see, e.g., Farr, 2000); the emergence of the joint-stock company (see Rosenberg and Birdzell, 1986); rules to address governance of common pool resources; and numerous examples in business and finance, such as accounting and payment systems. Of course, it has been the case, with the increasing reach of the state, that many institutional and organizational arrangements that emerged via spontaneous order motivated laws and regulatory and oversight regimes of the central political authorities.

In Asia, apart from the important role played over the centuries in areas such as the development of markets, money and of institutions to govern the exploitation of common-pool resources, one of the most interesting recent institutions due to spontaneous order to have come out of that region is the Grameen bank approach to lending to small (micro) borrowers who cannot meet the collateral requirements of formal financial institutions and have high administrative costs associated with their loans. This idea has inspired other group-based lending arrangements, even in Africa, with varying degrees of success (see, e.g., Masanjala, 2002). In Africa, also, spontaneous order has been important, historically, in economic interactions and made positive contributions to the development process. Of particular note, spontaneous order has been important in the development of markets, long distance trade (most notably trans-Sahara), and the evolution of property rights, especially land rights [see, e.g., Johnson (1972), Isichei (1997)].

Not all spontaneous order unambiguously contributes positively to the long-term development process. For example, in recent years, particularly the period since 1978, African citizens have had to deal with poor governance at the political level and have resorted to spontaneous order—in many cases, basically to substitute for a failed state. No doubt, many of the mechanisms of spontaneous order under such circumstances have tremendous social value (increasing trust and cooperation and developing organizational skills) and will, as particular organizational mechanisms, probably survive long beyond the period of state collapse and even sow the seeds for more complex organizational structures. Typically, though, these kinds of coping behavior result in wasteful investments and practices, with no clear long-run economic benefits similar to the kind of spontaneous order illustrated earlier. For example, private residential electricity generators in some African cities are a consequence of state ineptitude and could be avoided with more efficient state policies. In general, the spontaneous order associated with coping behavior in the context of state failure, or simply poor state governance, has other obvious problems for economic development: specialization tends to recede; market exchange and financial market development are hampered; the efficiency of investment is lowered; investment in human capital declines; and law and order often wanes.

Spontaneous order has also had to come into action, not because of state collapse, per se, but rather because of rising demands for services normally provided by the state—in areas such as education, health, and law and order —which the state is unable to satisfy at reasonable cost. It is for this reason that, in a number of African countries, many basic services have at times been provided in the context of spontaneous order (see the papers in Semboja and Therkildsen, 1995, for the cases of Kenya, Tanzania, and Uganda). Here, again, this sort of spontaneous order—filling-in for the state's failure to adequately supply while not making efficient provision for alternative sources—is not the sort that one associates with sound economic development. Indeed, economies of scale may be lost and the low-cost producer may not be supplying a service, so that some efficiency losses are occurring in the system as a whole. Another way to look at it is that disorderly privatization, even if temporary, is taking place in the provision of the services, because the state does not wish to formally privatize.

Factors hindering cooperation for spontaneous order

Cooperation for spontaneous order can be adversely affected by low generalized trust, ethnicity, and collectivism. Low generalized trust is the feeling that one can't really trust anyone, outside of a few close friends and relatives, to be honest and to put in adequate effort, in business relationships; in other words, there is an expectation of rampant corruption and free-riding. This could be aggravated by difficulties in constructing effective monitoring and sanctioning devices to use against dishonest persons and free riders, as when for example the legal system is inefficient and corrupt and socio-cultural mechanisms don't work effectively. The consequence is that agents find it optimal to assume that everyone else outside of some small circle of friends and relatives would be one type of agent (or partner) in a cooperative effort, namely, untrustworthy, and that dishonesty and free-riding will be costly to monitor and punish. In such a context, business ideas will remain small-scale with heavy emphasis on supervision, by the owner, of any employed staff.[20]

In an experiment conducted in 24 communities in Zimbabwe, Barr (2003) finds a positive relationship between trusting behavior and the expectation of trustworthiness. An implication is that there could be a vicious circle involving the level of generalized trust, trusting behavior, and the expectation of untrustworthiness, so that in fact generalized trust diminishes over time. To counter this, in order to foster economic development, a community must find exogenous ways to increase trusting behavior to promote the expectation of trustworthiness and hence generalized trust. Getting the community to understand the link(s) from trusting behavior to generalized trust to cooperation and finally to economic development would help; so also would the existence of feasible ways to begin the process and get onto the virtuous circle involved. Clearly, other things being equal, the desire for economic development can be a strong motivational factor, in the community, for trusting behavior.[21]

Apart from low generalized trust due to corruption and free-riding, other factors hindering cooperation are ethnicity and collectivism. Ethnicity is complimentary with low generalized trust, whilst collectivism results in high trust within ethnic groups (that is, group solidarity) plus heavy distrust of persons outside one's own ethnic group. In a study of the informal economy in Nairobi, Macharia (1997) found that kinship was rated by the respondents as the most important resource in developing a business—even more important than capital. The kin provides training (via apprenticeship, for example), advice and

---

[20] In dealing with the constraints to indigenous entrepreneurship in Sierra Leone, for instance, Kallon (1990) found that dishonesty was one of the factors of great concern to the entrepreneurs. "Consequently, 'policing' the firm in order to make it difficult for those who are predisposed toward dishonesty to undertake any fraudulent activities was the only way they could handle this problem. They did this by getting more intimately involved in the minutest details of their operations" [Kallon (1990), pp. 195-6].

[21] As Knack and Keefer (1997) state: "Trusting societies not only have incentives to innovate and to accumulate physical capital, but are also likely to have higher returns to accumulation of human capital." In addition, "trust and civic involvement are linked to better performance of government institutions..."

information, and financial help. Also, ethnic identity influenced the allocation of premises on which to do business. In general, ethnic identity and trust building were found to be closely linked, and "ethnic identity influenced, and to some extent determined, the transfer of skills and technology. This made it difficult for others from different ethnic groups to enter certain trades and subsectors"(Macharia 1997, p. 135). In his book on entrepreneurship among the fula in Sierra Leone, Alusine Jalloh (1999) discusses how business relationships that required trust and involved substantial capital were confined mainly to family members and kinsmen. This was extremely important as credit and other relations were informal and unwritten and the courts were not used by the fula to settle disputes. Even in employment there was a "kinship-centered" approach, which minimized losses through theft. Jalloh underscores, nevertheless, the limits of trust: namely, there was an "owner-centered approach to decision making" [Jalloh (1999), p. 92].

Thus, even the high trust within the ethnic group is, in today's Africa, abated by widespread corruption, which hinders trust of even one's own kin and ethnic group members. Urbanization and the possibility of emigration abroad seem to have aggravated the situation. For, in today's world, some individuals may be willing and able to break away from their families and their ethnic groups and avoid collectivist sanctions, if the material rewards of cheating and exiting the group are sizable enough. Consistent with this sort of development, declining trust and cooperation within ethnic groups is sometimes blamed on "westernization." For instance, Bethlehem (1975) and others have found that in many African countries: "people untouched by westernization are much more cooperative and trusting than people who are westernized." These researchers have found overwhelming support for the hypothesis that "the more westernized adults are, by reason either of education, engaging in a western occupation, or of living in town, the less cooperatively they will play in the Prisoner's Dilemma game." This would seem to imply that a "problem" of the typical African country is finding ways to increase cooperation, by increasing trust across ethnic groups, without diminishing it within groups, so that in fact generalized trust increases for the country as a whole.

Both theory and available empirical evidence lend support to the hypothesis that ethnicity will be less of a hindrance to cooperation in modern, formal institutional and organizational settings than would corruption and free-riding. Modern business organizations tend to concentrate in and around urban areas. Ethnicity tends to be lower in the urban environment than in the country as a whole. For example, Collier and Garg (1999), in a study of the effect of ethnic affiliation on wages, in the Ghanaian labor market, find no evidence of group favoritism (for the dominant group members) in the private firms in contrast to the government sector where a wage premium (favoritism) was detected. In other words, self-interest made it worthwhile to pay according to productivity in the private firms, while lack of internalization of costs and benefits allowed the government managers to indulge their taste for ethnicity. Hence, progress towards building large complex private organizations and coming up with institutional innovations and adaptations, via spontaneous order, for accelerating economic development, will occur, other things being equal, as improvements take place in the enabling environment and in the capacity of organizations to institute low-cost information and management structures to reduce the payoffs from free riding, dishonesty, and disloyalty. In addition, there will continue to be other types of inter-ethnic cooperation based on self-interest, for example, ethnically based enterprises dealing across ethnic lines in open markets.

Enabling environment: the role of civil society leadership and the state

I have argued, so far, that both theory and empirical evidence have shown that self-organization, due to cooperation founded on trust or self-interest or both, is possible and prevalent in societies across the globe. In many developing countries, leadership in civil society can help greatly in promoting cooperation, thereby fostering development-enhancing spontaneous order. The relevant actions would involve promoting mutual respect among ethnic groups where these are important, generalized trust, and self-help organizations, while promulgating the message that orderly and effective self-governance is possible.

The state can foster spontaneous order by its provision of a favorable environment for the appropriate cooperation to flourish. This is especially true for cooperation founded on self-interest. The enabling environment of the state will include, most notably, security, enforcement of contracts and property rights, and solid macroeconomic fundamentals. A sound commercial legal framework, reasonably well-functioning financial markets, and sound physical infrastructure, all of which could, at worst, evolve via spontaneous order, could also be part of the environment supplied by the state. Furthermore, state policies that resolutely address ethnicity (see, e.g., Johnson, 2005b, and Chapter 5) and corruption problems would constitute important positive contributions to this enabling environment.

For spontaneous order to thrive, at any level, some *pact of mutual respect and toleration* among ethnic groups in a country is a precondition. For such a pact, transforming leadership at the level of civil society would help by promoting mutual respect among ethnolinguistic groups. The civil society leadership could begin by educating their followers: that ethnic conflict can have serious economic costs, and hence that it is in the individual and group self-interest of all citizens to prevent disruptive ethnic conflicts and to reduce ethnicity; and that there are feasible ways to do so.

Similarly, promoting generalized trust will involve encouraging and supporting ethnolinguistically diverse voluntary associations, and educating fellow citizens about the benefits of social capital and generalized trust and how to build them via both individual and collective action. The civil society leadership will impart on to their compatriots the awareness that generalized trust is in their individual and national economic, cultural, and political self-interest.

It could also be pointed out by the civil society leadership, to their compatriots, that voluntary associations were extremely instrumental in the political mobilization efforts in the struggle for independence. Wallerstein, several decades ago, elaborated on the functions performed by the voluntary associations that sprung all over colonial Africa. Among these, he mentioned that the voluntary associations were an effective mechanism for crossing kin barriers and creating national groups. As training grounds for leaders, both in the technical skills of running an organization and in the substantive appreciation of political ideas, he noted that the associations "served as communication networks through which new ideas, even forbidden ideas, could circulate" [Wallerstein (1964), especially pp. 330-5].

Despite the risks it poses to building generalized trust, narrow group solidarity can be useful in certain circumstances, and I would argue on balance that there is a case for fostering it in the context of promoting self-help community development projects. These are usually small-scale projects, especially infrastructure and human capital, which often tend to benefit a particular local community. Examples would be community beautification and cleaning projects, small (feeder) roads, bridges, school buildings, hospitals, community centers, and wells. Civil society leaders could promote these cooperative activities as well.

Self-help organizations are typically formed to select projects and mobilize persons of the community to help in the finance and implementation. In some African countries these kinds of organizations have become extremely important in recent years, particularly in the provision of basic services such as health and education, mainly because the demands for these services have outstripped the ability of the state to provide them without substantial local community participation. The organizations involved in self-help projects are often termed nongovernmental organizations (NGOs) and people's organizations (POs) [see, e.g., the papers in Semboja and Therkildsen (1995)]. The POs are the ones that usually have substantial local community participation in all stages of the project as well as in the finance. NGOs contribute technical assistance and/or finance but typically as outsiders.

Civil society leaders can play an essential role in the activities of the POs. In this effort, they will find it easier to work with groups whose memberships comprise persons who feel a significant measure of solidarity towards one another. Solidarity facilitates the mobilization of local persons in support of projects benefiting the community at large. It also motivates the wealthier members of the community to accept a greater financial contribution to infrastructure projects than the poorer members, irrespective of the distribution of the benefits. Indeed, with sufficient solidarity, the wealthier members even make substantial contributions to projects from which they expect to derive insignificant or no direct benefits (such as school building projects when they do not have and are unlikely to have children of their own).

From a development standpoint, there is certainly a role for civil society leaders to play in preparing and managing self-help projects to address, among other things, literacy, primary and secondary education, basic hygiene and primary health care, and enhancement of technological capability involving elementary mechanical and modern technical skills (trade schools). Civil society leaders could also perform some entrepreneurship by arranging use of outside volunteers to assist well-organized and disciplined self-help groups. In general, successes of communities would be correlated with the effectiveness of organization (for energizing community members and making decisions on projects and funding), resource mobilization, and project management capability, all of which would benefit enormously from good transforming leadership.[22] This means that there is always a risk that self-help organization programs could exacerbate community, regional and ethnic inequalities. But this is good for energizing communities that don't want to be left behind in the development process. Also, resolute policies to reduce ethnicity in general would help mitigate the negative effects on ethnicity of competition for state and NGO resources to help implement self-help community development projects.

[22] This hypothesis is consistent with the evidence; see, e.g., Thomas (1985).

Finally, civil society leaders in the African continent could be at the helm of those explaining to ordinary citizens the interaction of self-interest and the enabling environment in facilitating cooperation and spontaneous order; the leaders should make use of the research of economists and other social scientists. This would help energize ordinary citizens of these countries to demand from their governments good economic policy environments.

Authoritarian Order

Whereas spontaneous order is an outcome of private cooperation, without central direction from the body politic, there is order that is centrally directed, which one can designate *authoritarian order*. Authoritarian order occurs when the individuals and groups in the society, via a generally accepted *decisionmaking process*, grant the *authority* to a central body or individual to coordinate the institutional and organizational activities of the individuals and groups and to enforce the rules and oversee the organizational structures that flow from such coordination. Under authoritarian order, the emergence of institutions is no longer spontaneous and rules are not necessarily self-enforcing. Instead, the *process of change* is coercive—rules, regulations, and orders being prescribed and enforced by the state. But both self-interest and trust are important in fostering cooperation to make authoritarian order work with low social cost relative to benefit.

Self-interest and trust

Authoritarian order in successful development efforts is typically founded on collective self-interest and facilitated by focal points, appropriate legitimation processes, and transforming political leadership. *Collective self-interest* typically arises in the face of exogenous constraints, that is, forces emanating from outside the community or from nature that make it the self-interest of the leaders and the followers of the community to pursue certain objectives the achievement of which can be accelerated by authoritarian order. These constraints could be factors which threaten the political or economic survival of the community or they could arise from international competition that endangers the self-esteem of the community vis-à-vis some other community with which it competes. Such constraints provide the incentive (make it in the self-interest of the community) to seek rapid economic development or progress that cannot wait for the slow evolutionary process of spontaneous order.

Authoritarian order succeeds in the objective of speeding up the development process when the authority is headed by capable *transforming political leadership* (see Burns, 1978, Johnson, 1986, and chapter 7). In the present context, the *focal points* would comprise values or beliefs prominent in the cultures of a society. The leadership must demonstrate that the content of the economic program does not violate those values and beliefs. Even more importantly, the leadership must convince the followers that the contribution that each individual or organization is being asked to make towards the implementation of the program, that is, any constraint on behavior, is strictly in conformity with the cherished values of the society. Moreover, the leadership must get the followers to agree that implementation of the program would advance the interests (including values and beliefs) of the society at large.

All this means that, for smooth implementation, the program should be *legitimated* by the populace. Legitimation involves citizens' consent without coercion. Such consent comes via several procedures, namely, open discussion and deliberation, voting, and overwhelming demonstration of support in Parliament, in the newspapers, and in civil society voluntary organizations (for further discussion of the issue of program legitimation, see Johnson, 2005a, and Chapter 4).

Trust also plays a very important role in cooperation for authoritarian order, namely, trust for the political leadership (and the authorities in general) by the populace and generalized trust within the populace. Thus, given the self-interest in cooperation for authoritarian order, and given the general trust by the populace in the political leadership and the government bureaucracy, the greater the degree of generalized trust within the population, the greater will be the willingness to cooperate to agree on a program of action and to fully implement that program.

East Asian examples

The successful high-performing latecomers to industrialization and development, from Germany to certain East Asian countries — notably Japan, Korea, Taiwan and Singapore — are classic examples of how cooperation via authoritarian order works and can prove highly efficacious in accelerating economic development. I shall briefly discuss the example of three of the East Asian countries.

For the East Asian countries, the self-interest, and hence incentive, of the political leadership to mobilize the population to cooperate and implement good policies for development came from the need for survival, both economically and politically. Consider the case of *Singapore*. It became a self-governing state in 1959. In September 1963, it joined the Federation of Malaysia. Soon it became clear that "[t]here were fundamental disagreements over policies between Singapore and the federal government" (Lew Kuan Yew, 2000, p. 3). On August 9, 1965, Singapore was expelled from the Federation. As Lee Kuan Yew writes (2000, p.4):

> "We faced tremendous odds with an improbable chance of survival. Singapore was not a natural but man-made country, a trading post the British had developed into a modal point in their world-wide maritime empire. We inherited the island without its hinterland, a heart without a body."

The structural problems of a small country, with no hinterland (Hong Kong, for instance, had China and was still a British colony) or not much in the way of natural resources to talk about[23] and losing its role as entrepôt of its region (which included Malaysia and Indonesia), and with two million people in a crowded and small space, were not the only problems Singapore faced. The British closed their bases and pulled out in late 1971. Singapore lost the economic benefits of the bases and British military spending (estimated at some twenty percent of GDP at the time). The country also had to build a military from scratch, as Lee Kuan Yew (2000, p. 6) put it, "to defend this piece of real estate."

Lee Kuan Yew rejected the suggestion of a common market with Malaysia, because politically it would not work. The leaders of Singapore knew that they had reached the limits of their entrepôt trade. They tried tourism; it helped but it was not enough to satisfy the growth and employment demands. Somehow they had to industrialize.

According to Lee Kuan Yew (2000, p. 57-8) "After several years of disheartening trial and error," the Singapore authorities "concluded that Singapore's best hope lay with the American multinational corporations (MNCs)." "American MNCs brought higher technology in large-scale operations," than for instance the Taiwanese and Hong Kong entrepreneurs, "creating many jobs." He settled on a two-pronged strategy. "The first was to leapfrog the region," and link up directly with Europe, America, and Japan, by attracting their manufacturers "to produce in Singapore and export their products to the developed countries." The second part of the strategy "was to create a First World Oasis in a Third World region." "If Singapore could establish First World standards in public and personal security, health, education, telecommunications, transportation, and services, it would become a base camp for entrepreneurs, engineers, managers, and other professionals who had business to do in the region."

Lee Kuan Yew adds (p. 58): "This meant we had to train our people and equip them to provide First World standards of service. I believed this was

---

[23] The only thing Lee Kuan Yew (2000, p. 8) could point to, in this regard, was "a natural world-class harbor sited in a strategic location astride one of the busiest sea-lanes of the world."

possible, that we could reeducate and reorientate our people with the help of schools, trade unions, community centers, and social organizations." Thus the strategy entailed much social engineering, which went with a price to be borne by the population at large. The reeducation and reorientation were all part of the process of legitimating the strategy to facilitate its implementation.

In *Korea*, also, there was a strong desire to come up with sound economic policies fast, because of the ideological and military competition with the communist North, in the face of American plans "to terminate grants by 1965 because Korea was considered hopeless in terms of economic development" (Chung-yum Kim, 1994, p. 30). In *Japan*, it was the prospect of losing their independence in the face of obvious threats by the powerful nations of the West that inspired the Meiji Revolution or Restoration (1867-8) and the modernization of Japan under the slogan of 'Japanese Spirit and Western learning.' As Morshima (1982, p. 96) put it: "The consistent aim of successive governments from the Meiji Revolution onwards was to build Japan into a strong country with a top class military capability and a top class industry—a country which could not be defeated by the advanced nations of Europe and America."

Important for the political leadership in eliciting the appropriate cooperation were focal points embedded in *Confucianism*. Morishima, for example, states that Confucianism "taught the Japanese people that frugal behavior was noble behavior" (Morishima, 1982, p. 86). He also discussed the relationship between Confucian culture and the Japanese development strategy as follows.

"Confucianism in Japan stresses (1) loyalty to the state (or lord), (2) filial piety to one's parents, (3) faith towards friends, and (4) respect towards one's elders. Therefore, according to the Confucian ideology it was quite natural that a nationalist-capitalist economy should develop based on a seniority system and lifetime employment" (Morishima, 1982, p. 86). In the Confucian world "individualism was suffocated. Nevertheless, Confucianism was intellectual and rational, and compatible with modern science" (Morishima, 1982, p. 87). From

1878-1900 "the Meiji government successfully achieved 'take-off' in the Japanese economy" (Morishima, 1982, p. 87). Moreover, "in Confucian political thought, those who play the most important role in the society are bureaucrats, who are strictly and competitively selected" (Morishima, 1982, p. 87). "The Meiji government was an advanced modern bureaucracy from the outset. It is therefore not at all surprising that Japanese capitalism started as state capitalism—an economy guided and driven by bureaucrats" (Morishima, 1982, p. 87).

Cho (1994, p. 10) notes, quite rightly, that loyalty "cannot exist in a vacuum; it is always situated in a network of incentives, rewards, patronage, coercion and constraints which must be considered in examining the full dynamics at work in Japan, or anywhere." In this regard, the legitimation processes utilized, as well as the culture of shared growth or fairness in income distribution that was promoted, enabled the authorities to attain the right combination of incentives to achieve the appropriate loyalty and cooperation from citizens to design and implement programs that fostered rapid growth and structural transformation of the East Asian economies [see Campos and Root (1996), Morishima (1982), and Lee Kuan Yew (2000)]. For instance, highly talented and motivated government bureaucrats were aided by deliberation councils, with substantial representation from the private industries and groups affected, in designing economic policies, including selective intervention policies of the government (see, e.g., Campos and Root, 1996). Important participation and feedback from the public was also solicited on a regular basis (see, e.g., Lee Kuan Yew, 2000, p. 132).

In this context, political leaders and government bureaucrats worked proactively to develop mechanisms (institutions and organizational structures) to facilitate smooth cooperation between labor and management, including by encouraging or exerting political pressure for fair wages and salaries and discouraging disruptive strikes and work stoppages. Sometimes this involved creating formal structures like the National Wages Council (NWC) of Singapore, set up in 1972, with representatives from unions, management, and government.

Every year, the NWC "reached a wide consensus recommendation on wage increases and other terms and conditions of service for the coming year that would be affordable and would promote further economic growth. Its joint recommendations were accepted as general guidelines, with variations for the different sectors, for all union-management negotiations" (Lee Kuan Yew, 2000, p. 88). Or the mechanisms involved leaning on management to treat workers fairly; for instance, Park Chung Hee at one time instructed the Ministry of Health and Social Welfare and the Office of Labor to insist that firms paying the lowest wages should be pressured to raise them to the average level of other firms in the same industry (Chung-yum Kim, 1994, p. 119). The cooperative arrangements between government and business, which were essential elements of the authoritarian order, gave leverage to the authorities in using such mechanisms when deemed useful to promote growth and stability.

Conclusion

To accelerate their development, African countries must often introduce new institutional and organizational arrangements to govern the economic interactions of their citizens. In this enterprise, whether they are imitating, adapting, or innovating, and whether they are self-organizing or they prefer to grant authority to a political center to coordinate their efforts, the citizens of the countries will need effective cooperation. In this chapter, I have argued that much of the institutional and organizational changes behind economic progress around the world have indeed occurred without any direction from the political center, but rather through cooperation among private individuals and groups. Such cooperation engenders an order traditionally dubbed spontaneous order. Generalized trust and self-interest underpin the cooperation engendering spontaneous order. Civil society leadership can influence the level of generalized trust. The government through its policies or benign neglect can affect incentives, facilitating exploitation of self-interest for spontaneous order.

There is another form of order that emerges from cooperation, namely, authoritarian order, which has been found useful by latecomers intending to speed up the development process. This order occurs when individuals and groups in the society agree to grant authority to a central body or individual to coordinate institutional and organizational activities and to enforce the rules and oversee the organizational structures that flow from such coordination. The emergence of institutions is no longer spontaneous and rules are not necessarily self-enforcing. Instead, the process of change is coercive—rules, regulations, and orders are prescribed and enforced by the state. But both self-interest and trust are important, as well, in fostering cooperation to enable authoritarian order to work with low social cost relative to benefit. I argued that authoritarian order succeeds in the objective of speeding up the development process when the authority is headed by capable transforming political leadership with the ability to utilize relevant focal points to motivate cooperation using socially accepted processes for program legitimation by the populace. The examples of Japan, Korea and Singapore were briefly discussed.

4

Country Ownership, Conditionality, and Economic Policymaking

Since the early 1980s, many persons—influential and non-influential—both within and outside the African continent have been attacking the international financial organizations and foreign donors, contending that those organizations and governments have adversely affected the ability of the African countries to design and implement policies appropriate to their circumstances. Thus, there has been criticism of conditionality, of the programs, and of what is regarded as inadequate ownership by African countries of their reform programs. In this chapter, I would like to argue that the international aid community, including the IMF for this purpose, can contribute to improving the policy environment in the African countries by supporting country ownership of programs and being resolute in supporting only countries that manifest a commitment to good policies. Supporting ownership will help increase demand for good policies within countries, while selectivity will tighten the exogenous constraints on African political leaders and help make them see the pursuance of good policies as being in their self-interest. In such a context, traditional policy-based conditionality is neither necessary nor helpful. [1]

In the rest of the chapter, I will argue that the essence of ownership is the acceptance of full responsibility for the consequences of a program, that ownership gives a country the right to insist on making the final decisions, without coercion, on the contents of a program, and that acceptance by a country of responsibility for a program must be credibly demonstrated. I argue that ownership matters because of the expectation that program design will be superior and that the country authorities will be resolute in taking the appropriate steps, especially domestic legitimation, to ensure full implementation of the program. I also argue that program success is correlated with degree of ownership, which in turn is correlated with program legitimation. I then discuss the rationale for policy-based conditionality, the context in which it is generally applied, and the criticisms levied against it, in particular, that it has not succeeded in bringing good policy environments in aid-recipient countries. Then the chapter turns to a discussion of selectivity as a device for allocating aid resources. It distinguishes ex post from ex ante selectivity, presents the case for ex post selectivity, which is currently fashionable among many analysts in the policy community, but then argues in favor of ex ante selectivity. Addressing the issue of operationalizing conditionality under ex ante selectivity, the chapter pursues the argument that reaching understandings on conditionality in this context would entail establishing existence of ownership, soundness of the program (policies and outcomes), and adequate implementation capacity. I suggest that if the approach (regarding rules and organizational arrangements) outlined in the chapter, is adhered to, there would be self-interest in the recipient countries in implementing and sustaining sound policies and there would be self-interest within the aid-giving organizations to insist on sound policies and satisfactory outcomes as a condition for future aid.

---

[1] An earlier treatment of the main themes pursued in this chapter can be found in Johnson (2005a).

Essence of Ownership

Johnson and Wasty (1993, p. 2) note, quite rightly, that "it is seldom made clear as to what constitutes adequate ownership..." In the context of World Bank supported programs, Johnson and Wasty (1993) use a four dimensional variable to reflect "the intensity of ownership." The first dimension is the "locus of initiative:" namely, who had the initiative in formulating and implementing the program, the degree of collaboration in working out the program, and whether or not the funding for the program was extended despite certain reservations of the country authorities (disagreements and reluctance to implement some aspects of the program). The second dimension is the "level of intellectual conviction among key policymakers:" namely, the degree to which there was consensus among policymakers on the nature and causes of the problem, the choices open for its resolution, and the approach to be taken. The third dimension is the "expression of political will by top leadership:" as reflected, for example, in "up-front actions" and public statements. The fourth dimension comprises "efforts toward consensus-building among constituencies," for instance, by eliciting broad participation in the program design and in launching a "broad-based public campaign" to elicit support for the program outside the central government.

Tony Killick et al (1998, p. 87) have put forward the following definition of government ownership:

> "Government ownership is at its strongest when the political leadership and its advisers, with broad support among agencies of state and civil society, decide of their own volition that policy changes are desirable, choose what these changes should be and when they should be introduced, and where these changes become built into parameters of policy and administration which are generally accepted as desirable."

I shall focus on country ownership, rather than simply government ownership, as the more complete form of ownership and the one which is desirable for ensuring smooth implementation of a program. 'Ownership' from the perspective of the typical African citizen, I believe, is more about (1) the right of the country representatives to be heard in the process of diagnosis and program design, and (2) the freedom and ability of the country to choose the program to be implemented, without coercion, than about (3) who designs the program. Of course, many among the educated elites in civil society in the African countries would prefer that their nationals design the programs, if they have the requisite technical skills; they would also want, over time, their own nationals to be fully equipped to design every program. In the short term to medium term, however, these same elites will not typically insist on a program being designed by local persons for the program to be deemed locally owned. Hence, there is no necessary correlation between the degree of active country participation in the program design (relative to participation of outsiders) and the extent or degree of country ownership. In brief, the line of causation runs from country ownership (ex ante) to participation in design and finally to implementation.

Broadly speaking, then, I say that country ownership exists when there is general belief by citizens of the country as well as by noncitizens that the country representatives freely chose the program to be implemented, and when there is at the same time general acceptance of the citizens of the country of full responsibility for the outcome of the program chosen. When a country "owns" a program it willingly accepts the costs of any failure. A country with a rational decisionmaking process will then act consistently with this belief and acceptance of responsibility. A rational decisionmaking process is one that is generally expected to result in a program that is in the best interest of the citizens of the country as a whole; in other words, an expected outcome of such a process is a program that maximizes the expected utility of the citizens, subject to unavoidable economic and other constraints.

A program that is owned would tend to be consistent with the general economic framework from which flow government policy of the country. In other words, although "expressions of political support" may be useful in assessing ownership and hence commitment to a program, the expressions must be credible. Ex ante, such credibility would be enhanced by looking at a country's policies in the recent past and by looking at current policies outside the framework of the program, when the program is not comprehensive. When the program implies major changes in economic framework of the government/country, then the country can use credible signals to demonstrate its belief that it owns the program. One such signal is, of course, active participation in the program design.

Ownership and Programming

A general view is that if a country "owns" a program, its commitment to implementation is stronger [see, e.g., Johnson and Wasty (1993), Killick (1997), Killick et al (1998), and Tsikata (2003)]. In addition, many have underscored that with ownership the program may be better in the sense of being more realistic in its objectives and in using instruments that could more assuredly attain the objectives. For both reasons, program success is expected to be correlated with degree of ownership. Johnson and Wasty (1993), in their statistical analysis of 81 World Bank policy-based lending operations during the period 1980 to 1988, in 38 countries, found "a significant degree of positive correlation between program success and borrower ownership." Program success is as classified by the Bank's Operation Evaluation Department: namely, each program's outcome is classified as highly satisfactory, satisfactory, unsatisfactory, or very unsatisfactory. Killick and his collaborators (1998, p.90) stated that in eighteen of twenty-one countries studied, "the extent of ownership, or its absence, was found to have exerted a decisive influence on the degree of programme implementation." They argue (p. 98) that "ownership has strong explanatory power because it is a proxy indicator of the extent to which the policy reforms in question are perceived by those who must execute them as being in their own, and their compatriots,' interests." In this context, they underscore (p.98) that "the objectives and interests of donor agencies and of recipient governments can rarely be expected to coincide."

Putting it somewhat differently, then, ownership matters because country authorities are expected to be resolute in taking the appropriate steps domestically to ensure full implementation. The most important steps are seeking proper domestic legitimation for the program and establishing appropriate institutional and organizational arrangements for effective monitoring of developments and full implementation (even in the presence of serious and adverse unforeseen developments).

Political legitimacy

Legitimation will prevent certain "political economy" factors from disrupting program implementation. Ivanova et al (2003) in an econometric study of the factors explaining implementation of IMF-supported programs found that "political economy" factors were the primary explananda. Other possible factors, *a priori*, namely, the effort of the IMF, the extent and structure of conditionality, and the initial and external conditions, did not "materially influence" implementation. Here the authors constructed three variables to gauge IMF support: (1) IMF effort, measured as the dollar costs of staff time allocated to a program; (2) number of IMF staff missions involved; and (3) the number of mission days. As they put it (Ivanova, et al, p. 28): "strong vested interests in parliament, lack of political cohesion, poor quality of bureaucracy, and ethnic divisions significantly undermine program implementation." For instance, although they caution drawing definitive conclusions from their study, they do find that "[f]or a country that enjoys perfect political stability and no special interests in parliament, the probability of program implementation is very high (96 percent).

Mecagni (1999) also found that some 20 percent (10) of 51 interruptions experienced in the implementation of programs with 36 countries supported by the SAF/ESAF facilities of the IMF, during 1986-1994, were due to "*political interruptions* serious enough to call into question the continuing authority of the government and, therefore, to prevent meaningful negotiations..." (p. 220). 'Political events' also played a role in the vast majority of the remaining interruptions "although not as disruptively as in the10 episodes where they were the overriding factor"[Mecagni (1999, p. 221)]. Program interruptions were defined "as either an interval of more than six months between different annual or multiyear IMF arrangements or a delay of more than six months in completing a program review" (Mecagni, p. 217).

Dollar and Svensson (2000) found that success in structural adjustment programs of the World Bank are mainly explained by political economy factors. In particular, success is associated with democratically elected governments and with political stability. High degrees of ethnic fractionalization and long-term incumbency of regimes are associated with failures, after controlling for other factors. Some donor (that is, World Bank) effort variables (notably preparation and supervision staff time) are highly correlated with the probability of success. But the variables are endogenous, and once the endogeneity is taken into account, the authors find no correlation between any of them and the success or failure of reform programs.

I have argued in Johnson (1994) that: "for effective implementation of adjustment programs it is necessary for the governments to have the legitimate authority to implement the programs." Without such authority, a government will not be able to galvanize the support, and hence cooperation, of the people..." When it does not have legitimate authority to implement a program, "a government may find that dependence on other forms of power (force, manipulation, persuasion) or of authority (coercion) will enable it to attain only a rather modest degree of implementation in the face of sabotage, indifference, nonparticipation, and minimum effort and compliance from the general population, despite large expenditure of resources."

Governments often start with a legitimation deficit for a program and fail to take appropriate steps to remove the deficit. Hence, Johnson (1994, p. 406) states:

> "To guarantee virtually full implementation of a reform program, the program designer must ensure that the government and its program managers have the authority to implement the program. When such authority seems absent or when there is sufficient doubt that the government has the authority, the program designer should advise that the government obtain the authority to implement the program; otherwise, the program designer cannot be assured that the program can be carried out."

Country ownership and legitimation of a program will, thus, be positively correlated. Johnson and Wasty (1993) state that "the following appear to be commonly associated with borrower ownership of the program: (a) political stability; (b) support of (or lack of opposition from) various constituencies; and (c) to a somewhat lesser extent, preconceived official attitudes toward or against certain kinds of reform" (Johnson and Wasty, 1993, p.7). In this regard, political stability is not necessarily related to the political regime, and, indeed, as Johnson and Wasty note, "there is no systematic evidence that a specific regime type intrinsically exhibits a greater degree of political will in support of reform" (Johnson and Wasty, 1993, p. 10). Support (or lack of opposition) from "pressure groups towards their government's pursuit of reforms" was "[p]erhaps the single most significant factor in government's ownership of the reform program" (Johnson and Wasty, 1993, p. 8).

The evidence of legitimation is ultimately citizens' consent without coercion, which comes via several processes—open discussion and deliberation, voting, and overwhelming demonstration of support (rather than a narrow majority) in Parliament, in the newspapers, and in civil society voluntary organizations. In this context, of major importance is institutionalizing a process of transparency and public deliberation.[2] Public debate would foster discussion of policy alternatives, including the short-term and long-term costs. Such discussion would also motivate genuine search for compromises among interest groups. Best

---

[2] See the discussion by Faruquee (1994) of a national debate in Nigeria of a suggested IMF-related adjustment program. Unfortunately, that process was not sustained over time.

of all, public debate would facilitate better appreciation by ordinary citizens of how the economy works and how good and bad economic developments arise. This would help in many ways, especially curbing unreasonable budgetary demands and enabling greater understanding of the value of organization, saving, and efficiency of investment.

In today's world, a search for evidence of legitimation would therefore look for signs of free and open public debate, parliamentary deliberation and voting, and referenda. If the need for ownership is to prevent policy reversal then the legitimation must probably entail more than simply majority approval and rather approach consensus, if possible, or at least some supermajority that ensures broad and stable support. That is, where decisions are taken by voting, super-majorities may be preferred to achieve a degree of legitimation which virtually ensures that, except in the event of very serious unforeseen adverse developments and policy constraints, there would be no policy reversal during implementation.

Participation and program legitimation

When open deliberation of economic policy is not institutionalized in a country, program legitimation can still be attained by encouraging broad participation of various interest groups and individuals in the design and implementation of the program. Indeed, this is one of the rational steps taken by a government that wants to ensure country ownership of a program, irrespective of the actual or perceived legitimacy of the government. Typically, in such a situation, the government is anxious to assume ownership of the program and uses broad participation of the citizens as a mobilizing tool to muster support, 'educate' citizens and ensure country ownership. Although this is always a rational step to take, it is even more so when the government has doubts about its own political legitimacy and hence cannot afford to introduce a reform program without broad-based support of citizens. In such a case, a government is perhaps not only concerned with preventing policy reversal but also with its own survival.

The description by P.V. Obeng (1996) of the case of Ghana and its Structural Adjustment Program of the 1980s is a good example of what is entailed. As Mr. Obeng put it, one of the benefits of the "involvement of all parties in the decisionmaking process" related to the structural adjustment program of the 1980s was that "as a people, we achieved a sense of ownership of the economic program, a greater acceptance of the consequences of the program, and a stronger commitment to implement."[3] As discussed in Chapter 3, the governments of what became the High-Performing Asian Economies also enhanced the quality and legitimacy of their reform and growth programs by promoting broad-based participation among citizens and organizations. As Campos and Root (1996)[4] argue in their book, "the East Asian leaders secured the support of economic elites without compromising sound policy through mechanisms designed to facilitate consultation, cooperation, and coordination."

Participation is, perforce, at different levels: expert, political, and social. The government could take the initiative to draw up a program and then actively mobilize public support and thereby obtain legitimation of the program. In the process, it could modify the initial draft program, to take into account the views and concerns of citizens at large. In this context, governments find useful five types of tactical moves, namely: (i) accepting, via consultation and advice, the views of outside experts; (ii) agreeing to the option of reversing or revising the program after experience with partial implementation; (iii) introducing measures designed to accommodate distributional concerns; (iv) incorporating safety net measures as integral elements in the program; and (v) ensuring consistency of the overall policy strategy with national cultural values.

---

[3] Also of interest here is Tsikata (2003), who compares ownership issues and experience as they arose in Ghana and Tanzania.

[4] Campos and Root (1996, p. 76). Famous among the "mechanisms" were deliberation councils, mentioned in Chapter 3, comprising representatives from the private sector and the public sector. Each council assisted the government in formulating policies "that would enhance the performance of a particular segment of the private sector (if not the private sector as a whole)" [Campos and Root, 1996, p. 79].

Use of experts from prominent public and private interest organizations could prove particularly useful to a policy reform minded government that has, nevertheless, lost credibility with the populace (perhaps because it took too long to come up with a serious program of action), or to a regime that has just taken over the reins of political office. Any type of regime can invite a group of experts to draw up a policy reform program, to assure the citizens of the "objectivity" and utilitarian nature of such a program, and thereby gain the necessary political support for implementation. The government could, alternatively, consult various interest groups (business, labor, agricultural, university professors, etc.) and seek their reactions to its draft program. In the process, the preferences of these groups become evident, giving the government the opportunity to come up with a consensus program that, at the same time, addresses the underlying problem(s) of the country.

Major policy reform programs in the African continent tend to get introduced in crises. In such circumstances, the citizens seem to grant authority to a government they consider credible to begin implementation of a program but with an explicit or implicit understanding that the program will be revised if it proves unpopular during implementation. This, unfortunately, has resulted in interruptions of many programs supported by the IMF, necessitating constant renegotiations.

Distributional conflicts could cause delays in implementing reforms. Typically, to find consensus solutions, the programs include various devices that address distributional concerns, in order to secure the support of various groups. To balance distributional concerns of various groups in a country, in the interest of obtaining consensus and limiting implementation costs, reform programs often include ceilings on wage increases, on taxation of certain groups, on the speed of price liberalization, and on the adjustment of prices of parastatal goods and services. The challenge for policy formulation has been to contain any associated allocative inefficiencies and prevent degeneration of certain policies into wasteful patronage activities. For example, taxes and expenditures outside the normal budgetary processes (extrabudgetary funds) designed specifically to favor certain groups in order to obtain their political support, or simply to favor them for social reasons, have eroded policies of fiscal restraint in some countries and made difficult the assessment of effective taxation and protection of different commodities and services, while further opening doors to corrupt activities.

Safety-net programs have become major ways by which governments stave off social unrest and obtain political support from what could be a large portion of the population (see, e.g., Stewart, 1995). These are poverty alleviation and income maintenance programs targeted to the lowest income groups of the population. Temporary public works employment programs or demand-based social funds are examples of safety nets. Ghana's *Programme of Action to Mitigate the Social Costs of Adjustment* (PAMSCAD), introduced in 1987 in connection with its Economic Recovery Program launched in 1983, was the first broad-scale attempt in the continent at safety net programming in connection with structural adjustment. The program included support especially for community projects, redeployment of workers, and basic needs of vulnerable groups. Unfortunately, the program got bogged down by logistical and other implementation problems (including lack of staff and accounting issues that delayed disbursement of funds). The general assessment of the donors and others was that PAMSCAD, which ended in 1990, did not significantly mitigate the social costs of adjustment. Lack of country ownership was thought partly to be blamed (see Stewart, 1995).

When governments want political support for major policy reforms, they sometimes need to demonstrate that the reforms conform to or do not violate fundamental values of the societies; for these values are among focal points for economic policy. Hence, if a government becomes unsure about the consistency of its proposed reforms with the values and ideological focal points of the society, it will probably need to launch a frontal intellectual attack on these focal points to convince the citizens of the country that the focal points are themselves inconsistent with achieving a satisfactory (high) level of economic welfare.

Ownership and policy soundness

I have argued that adjustment programs need not be designed locally but that for ownership and hence full implementation they should as a minimum be always legitimated by the populace at large. I now want to underscore that the programs must also be sustainable. If a program is going to be supported by outsiders—in particular by powerful creditors—then the outsiders must be convinced of the sustainability of the economic policies before they would give their support. The country authorities also need to ensure that, despite their authority and the legitimation of the program, developments along the way would not induce the populace to withdraw its support. To obtain the support of the outsiders would normally require that: (1) the policies are well founded in accepted social scientific theory and international experience; (2) there is credible commitment of the government to the policies; and (3) there is adequate capacity of the state and society to implement the policies. Commitment of the government would be revealed by appropriate signaling—especially evidence of legitimation and the very content of the program itself. Similarly, signals of the willingness and capacity of the state and society to implement the program would include the sequencing of measures to take due account of state capacity to implement, a credible state capacity building program, and state-society cooperative frameworks to prevent policy reversals.

Policy-Based Conditionality and Its Critics

Conditionality could be seen, charitably, as a set of understandings reached by recipient countries with their donors/creditors on the conduct of economic policy. It emerges from a bargaining process between donors and recipients, with the equilibrium set of conditions determined by several factors. In principle, the objective is to arrive at a set of policies voluntarily agreed by both sides that would resolve the macroeconomic and/or structural (institutional and organizational) problems of the country well enough to bring the per capita income growth rate much closer to its potential, lower inflation, and improve the balance of payments prospects.

Role of conditionality

The main objectives of the understandings are to increase the probability of prompt repayment of debt and sometimes even to ensure that the funds (including grants) do not support policies inconsistent with the values of the creditors. In other words, the creditors/donors typically want the funds to be used productively, and ensure that the recipient government is able to collect taxes and the country able to generate the foreign exchange to facilitate timely repayment of any debt assumed. In some cases, creditors/donors may also want to have the country graduate out of some types of borrowing (or unrequited receipts) from them. In principle, then, conditionality is all about promoting sound policies that resolutely address the economic problems of the aid recipient country. As Ahmed, Lane and Schulze-Ghattas (2001), put it in writing about IMF conditionality: "conditionality provides safeguards to the IMF that the money it has lent is being used for the intended purpose—to facilitate the adjustment process—and that the member country will be able to repay what it has borrowed from the IMF's pool of funds (to which all of its member countries have contributed)." In addition, the understandings are really also constrained by obligations of members not to pursue certain policies except perhaps for temporary emergency purposes—such as exchange policies inimical to multilateral trade and payments (see, e.g., Johnson, 1977a, and IMFIEO, 2002).

Collier et al. (1997) have distinguished five objectives of conditionality, namely, inducement, selectivity, paternalism, restraint and signaling. *Inducement*, which is the dominant use of conditionality, is the offer of financial support in exchange for the country authorities introducing a certain set of policies. To Collier et al, the aid donor is buying the policies and hence really owns them, not the aid-recipient country. *Selectivity* is where the maintenance of a good policy environment is used as a condition for aid. This means, in the context of Collier et al, that the conditionality cannot at the same be an inducement since no change in policy is called for. *Paternalism* is where the aid is conditional on its being spent on particular goods or services. It is obvious that this kind of objective is not relevant for macroeconomic or broad structural reform programs, which are the arena where the conditionality debate is most interesting.

A reform-minded government may want to use conditionality as a *restraint*, basically hoping that the reforms would be protected from reversal by domestic political pressures both during its term of office and after. This use of conditionality has some affinity with the role that IMF and World Bank conditionality supposedly have played in many country programs. Namely, the two organizations have been said to be willing to take the blame for unpopular policies and thereby provide cover for governments. It seems clear that a government which uses conditionality in this way cannot easily claim ownership for a program even if all the policies contained in the program are its own, because it refuses to take full responsibility for the outcome of the program. *Signaling* is when conditionality is used to provide information to the private sector that the donor has given its seal of approval to the future policies of the country authorities. This objective is more popularly expressed in the context of IMF and World Bank as the financial support having a 'catalytic effect' in attracting other financial flows to the country, especially from the private sector. The catalytic or signaling effect works, of course, only if the conditionality has a reputation of indeed inducing sound policies by governments.

Context of conditionality

If African countries obtained capital inflows only in the form of foreign direct investment (FDI) or loans from private markets, then the whole controversy over conditionality would be unlikely. African governments, of course, borrow as they do because they want concessional interest rates. One can highlight four contexts in which African countries borrow money that invoke discussions on conditionality.

The first context is where African countries borrow to abate reductions in consumption and investment as a result of shortfalls in income due to temporary shocks in the world economy (e.g., a temporary unexpected fall in demand for the country's exports) or in the domestic economy (e.g., following a drought, flood or some other natural disaster). In this first context, no major policy changes are ordinarily needed; conditionality fights are extremely rare in the circumstances.

The second context is borrowing for specific projects involving human and physical capital formation, particularly for infrastructure, health facilities, and educational buildings and materials. Again, these kinds of borrowing typically require no major policy changes, at least at the macroeconomic and structural levels, although specific pricing and taxation policies often come up for discussion and countries have often found themselves having to reach understandings on user charges, ear-marking of government revenue, and creation of special blocked accounts to lodge foreign exchange earnings for making the transfer of the loan repayments. Invariably, it is policy on user charges for infrastructure projects like water supply and roads that begin to bring in difficult conditionality issues even at this level. The effect on the poor is a major concern of the typical African country, while the effect on efficiency (avoiding waste and misallocation of the services) and on the sustainability of the overall government budget are the typical concerns of the lender.

Third, African countries borrow to finance the adjustment costs (to help prevent reduced consumption and finance increased investment) of short-term stabilization and reforms requiring policy changes of some significance. The rationale for conditionality would be that the country got into serious problems, which threaten its long-term growth prospects, because of poor policies in the past or because a permanent change has occurred in its environment to which it has failed to adjust. Both the country and the creditor(s) may agree that policy changes are needed; still, they have often disagreed on the detailed content of policy reform. The policy reforms needed here tend especially to involve macroeconomic variables, the emphasis being on getting absolute and relative prices right and increasing domestic saving. This is a bigger arena of controversy than in the first two situations, because the changes in relative and absolute prices as well as budgetary changes that take place will normally have real consumption and income distributional effects with social consequences [see, e.g., Johnson and Salop (1980)]. Moreover, there may be serious disagreements over the impact on development, and fundamental differences of views on the appropriate development strategy of the country typically become apparent.

These disagreements over development strategy become magnified even more in reaching understandings for borrowing in the fourth context, namely, to help finance major structural reforms. Here, typical policies on the agenda include privatization of state-owned enterprises; reform (usually meaning liberalization) of commodity, labor, and financial markets; reform (again, liberalization) of external trade and currency markets; agricultural sector policies with emphasis on price reforms and shutting down of state marketing organizations; civil service reform with bias towards reducing the size of the civil service; government expenditure reform, often with stress on containing the government wage bill relative to GDP; and reform of taxation and tax administration. Apparent is that the discussions on borrowing in contexts three and four are about economic governance of the economy as a whole.

Criticisms of policies

The international financial organizations (IFOs) insist on conditionality, in part because they want thc organizations to influence the policies pursued by the African countries. They believe that the organizations know exactly the kinds of policies that would change the development fate of those countries, if only the latter would fully implement the policies. Many Africans, on their part, seem to want greater control over policymaking even in the context of conventional conditionality, because in their view the policies they have had to adopt under conditionality have so far proved inappropriate to deal with their major economic problems, and sometimes have even had deleterious effects on ordinary persons.

Vociferous criticism of policies in connection with conditionality has a long tradition in the African continent. Mkandawire and Soludo (1999) provide, perhaps, the most coherent summary *in print* of so-called 'African perspectives' on structural adjustment programs (SAPs). They criticize the SAPs for downplaying the structural and global factors and overplaying the role of domestic policies in explaining Africa's poor economic performance. They also criticize the SAPs for having failed to engender sustained economic development, structural diversification, and poverty reduction in the continent. Instead, for them, the microeconomic and macroeconomic policies have hampered and sometimes even reversed industrialization, human capital formation, state capacity building, export diversification, and poverty alleviation.

Mkandawire and Soludo (1999) extensively discuss specific policies associated with SAPs. They attack policies such as privatization; emphasis on getting prices right in agriculture in contrast to other factors that influence agricultural production and productivity; opposition to selective intervention policies for industrial development and the consequent absence of a coherent industrial policy that go beyond the call for leaving matters to the market; emphasis on incentive neutrality in trade policy and discouragement of import-substitution policies to support export promotion; the stress on general financial sector liberalization including discouragement of selective credit controls and encouragement of market-determined real interest rates; and the failure to properly integrate poverty alleviation strategies in SAPs as opposed to what they consider ad hoc tacking on of initiatives to the core of the SAPs. The Mkandawire-Soludo criticisms mirror, *to some extent*, the perspectives of many critics outside the continent. [see, for example, Bird (1996), Goldsmith (2000), Helleiner (1994), Sender (1999), and Stewart (1994)].

Criticisms of conditionality

According to critics, conditionality as an attempt to buy policy change with financial aid ignores certain countervailing factors. Most notably, the aid by alleviating fiscal and payments pressures could daunt the incentive for policy change. This aggravates a time inconsistency problem, namely, that once the aid was received unless the government wanted the reform it could reverse it. In addition, when a government does not sustain the reform, it has not been typically punished, for reasons that include the fact that to cut off the recipient country from further assistance would aggravate its payments problem thereby threatening its ability to repay the very aid donors, where relevant (see, e.g., Collier, 2001).

Some critics see conditionality as very often essentially coercive. Tony Killick, for instance, states: "Conditionality is....characterized by the use of financial leverage to promote donor objectives." This is not meant to insinuate that the policies are necessarily bad for the recipient country, but only to emphasize that negotiations involving conditionality are not simply pure 'policy dialogues,' and that the conditions are not typically consensual between recipient countries and their creditors/donors, particularly where the international financial organizations are concerned (see Killick, 1997, and Killick et al., 1998).

The overarching theme is that as a matter of empirical fact, the critics argue, policy-based conditionality has not generally achieved its ultimate objective of ensuring sound policies, because the programs with conditionality are not sufficiently implemented, and this in turn is mainly related to the fact that the recipient countries do not own the policies and also do not get punished for failure to implement policies or for policy reversals. Policies of recipients change, the argument goes, for reasons that are exogenous to aid finance. As Killick et al (1998, p.165) put it:

> "in the general case, conditionality is not an effective means of improving economic policies in recipient countries. The incentive

> system, most notably the absence of a credible threat of punishment of non-implementation, is usually inadequate in the face of differences between donors and governments about objectives and priorities...."
> (Italics in original dropped).

Bird (1998, p. 107) argues that implementation of IMF and World Bank conditionality "lies on a knife edge." As he puts it:

> "There may be some governments that negotiate programs with little intention of carrying them through. There may be others where, although the intention is to implement the program, the effects of the program turn out to differ from what was expected, with the difference being either that there are higher net benefits[5] or higher net costs, and in these circumstances, governments dynamically adjust their behavior; noncompliance is the result. It is, therefore, unsurprising that poor implementation is a common feature of IFI-supported programs."

Collier (1997) also notes that because using aid as a means to buy policy reform, via the instrument of conditionality, has not worked, it has prevented countries with good policies from separating themselves within a set of countries that as a group, such as the African countries, have low risk-weighted return rating among investors because of poor policies on average. In a similar vein, Dollar and Svensson (2000) argue in general that their results "support the view that the best justification for policy-based lending is as a commitment technology for sincere reformers. However, the effectiveness of this technology is undermined if adjustment loans are given indiscriminately."

According to the critics, the poor relationship between conditionality and program implementation has meant, among other things, that agreeing a program supported by the multilateral financial organizations (notably the IMF and the

[5] The point here, according to Bird (1998, p. 106) is that if, for example, the balance of payments situation of the country improves—say because of improved income terms of trade—"the government has the opportunity to regain independent control over economic policy, and disengaging from the IFIs may now enhance the government's political prospects."

World Bank) has not served to raise the credibility of a country's policies in the eyes of potential investors. In other words, conditionality has not in itself engendered good policies and has had no perceptible catalytic effect in attracting private capital. If anything, it has had the effect of wasting resources on poor policy environments.

Rodrik finds "no evidence that multilateral lending has acted as a catalyst for private flows" (Rodrik, 1996, p. 190). At the same time he finds "some evidence that World Bank lending has focused on countries with brighter economic futures (once levels of indebtedness are accounted for)." This would seem to indicate that these loans have been assessed by the private sector, and correctly so, as having little or no information content in predicting where it is most profitable for them to lend and invest among the low- and middle-income countries of the world. Stijn Claessens in his comment on Rodrik's paper pointed out, however, that causality tests show that for many countries foreign direct investment (FDI) "is not related to any other capital flow" (Claessens, 1996, p.201). Indeed, he asserted that, in general, "FDI investors do not need much signaling, perhaps not even by multilaterals..." Moreover, the regression results of Rodrik in his view "make clear that the impact of multilateral lending should be measured not by subsequent private flows alone, but also by its developmental impact, including growth, poverty reduction, and increased domestic confidence (as reflected in investment, for example)" (Claessens, 1996, p.202).

Selectivity

Killick, in line with others, has argued for an approach to aid and adjustment grants and loans that virtually eliminates the need for hard-core conditionality (see Kahler, 1992, Killick, 1997, and Killick et al., 1998). Killick at al (1998, p. 11) think of hard-core conditionality as "measures that would not otherwise be undertaken or not within the time frame desired by the lender, promised involuntarily by governments in urgent need of the money to which the measures are attached." The approach suggested by Killick et al would be founded on four principles, namely, ownership, selectivity, support, and dialogue.

Proposals

Selectivity calls for "greater concentration of aid on governments with a demonstrated commitment to the pursuit of sound policies" (Killick et al, 1998, p. 179). Such a demonstration of commitment could, for instance, come from prior action. For, as Kahler (1992) shows: "prior commitment and policy action (taken before external support is offered) is a good predictor of successful implementation." Rodrik (1996) also supports concentrating loans on countries with good policy environments. Of importance to underscore is that programs selected for support would be owned by the country. Such an approach still would permit aid for some special reasons, such as for post-war (or post-chaos) reconstruction and rehabilitation or to support certain political and economic regime changes.

The challenge is deciding the extent to which selectivity should be backward-looking (ex post) and the extent to which it should be forward-looking (ex ante), the latter permitting a credible commitment to introduce and maintain a good policy environment to qualify a candidate country for selection. Collier (1997), for example, thinks it essential that selectivity be *ex post*, that is, backward-looking. Aid should flow to "already reformed policy environments instead of attempting to buy reform in bad policy environments." In his view (Collier, 2001, p.75), to condition aid "on policy *change* rather than policy *level* leads not only to inefficient allocations between countries, but also to inefficient allocations over time." A democratically elected government, for instance, that supposedly has a good policy level but is unwilling to change policies just before an election may find its aid finance squeezed at a very inappropriate time. He states (Collier, 1997, p. 72):

> "With *ex post* selectivity, donors would come in behind reforms rather than anticipating them. For the early stages of reforms, perhaps the first three years, the government would be reforming without aid, establishing a good policy environment. Governments which reformed in this way would unequivocally establish with investors that they were reforming because they believed that the reforms were needed. They would also have to justify the policy changes to their domestic populations in terms of their underlying sense rather than in terms of donor conditions."

Once a country is selected, 'support' in terms of financial assistance should be determined by the financing requirements rather than the policy reforms stipulated. In short, there should be de-linking of conditionality and finance. Support can also come in the form of technical assistance, in a form that enhances self-reliance in recipient countries and hence fosters ownership. In particular, the technical assistance would be demand-driven. The experts should also be independent and the recipient country free to choose, at it wishes, the supplier of the technical assistance.

'Dialogue' in Killick's framework would also foster ownership while improving economic policy. It would basically comprise analytical work and advice given directly by representatives of the donor, at the early stages of decisionmaking, for use by the authorities of the country as it sees fit in its decisionmaking. The dialogue would allow the donor to influence policy without imposing conditionality, and hence without coercion.

Skepticism

Khan and Sharma (2001, p. 17) criticize the ex post selectivity approach, among other reasons because "it would exclude a large number of member countries not having access to international capital markets from IMF lending, and this would be fundamentally inconsistent with the rights of all members to IMF resources under the Articles of Agreement." Unfortunately they discussed only a particular recommendation, which would have, inter alia, IMF financial support made at penalty rates. Most believers in selectivity do not argue with the current IMF interest rate policy. Also, as argued below, selectivity could be governed by rules that are forward-looking. Thus access of members need not be adversely affected, while the incentive to implement sound policies would, as otherwise a member would not be selected for financial support.

Khan and Sharma (2001, p. 17) also argue that selectivity "provides no guarantees against undesirable changes in the domestic policy stance (perhaps through changes in government), and thus may weaken the safeguards on IMF resources." It is difficult to see how traditional (policy-based) conditionality provides such guarantees after the funds have been disbursed, and the experience is that it does not. This is one reason why certain countries continue to return to the IMF repeatedly to borrow. They also argue (Khan and Sharma, 2002, p. 29) that there "is also the serious problem of what the IMF should do when a country's policies deteriorate. The disqualification of a country may itself trigger a crisis" This criticism would not apply to forward-looking selectivity. In addition, once a regime of selectivity is in place and known to countries, it is bound to influence their behavior, and one would tend to see fewer cases of policies deteriorating, since the Good Samaritan would no longer exist. Even the Independent Evaluation Office of the IMF sees greater selectivity as a tool that could be used to address the problem of prolonged use of IMF loans, "although this will always involve difficult judgments" (Goldsbrough et al, 2002, p. 37; see, also, IMFIEO, 2002).

A case for ex ante selectivity

This author also would support greater selectivity in aid giving. But well-designed *ex ante* selectivity can be superior to ex post selectivity. First of all, the thought process used to arrive at ex post selectivity is ultimately based on a simple but powerful finding: donors are unwilling to punish countries that do not keep their promise to pursue (introduce or sustain) policy reform. From that, the proponents leap onto the next step: a direct solution—encourage donors to punish those who do not keep their promises—is not possible, because presumably donors will not change their behavior, for reasons including the incentives of their staff to push money at recipients. That may be true. But then the question becomes: why do the proponents of ex post selectivity believe that they have any chance of convincing donors to adopt that approach? The question is extremely hard to answer, especially when one attempts to do so against the backdrop of the finding that much aid is not being given systematically to encourage or support policy reform.

In addition, ex post selectivity projects the future using only information from the past. This is unfortunate, especially since the economic policy environment depends crucially on the political environment. If a proponent of ex post selectivity finds out via perfect foresight that soon after a certain aid is disbursed, a change in the policy environment would occur, because of political developments, such a proponent, I believe, would prefer to hold the aid and wait, unless of course the aid is regarded as payment for past efforts rather for "keeping up the good work."

In my view, ex ante selectivity could be designed so as to be both forward-looking and backward-looking. A good predictor of the future cannot ignore information from the past, so it would incorporate the information used by ex post selectivity. Given recipient country ownership, selectivity (ex ante) would then be guided by a simple rule: the aid (financial support) would be given when the donor has reasonable belief that the funds would be effective in helping to solve the country's economic problems. The effectiveness of the aid would come from the fact that the program of the country contains sound policies *as a package* (not item by item) and outcomes, as assessed by the donor, and the expectation by the donor that the policies would be implemented, inter alia because they have been legitimated by the populace and the country has appropriate institutional and organizational capacity to implement them. Technical assistance would be given if the recipient country determines that it needs such assistance in specific areas to enhance its capacity to formulate and implement sound policies and if the country chooses the donor as the supplier of the technical assistance.

Reforming Conditionality: With and Without Selectivity

The general consensus is that the number of conditions attached to loans and grants has become too large. The IMF has perhaps been under greatest fire in this regard, particularly with respect to conditionality related to structural factors. The organization accepts this criticism and has been making effort to streamline conditionality [see, e.g., Khan and Sharma (2001, 2002)]. But simply streamlining is not enough. To argue in favor of traditional conditionality is to argue that conditionality improves the prospects for having sound policies and for ensuring implementation. There is general agreement that ownership not conditionality is the important element for effective program implementation. In the absence of ownership, programs have not typically been implemented. Policy-based conditionality, also, cannot guarantee timely repayment of loans and hence safeguards to IMF and World Bank resources; for it cannot guarantee the *sustainability* of sound policies (that is, an absence of policy reversal) after the funds have been disbursed. Only country ownership, because of its appropriate legitimation process, can prevent adverse domestic political developments and guarantee sustainability of policies. Thus, again, for timely repayment of the debt, country ownership is the essential requirement not conditionality.

The issue then becomes whether without conditionality the soundness of programs would decline. Perhaps IMF and World Bank conditionality could influence the soundness of programs if it influences IMF and World Bank effort in country program design and implementation. Hence, the question becomes whether desirable IMF and World Bank effort (say because of weak capacity of a government and the inability to obtain technical assistance and advice from other sources) will necessarily be adversely affected—that is, precluded from being supplied—by the absence of traditional conditionality. It is easy to see that this need not be so. The quantum of IMF and World Bank effort is not perforce determined by conditionality; only the *nature* of the effort should be so determined. Indeed, donor country effort (in preparation and supervision activities) does not seem to influence significantly the success or failure of programs. For example, in the case of World Bank's loans, Dollar and Svenson (2000) find no evidence, "that any of the variables under the World Bank's control affect the probability of success of an adjustment loan" (p. 4).

Floating tranches

It has been suggested that conditionality could be made flexible, by employing a device often dubbed 'floating tranches' (see, e.g., Khan and Sharma, 2001, 2002). The idea is that the lender—say the IMF—would agree with the authorities of the country on the policy measures but would allow the country some freedom to decide on the timing of the implementation of some of the measures; stipulated tranches of the funds would be accessible only after the particular policy or policies have been implemented. It is never suggested that the implementation of all policies would qualify for floating tranche conditionality, since timely introduction of some policies could be critical for the rest of the program and since sequencing usually matters in policy implementation.

Outcome-based conditionality

Another suggestion for reforming conditionality is to move away from 'policy-based' conditionality to 'outcome-based' conditionality [see Khan and Sharma (2001, 2002)]. By this is meant that conditionality could focus on certain intermediate and final targets and agreement on a time pattern for the achievement of specific quantitative levels of these variables. For instance, variables such as inflation, gross international reserves, or economic growth could be selected for outcome-based conditionality. Many outcome variables (related to foreign reserves, the budget, and credit, for instance) likely to be used in this approach tend already to feature in conditionality, even when not as performance criteria or even as structural benchmarks. Outcome variables such as growth (of gross domestic product) and overall balance of payments will not, for many countries, be available more frequently than on an annual basis and hence not really usable for conditionality tied to quarterly or semi-annual access to funds borrowed. Still the spirit of the suggestion could be captured by avoiding certain policy variables such as exchange rates, tariffs, interest rates, specific commodity prices, reserve requirements, and public sector wages as elements of conditionality.

Outcome-based conditionality with selectivity

Collier et al. (1997) favor a redesign of conditionality which selects countries to support on the basis of their policy environment and then conducting periodic assessment with the achievement of certain outcomes becoming the condition for continued financial support. For instance, future financial support could be made conditional on the achievement of certain levels of growth, after controlling for influences outside the control of the authorities. Outcome-based conditionality related to other objectives such as poverty alleviation could also be designed. In this context, review periods for assessment may need to be one-year or longer.

Gunning (2001, p. 136) states, among other points, that "outcomes-based allocation promotes accountability by signaling that donors have no involvement in policy choices, being interested only in results." Gunning, like other proponents, argues that outcome-based conditionality cum selectivity would also enable aid to play effectively the signaling and restraint roles denied it under the current regime of policy-based conditionality without selectivity. Namely, aid would provide credible evidence of sound policy environments and could be used by recipient governments to resist policy reversals, "by pointing out that such reversals would lead to a loss of aid" (Gunning, 2001, p. 136).

Credible evidence of ownership and implementation capacity

Consistent with what was said earlier in the chapter, in the discussion of selectivity, I would suggest replacing traditional conditionality with a different form of conditionality: namely, to qualify for aid (gift or loan) support, a country's representatives must provide adequate proof (credible evidence) to the donor that it (the recipient country) accepts full responsibility (ownership) for a program considered sound by both sides and that it has in place appropriate institutional and organizational capacity to fully implement the program. An implication is that in the interest of safeguarding its resources the lender (for example the IMF or the World Bank) must approve the country's program and establish proof of ownership as well as the existence of adequate implementation capacity. Funds would be disbursed on the basis of their total contribution to the reform effort of the country, rather than on the basis of some specific set of policy implementation schedule.

Operationalizing Conditionality with Ex Ante Selectivity

I have argued for ex ante selectivity. Agreeing conditionality in this framework would entail establishing the reality of ownership, soundness of the program (policies and outcomes), and adequate implementation capacity of the authorities.

Proof of ownership

The procedure for assessing ownership must be forward-looking. To conclude that ownership is real, one must have convincing evidence that effective ownership prevailed at the initiation of the program and that the probability of policy reversal due to political changes is very low, either because such changes are unlikely in the foreseeable future or because any new political leadership likely to emerge would continue to implement the program. Hence, the assessors must be armed with a theory of that state (predatory, interest group model, democratic and competitive model, etc.) and how the political institutions of the country work. This would, inter alia, facilitate a model of the structure and efficiency of the government as an organization (civil service bureaucracy, etc), and permit an overall assessment of both the commitment and the capacity of government officials and employees to implement the program. Intra-government rivalries and communication would be important elements in the above analyses and assessments.

The overarching concern is to make sure that, without coercion, virtually everyone in the country is committed to the policies in the program; namely, that there is national consensus on the policies. Without such commitment and consensus the risk of policy reversal cannot be estimated with confidence. The onus must be on the authorities (the government) to come up with the evidence of commitment and consensus. Knowledge of the system would enable the assessor to form a rational judgment on the credibility of that evidence.

Some guidelines are possible on the methodology of assessing the evidence. Indicators of the existence of ownership would comprise, as a minimum, a 'political legitimation indicator' (or test) and an 'economic model indicator' (or test). The former would consist of convincing evidence that the program has evolved out of decisionmaking processes that, in the past history of the country, have resulted in effective cooperation, among all major parties and interest groups, engendering collective agreement, without coercion, on major policy issues. Hence the elements in the evidence would depend on the specific circumstances of a country, including the political regime, ethnolinguistic composition, and consensus building mechanisms. The 'economic model indicator' would comprise convincing evidence that the program is consistent with past (especially recent) economic policies of the country. Apart from this backward-looking element, this latter indicator must also have a forward-looking aspect, which could include public pronouncements of the current government about its future economic policies and the institutional and organizational arrangements to implement those policies.

Soundness of policies

Ownership is not sufficient for ‘selection’ for support. The soundness of the policies would be also important. The policies of the program are sound if as a package they are assessed as adequate to achieve the objectives and if the objectives are considered reasonable in light of the economic circumstances of the country. Basically, for a macroeconomic program, the exercise would involve assessing the reasonableness of objectives—over some period of time (say three to five years)—such as per capita economic growth, balance of payments, external debt and debt service relative to GDP, and inflation. The past and prospective policies that affect these objectives would be assessed as well. This may involve evaluating both macroeconomic and microeconomic policies, such as interest rate policy or policies to control some monetary variable, real exchange rate policy, external tariff policy as well as policies affecting infrastructure, labor market and human capital, government efficiency, and microeconomic policies in important sectors such as agriculture. Neglect of the microeconomic policies would risk not being able to make an informed judgment about the likelihood of the package of policies being adequate to attain the economic growth objective, especially since microeconomic, including so-called sectoral, policies could neutralize the favorable impact of macroeconomic policies on particular sectors.

Alternatively, of course, it is possible to take an approach somewhat similar to the outcome-based approach to conditionality. This would involve agreeing the objectives and then leaving the country the freedom to decide the means to achieve the objectives, the means being perhaps subject to constraints due to certain international obligations such as requirements of membership in IMF or the World Trade Organization (WTO). In this case, country teams would not have any obligation to pass judgment on the adequacy of policies, and financial support would begin only after the country had achieved certain objectives. Since, in principle, financial support has positive effects on the targets, the initial level of the objectives would be set taking into account the absence of any financial support. A few African countries may find this approach more to their liking and in this author's view they should have the opportunity to use it, without compromising the requirement of ownership.

Country implementation capacity

Given ownership and soundness of the policy framework, the next logical step is to test for implementation capacity. Although implementation capacity has been taken into account in establishing conditionality associated with IMF financial support, still, in a few cases, low implementation capacity has played a role in program interruptions (see Mecagni, 1999). This often means that expected technical assistance to remedy capacity weaknesses did not materialize in time or was not as effective as projected. Capacity problems can arise in any area, but budgetary reforms and privatization have proved particularly troublesome for a number of the African countries.

Conclusion

A question that often arises is whether external forces constrain African countries' freedom to exercise ownership rights over their policymaking. In response, I would posit that if African political leaders create good policy environments and thereby put in place institutional and organizational structures to design and implement sound and legitimated programs, they can demand country ownership of their reform programs. With a good policy environment, the typical African country can take certain initiatives in exercising its ownership rights. In addition, whether in drawing up a program or in designing and implementing particular subprograms emanating from it, nationals would decide how they want to utilize foreign experts, governments, and international organizations. Most of these countries would not be reluctant to use foreigners for training and technical assistance. They would also selectively use foreign experts as advisors, although it would be important that these advisors participate in local capacity building rather than only in performing specific technical or analytical tasks.

In Uganda, for instance, Mutebile (1999) describes a capacity building program over which Uganda intended to have ownership. "A strategy and program of action were developed between 1991 and 1993 through consultations with all the major stakeholders, including government ministries, institutions of higher learning, technical education institutes, private sector organizations—such as the Uganda Manufacturers Association and the Uganda Bankers Association—accountants, members of the various consulting professions, and the donor community. These consultations culminated in Uganda's Capacity Building Plan, which was published in 1994." Apart from civil service reform and attempts to build the foundation for sound decisionmaking in government (good database, well-trained analysts and technicians, measures to attract and retain skilled Ugandans, supporting independent research institutes and programs outside government), a noteworthy aspect of the program were measures to foster what Mutebile calls "private sector capacity building," for example, "through United States Agency for International Development grants to the Uganda Manufacturers Association Consultancy and Information Services." Another noteworthy characteristic manifested in the program was that ownership not eschew requesting external finance or technical assistance—only that the authorities would determine the priorities and manage the process.

5

Ethnicity

Since independence, the leaders of African states have reacted to ethnicity—ethnic consciousness and mobilization for effective ethnic group demands on the state—in three major ways. There are those who have exploited it, to galvanize solidarity of their particular ethnic group, for their political ends. Some other leaders branded ethnicity as false consciousness, and in consequence decided either to ignore it or to take decisive steps to suppress it for being harmful to the process of modern nation state building [for a critique of these attitudes see, for example, Hameso (1997), Doornbos (1998), and Jerman (1998)]. But probably the majority of the political leaders have come to believe that ethnicity is a thorny socio-political reality of their countries, and have reacted with formal and informal initiatives (strategies) to manage this ethnicity in order to prevent or limit costly (especially violent) ethnic conflicts.

The major ethnic struggles in Africa are over control of the center (the state), in order to dominate decisionmaking within three arenas: (1) use of government power and authority; (2) government employment; and (3) income distribution among residents across geographic regions of a country. In the first arena, there is fear especially about governmental use of its instruments of force (military and police) and of its discretionary power to alter institutions and organizations. The second arena of struggle is big because of the importance of government in formal employment, while the third arena is especially prominent where mineral and petroleum resources are substantial and rather unequally distributed across geographic regions of the country.

Of importance are legitimated rules to control the center and the distribution of the benefits flowing from it and organizational arrangements to enforce the rules. Against this background, there are two main objectives of this chapter. First, I want to support the thesis that stable processes and rules can be found to reduce ethnic consciousness and mobilization for ethnic group demands (ethnicity) in African countries. The stable equilibrium determination process for constitutional design discussed in chapter 2 can be utilized to this end; the chapter demonstrates the existence of focal points embedded in the cultures of the societies, which could play a central role in the use of the process. Such a demonstration is important to support the claim that a slow evolutionary process is not inevitable to achieve important stable political and social institutions (including constitutions), despite the fact that the modern African countries were created out of societies brought together mainly by European colonization. As a result, attempts to manage ethnic relations should not merely focus on short-term power sharing arrangements among the groups, while ignoring or downplaying constitutional and fundamental organizational reforms utilizing processes that would promote the legitimacy and hence stability of such reforms.

Second, in the chapter, I underscore the importance of civil society agency in engendering appropriate constitutional reform. The intention is not to assert that such agents will promptly emerge in all countries. Rather, the speed with which such agents do emerge will greatly influence how quickly one observes the changes occurring, mainly via the effect on the popular demand for the reforms. The chapter outlines what persons will be doing when they are acting as agents facilitating the emergence of the rules. From a normative perspective, one could rationalize these as actions that persons who see themselves as potential or actual societal leaders should take to promote the demand for constitutional reforms utilizing stability enhancing processes.

The rest of the chapter is organized as follows. The next section, on ethnicity and group solidarity, makes the point that the road from group solidarity and selection to ethnicity and ethnic conflict is a long one. This is followed by a section discussing the popular consociational democratic solutions, outlining some of their costs and weaknesses. I then continue a major theme introduced in chapter 2, namely, that since independence African citizens have failed to establish their major political and social institutions via processes that underscore the pluralism of their countries. I give examples of experiments in recent constitutional reforms in the continent that fail to apply processes mimicking the stable equilibrium determination process described earlier. The two following sections then focus, respectively, on the nature of focal points embedded in the cultures, which should facilitate stable equilibrium determination processes, and the potential role of civil society leadership in helping to create enabling environments for the processes. The final section of the chapter concludes with comments on ethnicity, cooperation and economic policymaking. [1]

Ethnicity and Group Solidarity

Ethnicity as a topic, in Africa, is prominent particularly for those cases where violent conflicts have erupted, such as in Angola, Burundi, Democratic Republic of Congo, Mozambique, Nigeria, Rwanda, South Africa, Sudan, Uganda, and Zimbabwe [see, for example, Deng, et al (1996), Eller (1999), Glazer and Moynihan (1975), Lemarchand (1998), Ndikumana (1998), Prunier (1995), Rothchild (1997), and Zartman (1991, 1997)]. As Talcott Parsons (1975, p. 56) states, an ethnic group is "a group the members of which have, both with respect to their own sentiments and those of non-members, a distinctive identity

[1] The chapter follows closely the analysis in Johnson (2005b).

which is rooted in some kind of a distinctive sense of its history." As regards the distinctive identity, "common culture is probably the most important general core, but it is a culture which has some feature of temporal continuity often reaching into an indefinite past" (Parsons, 1975, p. 57).

Distinctive cultural identity among groups does not in itself necessarily engender ethnicity. Ethnicity fundamentally begins with solidarity among persons (for analyses of solidarity, see, e.g., Hechter, 1987, and Lindenberg, 2002). But the road from group solidarity and selection to ethnicity and ethnic conflict is a long one. Although research relating ethnolinguistic fractionalization and economic growth typically fails to control for this consideration, researchers, on the whole, have stressed that ethnicity is consciousness of difference and of salience of that difference, as well as mobilization and organization around that difference. In short, the members of an ethnic group, whose consciousness gives rise to ethnicity, constitute a segment of a larger social whole, and their consciousness engenders a movement with goals (Eller, 1999, pp. 8-16). Ethnicity itself gives rise to violent conflicts when there are circumstances (including adverse economic shocks) that cause groups to want to fight to achieve their objectives—perhaps because of a feeling of grave injustice or insecurity with no hope of fair treatment or remedy under normal due process, including within the extant economic "system."

Popular Approaches to "Managing" Ethnicity and the Costs

When ethnicity engenders periodic violent conflicts, it is generally accepted that one must deal with the *basic causes* of the tension or conflict. Here, Lemarchand (1998) and others have underscored the power of memory. In addition to addressing the underlying causes of a conflict, *process* is important in ensuring the sustainability of the outcome of negotiation or mediation, particularly when the intention is outright resolution of a conflict. Indeed, the process itself may influence the chances of reaching any agreement at all. For instance, in the Hutu-Tutsi problem in Burundi and Rwanda, credible and sustainable power sharing arrangements have been difficult to negotiate. Lemarchand sees the emphasis on collective guilt as a major obstacle. He writes: "The notion of collective guilt is the principal obstacle to national reconciliation. To hold all Tutsi collectively responsible for human rights violations is hardly more convincing than to assume that the hundreds of thousands of Hutu refugees in eastern Congo were all involved in the 1994 genocide" (Lemarchand, 1998, p. 11). Conflict resolution experts and intermediaries are also finding useful the method of *healing* used in South Africa.

Approaches

While alert to approaches to resolve violent conflicts, African countries have been experimenting with strategies and actions to prevent such conflicts, which could be classified into four types, along lines of consociational democracies discussed by Lijphart (1977, especially pp. 25-52), namely, grand coalition, mutual veto, proportionality, and segmental autonomy and federalism; the mutual veto has been at times replaced or supplemented by what one could call a "qualified majority" approach (see also the discussion of Rothchild, 1997, pp 25-58).

The *grand coalition* comes in different forms; essentially, though, it is coalition and power sharing at the center. A good example would be having representation (not necessarily proportionately) of all the major ethnic groups (or political parties, where these tend to be split along ethnic lines) in the cabinet (the political center). In practice, grand coalition formulae are not written into the constitution in African countries but are left to "enlightened" political leaders to implement "reasonable" power sharing formulae.

As to the pure *mutual veto*, the approach is typically to have an understanding or a norm whereby the government in certain cases will simply refrain from proposing a law or putting into effect certain desired government initiatives objectionable to some ethnic group(s), even though the majority of the population wants to proceed with the law or policy. A good example of the *qualified majority approach* is the 1999 Constitution of the Federal Republic of Nigeria, which specifies that, in the Presidential elections, for a candidate to be elected he or she should win a simple majority of the total number of votes cast as well as at least one-quarter of the votes cast in each of at least two-thirds of the states in the Federation and the Federal Capital Territory, Abuja. Indeed, both the mutual veto and qualified majority approaches could be used effectively to institute decisionmaking by virtual consensus, for certain laws and policies. A qualified majority approach works better being formalized, while the mutual veto can work smoothly even when it remains only a convention or an understanding.

Proportionality is a significant refinement and extension of the grand coalition approach. At the top level of government, proportionality could be introduced by specifying that certain major ethnic groups be represented proportionately in the cabinet. Alternatively, or in addition, the proportionality could simply be understood to mean that attempts would be made to ensure that all ethnic groups are fairly treated in the allocation of senior civil service positions and government financial resources (subsidies, scholarships, etc.), and that as much as possible the shares of ethnic groups would be proportional to their relative size in the population. In the limit, it becomes essentially a quota system. Of course, strict proportionality is likely to be impossible to achieve when the number of ethnic groups is large. Some method would then be found to combine groups to reduce the number for application of the principle. Alternatively, certain ethnic groups may simply be considered too small to warrant detailed attention in a proportionality arrangement. As in the case of the mutual veto, convention typically replaces law in the application of this principle. Hence, political leaders, even in the absence of explicit and formal arrangements to that effect, will often practice so-called "tribal balance."

Segmental autonomy involves giving local autonomy to an ethnic group to manage aspects of its society. This could involve giving it legal jurisdiction over some issues (e.g., domestic and "cultural" matters). Where the ethnic groups are regionally separated, this could take the form of regional autonomy over many legal, economic, and political matters. Increasing the scope and autonomy of local governments as an element in managing ethnicity has led to *federalism* in Nigeria and Ethiopia.

Costs and weaknesses

There are social costs associated with the above strategy and actions, which effectively tax the population as a whole, and some other serious weaknesses as well. First, in order to achieve ethnic balance, central government cabinets get bloated and their bureaucracies politicized. Indeed, positions get created that would not otherwise be there, such as special advisers, to ensure representation of particular ethnic interests at senior political levels. Second, local governments can proliferate in the attempt to satisfy demands for autonomy or equity in distribution of certain public goods.

Third, and related to the second, when the ethnic management techniques include federalism or segmental autonomy, the country can end up with too much government, from an economic efficiency standpoint. Namely, there is an incentive for every region dominated by a sizable ethnic group to demand its own local government, and every local government can end up with a large bureaucracy of offices and departments, and sometimes with locally supported bodies like universities and public enterprises that require subsidies to survive. The inefficiencies could be especially serious when the major taxes of the country get assessed, collected and distributed by the center, creating a common pool resource problem.

African countries have heightened their interest in constitutional measures of decentralization widely discussed in the academic literature [see, e.g., Brennan and Hamlin (2000), Frey and Eichenberger (1999), and Bardhan (2002)]. In that context, I agree with Brennan and Hamlin (2000, p. 260) that "the driving force in federal partitions is more often the desire to minimize the likelihood of conflict by satisfying the demand for local autonomy/identity, than to exploit possible efficiencies in the provision of local public goods." One problem in the African case is that ad hoc experimentation and bowing to the wishes of the ruling political faction have dominated decisionmaking on political and functional jurisdictional boundaries as well as governance arrangements for segmental autonomy. Hence, the decisions have not been much (if at all) informed by learned or free and open debate. In the recent decentralization moves in Sierra Leone, for example, which included the *Local Government Act 2004*, the country basically replicated the British experiment before 1961, in terms of the geographical divisions of regions and districts, while the Act itself is unlikely to prove effective in controlling corruption and encouraging efficiency in local government; in fact this author expects the Act to do quite the reverse.

Fourth, power sharing norms are highly unstable, in general, since enforcement regimes are typically weak at best or there is legitimacy deficit at worst. Hence, they often break down, and the political situation then degenerates into intensive struggles for power in which ethnic groups are used as instruments for increasing and maintaining political control. Kagwanja (2003), for example, discusses how a movement in Kenya, the *Mungiki*, which sprouted among the Kikuyu, was transformed from a moral ethnic movement to a politically tribal one. The idea of "moral ethnicity" is that ethnic identity provides "a space of relative autonomy from the centralizing ambitions of the postcolonial African state, moral community for cultural citizenship, and the focal point of resistance against tyranny." But the state managed "to penetrate, co-opt and fragment a movement based on moral ethnicity and to transform it into a disruptive force espousing political tribalism"(Kagwanja, 2003, pp. 28-29).

Fifth, with the traditional methods of managing ethnicity, a culture can develop in the economy with an overwhelming emphasis, in economic relations, on distribution to the detriment of production—pie sharing rather pie making. In such an environment, the management of ethnicity will not necessarily promote trust across ethnic groups, which over time is necessary for intensive, complex, and sustained cooperation.

Finally, in managing ethnicity, it is important not to employ strategies that implicitly assume that the current level of ethnicity will be given over the medium to long term. Indeed, ethnicity could decrease or increase spontaneously over time. I would conjecture, though, that the above attempts to manage ethnicity are likely to aggravate the problem and cause ethnicity to increase over time. The object of a concerted policy toward ethnicity, in the fragile national states of Africa, should be to reduce it over the medium to long term, given that economic growth and socio-political stability are important goals of the national communities that the citizens of the countries are vying to create.

Constitutional Reform

In Chapter 2, I argued that, at independence, in the typical African country, leaders (of the state and civil society) failed to take due account of the significance for future cooperation of the fact that their citizens really were members of several societies without a long history of emergence, via some evolutionary process, of their socio-political institutions to live together as citizens of one country. Unfortunately, the processes utilized in rewriting their constitutions since independence still have not been conducive to the emergence of evolutionary stable constitutions in the continent — constitutions which would reflect the values of the citizens, encompass the interests of future generations, and receive the voluntary consent of the current citizens.

African experiments in constitutional reform

There have been quite a few variations in the details of the processes African countries have utilized in changing/amending their constitutions since independence. The variations have been basically related to whether or not there is a constitutional convention or conference in addition to a constitutional commission; whether or not there is a referendum in addition to Parliamentary approval; and whether or not in the case of only Parliamentary approval the constitution must be passed by two parliaments, the first being dissolved after it approves the constitution. These days the pattern tends to be to have approval by Parliament of a draft which is then put to the people in a referendum. In every case, notably, the head of state has tremendous say in the selection of the members of the commission, convention or conference, as relevant, and the party of the President typically controls the Parliament at the time of discussion of the constitutional reform. Of course, if a Parliament does not exist at the time of the constitutional review, then the draft constitution will go straight from the commission or convention to the people. The drafters of the constitutions have also struggled with how to address multiculturalism in general and ethnolinguistic diversity in particular. Two recent examples are interesting as regards the processes utilized and the concern with ethnolinguistic diversity/ethnicity (more will be said later, in the chapter, on multiculturalism).

Kenya began a constitutional review process in late 2000, "meant to give the people of Kenya an opportunity to take part in the making of the constitution so that it reflects their wishes, aspirations, hopes and dreams for the future" (see, e.g., Hassan, 2001). The original intention was for the process to be guided by a Commission of "experts" appointed to draft a proposal for altering the extant constitution to be then debated by a National Constitutional Conference. The Commission finished its work and made recommendations for a new constitution based on analysis of views of the public collected through direct presentations and constituency constitutional forums; study of other constitutional systems; and consultations and hearings conducted by the Commission itself. The National Assembly (Kenya's parliament) had nominated the twenty-seven voting commissioners, who were formally appointed by the President; there were two non-voting ex-officio members—the Attorney General and a Secretary to the Commission.

The National Constitutional Conference (NCC) debated the preliminary draft to agree a proposed constitution. The NCC had 629 members, comprising the 29 Commissioners (with no voting rights at the NCC), 223 members of parliament, 210 representatives of districts, 41 representatives of political parties, and 126 civil society representatives from religious organizations, professional bodies, women's organizations, trade unions, non-governmental organizations, and other interest groups as the Commission determined. The Commission chairperson also chaired the NCC deliberations. It was specified in the Constitution of Kenya Review Act that all questions before the NCC should normally be determined by consensus. In the absence of a consensus, proposals to be included in the Constitution required at least two-thirds vote. Any such issue that could not be so resolved by the NCC was to be submitted to a national referendum; all registered Kenyan voters would be entitled to vote in the referendum. The final report of the NCC and a draft bill was presented to the National Assembly [see Kenya (2000)]. At the end of the process, including input from the National Assembly, the draft Constitution was rejected in a referendum in November 2005, following a bitter campaign between the 'yes' and 'no' camps. Apparently, the voters did not approve of changes made by the Parliament to the draft that had been given to them by the NCC. In early 2006, the President re-started the process by appointing a 15-member Committee of Eminent Persons to evaluate what went wrong and advise on how best to proceed with the constitutional review exercise. The evolution of the process still remained uncertain even as 2006 was coming to an end. Fortunately, the point of our discussion here is not likely to be affected, irrespective of when the process is finally completed.

That point is that, despite all the impressive precautions taken to ensure that the Constitution which emerges from the process will have widespread support and in the long-term national interest, the role of political office holders in the selection of Commissioners and NCC members prevents the process from being confidently described as a stable equilibrium determination process. In particular, there was no direct national election to membership of the NCC.

In *Ethiopia*, in July 1991, a national conference of 400 delegates, representatives of different political and ethnic groups, adopted a charter and formed a coalition transitional government. As Mengisteab (1997, p. 124) put it: "The transitional government of Ethiopia....quickly recognized the unconditional right of every nation in the country to self-determination, including the rights of self-governance, cultural autonomy, as well as secession." By "nation" Mengisteab is talking, of course, about what I would call ethnolinguistic society. The federal constitution that included these principles was drawn up and came into force on December 8, 1994, with 9 ethnolinguistically based states, each with a constitutional right to secede.

Although respect for cultural diversity is important in promoting civility in society, it is doubtful that political ethnification of the Ethiopian type is a sustainable solution that would, inter alia, maintain the integrity of the Ethiopian national state, unless a strategy is developed to reduce ethnicity over the longer term. In addition, as pointed out by Eva Poluha (1998), one should not assume in general that ethnic groups do not change over time; that people of the same ethnic group necessarily live together, geographically; that persons of the same ethnic group all have similar interests politically; and that ethnic group rights are more important than individual, class, or gender rights.

Focal Points for a Stable Equilibrium Determination Process

Focal points embedded in the cultures, relating to political institutions, distributive justice, and societal civility will facilitate constitutional reform utilizing a stable equilibrium determination process. As stated in Chapter 3, focal points are clues that provide keys or starting points to possible solutions to a problem—especially a coordination problem. The relevant focal points here would be those prominent in the basic cultural beliefs and behavior of the local ethnic groups. The stable equilibrium determination process should permit the potential focal points to come into play to facilitate the emergence of an evolutionary stable constitution. To give concreteness to the discussion, I illustrate with focal points that I believe would be pertinent across the bulk of the Sub-Saharan African continent.

The political constitution

By all accounts, the political institutions in most pre-colonial African societies reflected the will of their citizens (see Ayittey, 1991, pp. 71-272). In numerous pre-colonial African societies, the main challenge for political institutions was, typically, how to maintain the stability of the community while ensuring a reasonable degree of individual autonomy and liberty. The issue was not so much one of order versus anarchy (the Hobbesian challenge) or one of freedom versus oppression (the Lockean problem). Outside a few exceptions, order was not maintained by some strong central authority but by the voluntary cooperation of the members of the community. Also, freedom in most of those societies was not being guaranteed by some notion of individual rights but rather by the degree and nature of autonomy and liberty that individuals effectively demanded to remain members of the community. For the most part, therefore, a stable equilibrium emerged: the political unit that often resulted was one in which community interests were prior to those of individual interests but at the same time the individual was assured of enough autonomy and liberty to want to remain in the community voluntarily. It is no surprise that the equilibrium size of this basic political community was often very small, comprising predominantly persons with close kinship ties. Still, this is one type of mentality that persons with values from pre-colonial societies would have brought to the table at the dawn of independence, in any open constitutional discussion on the modern state. I briefly examine other aspects of this basic mind-set, which I believe was also present among persons from more complex societies—for example, centralized fairly large states—and in stateless societies.

Common to the basic political communities was respect for the adult individual as a responsible agent and a fundamental belief in the equal worth of all humans, and hence a conviction of the appropriateness of equal consideration of all persons in the community. Such Africans also had a strong regard for hierarchy. From those foundations (equal worth of all humans and respect for hierarchy) sprung certain views on rights, decisionmaking procedures, and obligations of all persons, which dominated their attitudes in designing their political institutions. Fortunately, even those cases of the 19th century—like Dahomey, the Zulu Kingdom, and Ashanti—where strong centralized states emerged, subscribed to these two principles. What then are the basic ideas that could have comprised the focal points, under the stable equilibrium determination process, to begin the evolution of stable political institutions in the majority of the African countries at the dawn of independence, which I believe would still be relevant as focal points today?

As regard *rights*, first, there is the right to be heard; in the basic pre-colonial African societies, this was evident in all aspects of conflict resolution, whether in informal settings, such as within the family or the neighborhood, or in formal settings such as in the courts, in meetings of the elders, advisory councils, or the towns and villages. In all these settings, the approach was to hear all sides of an argument or dispute fairly and openly before reaching a decision. The right to be heard, indeed, seems a common occurrence in human societies. Stuart Hampshire (2000), for example, has argued that adversary reasoning (public and private) in conditions of uncertainty is a universal feature of human behavior. So also is the creation and recognition of institutions within which such adversary reasoning takes place. From these he derives a view of justice as fairness in procedures—equal hearing of contrary views, institutionalized, and without domination or threat of force or imposition, by such tactics, of one conception of substantial justice. Here, I am talking about what may be termed "political justice."

As regards *decisionmaking*, the basic African political system showed a preference for unanimity in small groups, such as the Privy Council of a chiefdom, and for consensus in larger group meetings, such as the village assembly. Indeed, a small minority that found itself in disagreement with the overwhelming majority was often free to leave and form its own village—hence the dominance of kinship ties among the members of many of the political units. Alternatively, one may argue that it was thc small size of those societies that made unanimity and consensus on ordinary (as opposed to constitutional) issues stable in the decisionmaking apparatus. But one virtue was that unanimity and consensus reinforced the approach of hearing all sides, because that allowed a solution to be found that secured the support of all, which made enforcement less costly than otherwise. Little wonder that the Constitution of Kenya Review Commission tried to be diligent in listening to the people in cities, urban centers, and rural areas, individually and through organizations and groups.

The above rights and decisionmaking procedures left precolonial Africans with an *obligation* of obedience to the consensus of the group, an obligation that emerged out of a societal equilibrium process, and hence the freedom in extreme cases for persons who disagreed with the vast majority on some fundamental issue to leave and form their own political community.

With respect to *institutions and the organization of government*, focal points for a stable equilibrium determination process in a typical modern African state at the dawn of independence would, no doubt, have included various pre-colonial African conceptions of the state and its role; devolution of authority; the role of chiefs in general; incentives and disincentives related to governance; as well as the practical organization of their own pre-colonial governments that survived colonialism or that they remembered from the past (before colonialism) [see, e.g., Boahen, Ajayi, and Tidy (1986) and Ayittey (1991)]. There is no intention to get into the details here, but only to draw attention to the types of topics that would have influenced the discussion. Finally, at independence, the new states would certainly have included ideas for the constitution brought to the table by the western educated Africans. Hence, individual rights to freedom of speech and association and freedom from arbitrary arrest and detention, as well as equal protection under law—in a context in which no particular conception of the good was officially promoted—were clearly desired by the majority of the urban African (detribalized, evoloués) elites at the time of independence. As focal points in any attempt to draw up a constitution, these liberal political philosophical values are even more relevant today, because they are now widespread among the individuals of the various societies.

Distributive justice

A discussion on norms for distributive justice would address the fundamental question of what should determine an individual's share in the benefits and costs of producing any given bundle of commodities and services in the country. The basic question would become: what is a fair share for an individual? In principle, over time, an evolutionary stable approach to this question consists of the members of the community agreeing norms for guiding autonomous individuals and groups cooperating with each other in various activities throughout the society (see, e.g., Young, 1993a, 1993b). These norms will guide contracts and exchange throughout the economy. In addition to mere static norms, there would also be norms relating to continuous assessment of the fairness of the distributive regime and the processes for modifying existing norms.

Norms typically would influence the nature of more formal rules where these are desired. The body of norms, rules and laws existing at any time, related to distributive justice, would be generally obeyed with relatively low enforcement costs, as long as they reflect the shared understandings of the community. Once again, of importance in this process would be focal points comprising overlapping salient elements of the norms of distributive justice in all the ethnic societies concerned.

One salient feature that appears common to most African societies is a *meritorian* conception of distributive justice, with very similar approaches as to what a person deserves. The general criteria for determining what one deserves are generally clear, and the formulation tends to be such that the conduct or action of merit is observable, so that what is deserved can be quantified. In the traditional societies, this meritorian approach is considered fair, impartial, and just, irrespective of the implications for the outcome of distributive shares in the output of a group. The approach is not incentive-based from a social perspective—that is, what is merited is not ultimately justified by the good consequences for society [see, e.g., Sen (2000) on the incentive-based justification for reward on merit]. There is also no confusion between distributive justice and being humane. A person who justly deserves something is free to give some of it away, voluntarily, to someone else, for humanitarian or other reasons—for example, instrumental reasons such as insurance against misfortune when a similar gift from someone else would be anticipated. The basic criteria determining merit are:(1) being first, and (2) the direct product (outcome, good or bad) of a person's efforts (labor, management, etc).

That *being first* entitled one to certain rights was, historically, an important overarching principle in African moral systems. This typically established a hierarchy. Depending on the context, sometimes being first was related to age (being first in this world) and at other times to the first comer to a locality—the first to settle an area of land or clear the bush. At still other times it was related to a find—the first to locate something valuable.

This necessity to legitimate via the criterion of being first often engendered interesting stretches of the imagination and logic. For example, rights to chieftaincy and indefeasible usufruct rights to land would typically be restricted to those who could claim to be descendants of the first comers to the community concerned. But with a thorough examination one could sometimes find that the first comers were not necessarily the first to settle the land but the first in the sense of "founders" of the current political and social structure (the current community), which could mean that they conquered whosoever were there before they arrived. In such a case, it was not unusual for those with the appropriate first comer rights to claim that they came and found some people who then ran away (see, e.g., Kopytoff, 1987).

A traditional pattern of land rights can be used to illustrate the importance that Africans placed on the meritorian approach to distributive justice. An example of such a land tenure system is found in much of Sierra Leone today [see Johnson (1972, 1974, and 1976)]. In this system, the land is typically owned by extended families, although at times the whole community owns some parcels communally. Each individual in a family would have the right to request a piece of extended family land for farming. The land concerned cannot be sold but can be leased, loaned, or pledged. The fruits of a farm would belong to the person who farmed it. If, as often happens, he or she had obtained the help of others for activities such as clearing or driving away pests, then the helpers would be rewarded by the farmer sharing the fruits of the farm with them—as the farmer deemed fair. Also, extended family or village ownership of land does not mean that other members of the extended family or village are by right entitled to any of the individual farmer's produce.

In a meritorian approach to distributive justice, the agent cannot claim that he or she deserves a good without demonstrating that the good is due to his or her action. Hence the agent cannot, for example, claim that he or she deserves, by right, a good that people know to be due to nature. For instance, in the land tenure system discussed above, this often leads to others in the community being allowed to pick fruits freely from the trees standing in another's land as long as the person picking the fruit intended them for own consumption, rather than for sale, and as long as the trees were not the product of the work of some other person, who would then really deserve the fruits.

The obverse of the above is that in a meritorian conception of distributive justice, as long as someone can demonstrate that she has been conscientious and sensible in her actions and efforts, she would not be seriously blamed for an unfortunate outcome. Perhaps, this is one reason why Africans in "traditional" settings are so quick to assist each other, at no explicit cost to the aid recipient, in times of adversity in production.

Societal civility and multiculturalism

The *right of exit* of individuals and groups in numerous pre-colonial African societies would appear to be the prime candidate for a focal point in any discussion that might have taken place at independence on formulating an effective social contract on cultural matters. More specifically, as stated earlier, in numerous pre-colonial African societies, when the practice of governance in a locality incited the disaffection of certain individuals, or when certain groups lost a fight over some important matter of principle, they had a right (which the rest of their society members sometimes encouraged them to exercise to prevent undue conflict) to leave and form a new political community.

In our present context, the focal point that would directly emerge from this principle is that citizens would want to create a national state such that the membership comprises persons who even if they were free to leave the country would voluntarily choose to stay. In such a country, the ethnic identity of some significant group could not be a serious disadvantage, since otherwise that group would not voluntarily choose to stay if free to leave. Hence, the claim here is that the pluralistic society that emerges under the guidance of some stable equilibrium determination process would be one in which ethnic identity would not hurt one greatly.

Although the power holders in Ethiopia may have no intention of allowing the country to break up, the approach they have taken has as its guiding spirit exactly this sort of ideal of trying to create a multi-ethnic society in which the various groups (members) feel they have a right to exit but willingly choose to stay. The positive that *might* emerge is that most of the ethnic groups may come to adopt a *trigger strategy* in which they agree to cooperate to find solutions to problems until they discover that others do not want to cooperate. In the process they may, inter alia, create an environment of "civility" and genuine pluralistic solidarity (see below).

As an element, perhaps, of the right of exit, but nevertheless useful to keep separate, I would argue that, in today's Africa, a *desire for cultural diversity* (multiculturalism) would be a focal point. That is, citizens would require that individuals have a large degree of freedom to pursue the good as they see it, particularly in the spheres of religion, the arts, and philosophy. In short, substantial *autonomy* as regards one's conception of the good would be appreciated by all as desirable.

Some degree of cultural diversity is consistent with the historical traditions of the societies, while modern African national states have further promoted such diversity. But the scope remains to be determined in a number of areas, as could be seen, for example, in the conflicts in Nigeria over Sharia law. Constitutional reforms, which use processes that mirror the stable equilibrium determination process of Chapter 2, would appear inevitable if solutions are to be found that go beyond mere easing of tensions.

My reading is that the approach to *multiculturalism* within countries has come to be guided by three central principles, namely: (1) that recognition focus on cultural communities rather than on ethnic groups per se, unless this is unachievable; (2) that each individual should have the right of free association and choice of his or her cultural community in any cultural area of activity; and (3) that cultural communities have the freedom to change the content of their particular cultural activities over time according to the revealed preferences of the cultural community members concerned, subject of course to constraints set by the need to maintain public order as determined by the larger community of all citizens of the country via the laws of the country. I see these three principles being applied in the simultaneous recognition of western/Christian, indigenous, and Moslem laws and customs in the areas of marriage, inheritance, land tenure, and religion. In that context, one observes cultural communities that cut across ethnic groups, with the alignment of ethnic groups not necessarily the same from one cultural area to another. In brief, the tradition of promoting multiculturalism with public recognition of ethnic groups only when ineluctable is embedded in the practices of the countries. Still, questions of legal status of certain cultural practices, and jurisdictional issues relating to individual rights versus group (ethnic or cultural) rights, given the legal status of a cultural practice, remain to be clarified via constitutional reforms. The urgency of the need to clarify the legitimate rules of the game in establishing jurisdictions is heightened by the fact that the details in the approaches to legal status and individual versus group rights tend not to be uniform across all cultural areas.

Where cultural differences in a particular area of activity (e.g., language) are marked along ethnic lines, the approach to public recognition has been guided by the principle of equal worth of the humans that make up the cultural community concerned. Nevertheless, the level of public recognition and the rules of the game in the competition for survival of the cultural activities (particularly those related to language) are not typically guided by evolutionary stable constitutions and hence are critically influenced by whosoever controls the state, heightening ethnic struggles for such power and instability in public policy.

Agency for an Enabling Environment: Leadership in Civil Society

Persons who regard themselves as leaders in civil society can become mobilizing agents for evolutionary stable constitutional reforms that facilitate reduction of ethnicity if they: (1) actively promote stable equilibrium determination processes; (2) educate the public about the existence and nature of focal points to facilitate such processes, and (3) help to bring about the kind of environment that makes for good inter-ethnic relations. In such a context, I have, in Chapters 2 and 3, already discussed the agency role of civil society leadership in promoting mutual respect and generalized trust among ethnolinguistic groups thereby promoting cooperation for constitutional reform and spontaneous order. I shall here say a few words on the implications for pluralistic solidarity in the community at large, which can be important not only for the emergence of cooperation in general but also for reaching agreement on economic development enhancing and socially efficient authoritarian order.

Mutual respect and generalized trust should help civil society build an atmosphere of meaningful dialogue and communication to develop cultural bonds and what has been termed "pluralistic solidarity" among persons in the country, irrespective of their ethnicity. The idea of pluralistic solidarity is that there is both pluralism and solidarity. The solidarity comes from a shared identity—an identity that bonds the different groups in the community. Pluralistic solidarity "sees the development of public reason as one that emerges out of the dialogue among various communities and traditions where these communities and traditions have the necessary resources to engage each other in a dialogue" [Addis (1997), p. 133].

With pluralistic solidarity and mutual respect, the typical country would go from a world of ethnicity to a world of diversity in which the focus would be on the individual and on associations of individuals rather than on ethnic groups. In such a world, there would be respect for different cultural perspectives and lifestyles in those aspects of culture kept outside the realm of national collective action and regarded as belonging to the private domain. But there would also be a core set of values to which every citizen, in principle, would subscribe and hence that bind the whole group of citizens.

Persons likely to emerge as leaders in the civil society of the typical African country, for the above-mentioned tasks, can be classified into two types: the strictly *self-interested* and *altruists*. Persons acting in self-interest will see reduction of ethnicity as good for their material well-being, say because they can employ persons in their business in light of their productivity and not have to worry about social ostracism within their own ethnic groups for not discriminating in the labor market. For the self-interested, reduction in ethnicity would be a spontaneous innovation [see Goff, McCormick, and Tollison (2002)]. The theory of innovation would lead one to the view that, with an enabling socio-political environment, the best managed and strongest performers among firms would take the lead in this innovation. The political and civil society leadership actions of concern in this chapter will thus enhance the incentives for the spontaneous innovation "reduction in ethnicity," namely, by changing the political and social environment in which individuals and firms make decisions on their cross-ethnic relations.

The *altruists* are people who have social preferences and are willing to act in ways other than simply those ensuing from self-interest. In the words of Fehr and Fischbacher (2002): "A person exhibits social preferences if the person not only cares about the material resources allocated to her but also cares about the material resources allocated to relevant reference agents." The relevant reference agents "may be the colleagues in the firm with whom a person interacts most frequently, or a person's relatives, or the trading partners, or a person's neighbours" [Fehr and Fischbacher (2002), p. C2]. Adding together the altruists and those acting in self-interest, as in Chapter 2, one can envisage the civil society leadership coming from any of three types of groups, associations, or organizations: business groups, policy analysis centers/institutes, and civil society governance groups. Effectiveness of this leadership will demand renewal within civil society itself, including improved democratic governance within civil society organizations and a greater willingness to engage the state as opposed to disengagement because of frustrations with the state [see, e.g., Ake (1993), Diamond (1999, Chapter 6), Ikelegbe (2001), and Aiyede (2003)]. The leadership must also be trusted by the rest of society as comprising persons that are resolute in keeping their organizations and networks autonomous from particular groups (cliques) or individual leaders (avoiding cult of personalities).

Conclusion

Studies that have demonstrated that ethnic diversity is detrimental to economic growth in the absence of strong institutions which foster sound economic policies and promote political rights (the latter themselves indirectly also promoting sound economic policies) really must mean that ethnic diversity is not detrimental to growth when the ethnic groups are somehow able to *cooperate* to develop appropriate political, legal and social institutions that are favorable to economic growth [see, e.g., Collier (2000b), Easterly (2001a, 2001b), and Easterly and Levine (1997)]. Why such cooperation occurs in some environments but not in others is a question of great importance. Clearly, of significance would be the history of how these different societies (ethnic groups, in our context) came together in the first place. If they came together voluntarily, for example to defend against a common enemy or strengthen their commitment in favor of a common cause (such as ideology or religion), then cooperation is likely to take off very positively from the start. If before they came together they separately had institutions that were similar and also favored sound economic policy environments, then cooperation is likely to be sustained and to increase virtually spontaneously over time. In contrast, if the groups came together via conquest, the evolution of cooperation might be a very slow and painful (including bloody) process.

In the absence of agency to demand appropriate constitutional reforms and create an enabling environment to foster reduction of ethnicity, African countries may indeed have to go through such a long and painful road to reduction of ethnicity, with adverse effects on political stability and economic development. I would conjecture that this evolutionary path would be influenced by random crises, democratization attempts and processes, and per capita income. As evidenced by the recent experience of Benin [see Decalo (1997) and Magnusson (2005)], economic crisis can bring about spontaneous cooperation within the civil society to make constitutional changes. This gets the various ethnic groups to work together and in the process build goodwill and gain learning experience in putting aside ethnic prejudices for the larger public interest. In 1989, in the midst of a national crisis following years of economic mismanagement and military rule, the President of Benin convened a national conference of diverse interest groups in society to find a consensus on ways to solve the economic problems. The conference participants decided to go for a full regime change. They declared sovereignty for the convention, selected their own chairman for the meetings, forced the President to a figurehead position, set up an interim government with an executive prime minister, and drafted a constitution which was approved in a referendum in 1990. This manifested a remarkable degree of cooperation, and although it did not usher in a complete break with the past in terms of ethnic tensions, and did not eliminate voting in future elections along ethnic lines, it did lay the foundations for inter-ethnic cooperation that have been good for the democratization process in the country. Clearly such cooperation in crises will promote reduction in ethnicity over time.

Cooperation across ethnolinguistic lines, and thus reduction of ethnicity, should also benefit from increases in per capita income due to factors other than reduction in ethnicity, particularly in the context of increasing democratization. For such co-evolution (income growth and democratization) should cause individuals to have better economic security, including increased ability to withstand economic shocks, at the same time that they are observing a system in which they feel they can have greater trust of being able to obtain fair treatment under normal due process. Thus agency for increased demand for good economic policies should have a salutary effect on reduction of ethnicity.

Still, agency aimed directly at speeding-up the reduction of ethnicity is possible and superior to waiting for the slow evolutionary process, with its attendant risk that ethnicity may in fact increase in the near term in many countries. Economic policymaking in sub-Saharan Africa has indeed been greatly influenced by ethnicity—including via policies to manage or, even worse, to exploit ethnicity. In the process, ethnicity has been promoted, not abated.

Economic policymaking would differ significantly between a country that is working to reduce ethnicity rapidly over time and one that is satisfied with merely managing ethnicity at its current level. In the former, policymakers would be free to work resolutely to integrate the economy, open up markets, and to strictly apply economic efficiency principles in government investment, employment, and resource allocation decisions. A meritorian approach to distributive justice would also be facilitated in such an environment. In contrast, economic policymaking in an environment of managing ethnicity in Africa has found it very difficult to be strict about government efficiency and to take a meritorian approach to distributive justice. In fact, the bloated cabinets and bureaucracies and other management costs, mentioned earlier, have proved an enormous tax burden on citizens and noncitizens alike of African countries trying to manage ethnicity. A collectivity would find it easier to define and maintain standards for good governance in the public sector in a country that seeks to reduce ethnicity than in one satisfied with managing ethnicity at its current level.

6

Government Corruption

A reasonable definition of corruption remains one provided by McMullan many years ago. He considered someone corrupt "if he accepts money or money's worth for doing something that he is under a duty to do anyway, that he is under a duty not to do, or to exercise a legitimate discretion for improper reasons"(see McMullan, 1961, pp. 183-184). I will consider government corruption to exist if there is a diversion of state revenues and of national income flow in order to augment the private wealth of the members of the government, when the latter are not legally entitled to do so.

An important point made by a number of writers (see, e.g., Szeftel, 2000) is that corruption in Africa has been used as a private accumulation device of the "petty bourgeois" who can be viewed as the "robber barons" of modern day Africa, confronted with the realities of today's world economy.[1] Clearly, this makes urgent, inter alia, cooperation among individuals in the societies to build strong institutions and organizations in the struggle against corruption. Otherwise,

---

[1] For Szeftel (2000, p. 304, note 4) the term "petty bourgeoisie" is used "as a holdall category to cover the various elements (the middle classes, professional elites, intellectuals, small business interests, commercial farmers and so on) who make up the inchoate 'bourgeois society' that has been struggling so painfully to find its feet in Africa for more than half a century." Rowley (2000) also argues that since the new African leaders, following independence "had no entrepreneurial experience," they used "government power as a basis for the personal accumulation of wealth."

much social conflict over attempts to capture government and reap the profit of the robber baron will be the order of the day for the foreseeable future. Maybe this is the fate of certain countries, but at least one should understand why [see, also, the papers of McGuire and Olson (1996) and Olson (1997)]. More optimistically, it may be possible to find ways to avoid this fate by addressing corruption directly. In addition, measures may exist to neutralize some of the adverse effects of corruption until it declines over time with evolutionary forces. In this chapter, I discuss the causes and origins of government corruption in African countries, the issue of agency for control of corruption, the welfare costs of corruption, and issues in the design and implementation of government reforms to control corruption.

The Problem and its Determinants

Empirical evidence leads us to the conclusion that corruption declines as income per capita increases over time (Treisman, 2000, and Paldam, 2002). But the theory is unclear. It is possible that rising income per capita tends to be accompanied by a number of developments—both as cause and effect—that would, on balance, tend to reduce corruption. As income increases, the opportunities for economic agents to accumulate wealth and raise capital for investments tend to multiply, reducing the need to use theft from government as a means to raise capital; democracy increases, and hence eviction from office as a disciplining device for corruption becomes more effective; the legal system becomes more efficient in punishing corruption; inter-ethnic cooperation improves, muting the adverse effect of ethnolinguistic diversity on development of institutions that control government behavior; and, after controlling for ethnolinguistic diversity, the quality of government and government efficiency improve (see La Porta, et al., 1999, and also Collier, 2000a), with positive effect on reducing corruption.

Of course, although government corruption causes a decline in economic efficiency of resource use and discourages certain highly productive investment, it is still possible to grow rapidly with corruption, as the history of the world must surely attest, even if in the period of low per capita income this growth is not as fast as the potential because of the adverse effects of the relatively high corruption at that stage of development. In other words, corruption causes countries to operate below their potential (inside their production possibility loci). But although perceived corruption discourages investment, and hence growth,[2] it does not necessarily dominate the positive effects of other factors (such as taxation, interest rates, inflationary expectations, and political stability) on investment and growth. It is certainly desirable to get rid of corruption as quickly as possible. But the above consideration implies that it is possible to create a sufficiently good economic policy environment, even in a corrupt country, which fosters rapid economic growth and ipso facto has a favorable effect in reducing corruption in its wake (given that corruption tends to decline with income).

Africans, in their private homes and public places, have corruption as one of the most popular subjects of discussion. In the agenda of political campaigns, reduction of corruption often ranks highest, and more often than not opposition parties would accuse the government in power of being corrupt. Such discussions bring out four main views on the determinants of corruption, irrespective of the country and the economic and political circle.[3] Based on my experience, when it comes to the government bureaucracy, low salaries of government employees, including top civil servants, is the most frequent explanation given by Africans, coupled with low per capita incomes of the countries, which constrain the ability of the government to pay "reasonable" salaries. The second factor frequently mentioned and applicable especially to the top political leaders but relevant for all

---

[2] See Johnson (1975) and Mauro (1995). Mauro's paper is an empirical study of the relation between perceived corruption and investment, and hence growth.

[3] Leys (1965), McMullan (1961), Myrdal (1970), and Van Roy (1971) are among those who long ago addressed the question of what determines people's moral attitude towards corrupt acts, whatever the country, but especially in developing countries.

government personnel is pressure from those in society with whom persons in power have strong loyalty bonds. Alternatively put, persons in office face pressure, from society and from the nature of politics in the countries, to divert governments funds and grant favors (jobs, contracts, welfare benefits, etc.), at the expense of the state, to help their political cronies, families, friends, and persons from the same town or village. Hence, government employees face weak autonomy from society in the performance of their jobs.

The third factor popular in explaining government corruption, especially at the highest levels, is weak (political and legal) institutions, including the absence of sacrosanct democratic institutions. In brief, consistent with the discussion in Chapter 2, government corruption is an outcome of the weak institutions established at the dawn of independence. For not only were the institutions weak to begin with, but typically the institutions have been further crippled over time, partly by corruption itself (hence via a vicious circle) and partly by authoritarian regimes. Thus the President, cabinet ministers, civil servants, the legal system (courts, police, etc.) may all have become corrupt because initial rules were not appropriately designed and enforced, which then helped breed more corruption and the further weakening of the rules themselves. Finally, low morality is an explanation that shows up when someone is thought to be excessively corrupt (trying "to eat everything from the pot").

No doubt, to reduce corruption appreciably in African countries, one would need to address, as relevant, the four factors just mentioned. For example, reducing ethnicity as discussed in Chapter 5 should weaken loyalty bonds and hence reduce corruption emanating from that source. In addition, for a complete strategy addressing corruption in the public sector, salaries also will need to be adjusted in countries where they are indeed very low by any reasonable standard, after controlling for the general levels of per capita incomes in the country. Certainly, also, institutions must be introduced or strengthened as necessary.

But from the perspective of ultimate causes, I would add to the above the absence of citizens' loyalty to the state and of legitimated (generally agreed) anti-corruption norms in the typical African country, as important in explaining government corruption and hence needing attention in any attempt to address the problem. Absence of loyalty is, in turn, the result of an absence of a feeling of ownership of the state by societal persons at large. Once again, one ends up with this underlying nemesis of sub-Saharan Africa—the origin of the institutions and organizations of the state from the first moves made by the citizens at the dawn of independence.

The absence of loyalty to the state and of legitimated anti-corruption norms leave government employees with no guilt in stealing from the state and make difficult (particularly in the face of high ethnicity) cooperation for establishing the kinds of institutions and organizational structures that would facilitate control of corruption in government. People's effective morality (given the agreed norms of the society), and hence their taste for duping the government, will change as they become loyal to the state. Whatever morality shortfall remains would then need to be dealt with by institutions, which would be created by the kind of cooperation that itself would follow a feeling of ownership (of the state) by the vast majority of the citizens. Institutions would be very difficult to maintain and keep effective without some assistance from loyalty to the state and agreed anti-corruption norms of the society. For instance, whistle-blowing cannot then be considered normal behavior by government employees—to be applauded instead of being frowned upon.

From a policy perspective, any coherent government strategy to reduce corruption would need legitimation from society as a whole as well as a credible commitment from the political leadership and the economic and societal elites of civil society, if the program is going to be resolutely implemented. The widespread notion that low salaries and per capita incomes are the most important factors fuelling corrupt practices in most of the countries has also made very difficult to achieve, in many African countries, genuine and sustained drives and commitments to reduce corruption, most notably in the government bureaucracy. This attitude is buttressed by a view that there is corruption everywhere in the world and that corruption often helps get things done (the oil-in-wheel approach to corruption). Of course, excesses are deplored, which explains the recurring anti-corruption protests, changes of leadership, commissions of enquiries, confiscation of property, imprisonment, and occasionally even execution;[4] yet the problem persists. The excesses may be bewailed, but a firm credible commitment to make corruption in government insignificant is not sufficiently widespread in many African countries.

Controlling government corruption has also suffered from a failure by Africans to really appreciate the costs of corruption to the economy and to society as a whole. It seems clear, then, that any anti-corruption campaign would benefit from de-emphasizing the moral and the distributional aspects of corruption and emphasizing, instead, the economic growth aspects. The morality argument is not very convincing to people who believe that corruption can't be helped because of low incomes. The latent and often transparent attitude that corruption involves distribution from one group of citizens to another also tends to lead to the conclusion that government corruption is adequately addressed by changing leadership, "so that others might eat."

It is, therefore, particularly useful to educate the African public about the socioeconomic costs of high-level corruption. That way, ordinary citizens could begin to see corruption as not merely a distribution problem. It is really important that the attitude, which one encounters so often in many African countries, of "X has eaten enough now let someone else take over and enjoy also," should be understood as really damaging to the development process in the continent. Once this happens, it would become easier for agents of reform to be certain that any effort on their part has a good chance of resulting in an institutional and organizational framework that could effectively fight corruption.

---

[4] Perhaps the most notorious example of executions for alleged corruption are those ordered by the Armed Forces Revolutionary Council of Ghana, led by Jerry Rawlings, which had former military leaders of Ghana—General Akuffo, Lieutenant General Afrifa, and General Acheampong—all executed in 1979 for illegally amassing wealth during their tenures in office.

Agency and Control of Corruption

If citizens feel a sense of ownership of the state, and hence loyalty to it, and if legitimated norms governing behavior in a wide range of interactions have emerged in the community at large, it would be *relatively* easy to agree on what constitutes corrupt behavior and to develop formal institutions (that is, rules) to contain such behavior in government. Indeed, a generally accepted anti-corruption norm could then be formalized via societal cooperation or by some authority and enforced via spontaneous or authoritarian order or both.

Principal-agency

It would then be possible for the individuals in the country, via some legitimated process, to devise a contract which they offer an agent. The contract would grant the agent authority to enforce a legitimated (widely accepted) anti-corruption norm over any set of activities she finds beneficial to do so.[5] The agent would be knowledgeable of the population and of the socio-economic environment of the country. In other words, to facilitate her task, society would give the agent two kinds of resources: (1) *authority* to impose the anti-corruption norm, and (2) *resources* for enforcement. The agent will accept the contract if it satisfies her participation constraint, given that the other terms of the contract are incentive compatible (that is, in her self-interest and within her ability given the resources available to her).

The contract would specify that the agent must produce a minimum gross payoff to society from reducing corruption; in principle, this could be measured as the additional real output from the anti-corruption activity of the agent. The additional output would ensue from additional resources (labor and capital) used productively domestically over what would have happened in the absence of the

---

[5] Although the agent is characterized as a "she," one could just as easily have decided to talk of 'agency' and an "it."

reduction in corruption. The contract would also include a tax rate, used to finance the payment to (the budget of) the agent, and the punishment of the agent, by society, for failure.

Societal constraints

Society has three issues the resolution of which would greatly reflect its demand for agency, namely: (1) it must set a rate of taxation high enough to collect funds equivalent to the minimum required to convince a worthwhile agent to do the job—that is, to cover agency cost; (2) it must set the minimum performance target for agency; and (3) it must decide on the punishment for breach of contract and implement it. I would hypothesize that the difficulty of finding solutions to all three of these issues is aggravated by high ethnicity and by low incomes.

Ethnicity hampers cooperation necessary within society to agree solutions to the issues. As discussed in Chapters 3 and 5, with a high degree of ethnicity, norms of civic cooperation, trust, and associational networks that favorably affect cooperation will tend to be mainly intra-ethnic. As a result, in such a society, transaction costs (information, mobilization, and negotiation costs) to agree any kind of institutional or organizational change in the society tend to be rather high.

Low-income persons will tend to find it difficult to comprehend fully the macroeconomic cost of corruption and the majority of them may consider financial contribution to enforcement of an anti-corruption norm a luxury they can ill-afford, especially when each person feels he or she has the option of either joining in the corruption or leaving the country. This is one reason why so many African countries seek external aid to finance their anti-corruption activities. This attitude is further complicated by the failure to perceive the social dilemma aspect of corruption and the tendency to view corruption mainly in distributional terms.

In the fight against corruption, citizens will most likely need to come up with the budgetary resources for enforcement even before the gains begin to be realized. In low-income countries, the discount rate of citizens may be quite high, adding to their reluctance to make financial contributions to fighting corruption. Low-income countries also tend to lack adequate instruments to penalize breach of agency agreement—instruments such as free and open democratic elections and a well-functioning legal system. Indeed, because the absence of political freedoms help slow down the adoption of policies to control government corruption (via explicit or implicit agency contracts and their enforcement), a positive correlation between per capita income and political rights could help induce an inverse correlation between per capita income and government corruption, other things being equal.[6]

Agency under spontaneous order

Selected members of society can come together, take charge as it were, and set up an agency or even several agencies to spread an anti-corruption norm and monitor government corruption. Budgetary funds for their work would then be built up from voluntary contributions collected via dedicated fund-raising campaigns and donations. The agency or agencies can fashion the norm and involve citizens to resist, monitor, and report corrupt acts and then the agency or agencies will pressure the government authorities to punish corrupt officials. Such agencies become watch-dog organizations. They are feasible, inter alia because corruption typically involves counterparties outside the government.[7] If the agency performance of a watch-dog (civil society) organization falls below expectations, societal persons will simply reduce their contributions to its budget. This disciplining device can be very effective; the agency will simply be forced to fold if its performance is sufficiently poor.

---

[6] The empirical evidence does seem to indicate that up to a point increased political freedom is beneficial to rising per capita income but that political rights (democratic rights) tend to increase with per capita income [see Barro (1996)].

[7] This fact has given rise to several interesting models in the corruption literature. See, for example, Lui (1985), Mookherjee and Png (1995), and Polinsky and Shavell (2001).

One would conjecture that such an approach (agency via spontaneous order) would work especially well for corruption where the problem of free-riding (noncontribution in assisting with enforcement of the anti-corruption norm) is not a very serious problem. The set of transactions would, in such cases, have certain characteristics of which three are noteworthy. First, those who benefit directly from reduction in corruption in those types of transactions would tend to outnumber substantially those who benefit from the corruption. Second, this difference in numbers would not be counterbalanced by financial power distribution between the gainers and the losers from the anti-corruption norm. Third, there must be insignificant uncertainty among the population as to the gainers and the losers from enforcement of the anti-corruption norm.[8]

Many types of transactions and corrupt activities would qualify, e.g., bribing of regulators of health and safety standards, or of suppliers of government services for which scarcity is not a serious problem—such as issuing of passports. Many others would not qualify, particularly those involving payment of taxes and fees to the public sector, such as customs duties, traffic fees, and income taxes. Spontaneous order organizations can also serve as anti-corruption agents of society in these areas as well, but their role would be somewhat different as suggested below.

The government as agent

Normally, it is natural to expect government itself, both the political leadership within it and as an organization, to be the main agent of society in the fight against corruption. Sometimes governments would, in this role, create at least one special watch-dog agency within it to enforce the anti-corruption norm, as formalized into laws, implementing rules, and codes of behavior.

---

[8] Fernandez and Rodrik (1991), for instance, show that there could be a bias towards the status quo (and hence against efficiency-enhancing reforms) when some of the individual gainers and losers cannot be identified beforehand.

When government is the agent, an implication of the above framework is that society needs to spend time negotiating a contract between the government and itself containing just two elements—the minimum payoff from anti-corruption effort and the tax rate to finance the effort. Then society should have the ability to enforce the contract—to hold the government accountable. The government would be given instrument autonomy, subject to the laws of the country. There would be no need to spend time and effort policing the government's day-to-day activities in this area.

There are two advantages of government being the agent, both ensuing from its legitimate power (that is, authority) to compel obedience by force. One advantage is the ability of government as an organization to assess citizens and compel them to make contributions to the budget. In that case, society just needs to sanction the tax rate and leave the government to go about the process of collection; hence something for tax administration would normally be added to the tax level. The second advantage the government has is its ability to enforce the anti-corruption norm, again via its legitimate control over instruments of compulsion. In such a context, free-riding will itself become an element of corruption punishable by government.

Against these advantages must be considered the possibility that the government leadership (the political group or party in power) itself may be corrupt, which is the case in many African countries, reducing the agency effort by government, with negative impact on the size of the payoff to society from funds given to government to fight corruption. When, in addition, it is difficult for the society to punish poor agency or breach of agency contract (explicit or implicit), society would need to search for supplementary approaches to the agency problem. One such design would involve a nongovernment watchdog agency as mentioned above, with that agency policing the efficiency of government agency, even if it also does some direct agency of its own. In other words, in the face of high-level government corruption, spontaneous-order agency organizations may be unavoidable, if a substantial reduction in corruption is to occur. Unfortunately, once again and for the same reasons discussed before, low incomes and ethnicity will tend to hamper the willingness and ability of African societies to cooperate and facilitate such an approach.

African societies and the control of government corruption

One implication of this analysis seems to be that any "failure" to control corruption is a "failure" of society at large to devise an appropriate agency contract and enforce it resolutely. Ethnicity in particular simply aggravates the culpability of society. Essentially, the argument so far is that the failure to cooperate, among other reasons due to ethnicity, to devise and enforce an agency contract to control corruption leaves wide open the *opportunity* for corruption. But there is more. The equilibrium amount of government corruption will tend to be greater in a society with high ethnicity than in a society with very low ethnicity, also because the *incentive* for corruption would be greater in the former than in the latter.

The greater incentive in the high-ethnicity society arises from two sources. First, because of group solidarity (strong loyalty bonds), an individual's utility is greater the higher the average consumption level of members of his or her identity group relative to consumption levels of other groups. Hence, he or she is willing to take risks and bear costs to effect wealth transfers from other groups to his or hers, via corrupt practices, and to share the corruption revenue more readily with members of his or her identity group than with those of other groups. Second, per capita and total wealth of a group affect the resources potentially available to that group to fight battles with other groups and hence the ability of the group to survive and grow in numbers and to increase its wealth relative to that of other groups. Hence, there are strong reasons to believe that reduction of ethnicity would have favorable effects on government corruption.

In African countries, therefore, over the long run, corruption will decline with: (1) the evolution of a sufficient sense of ownership of and hence loyalty to, the state; (2) reduction of ethnicity; (3) the emergence of clear legitimated anti-corruption norms to guide development of rules relating to corrupt behavior in government; and (4) rising per capita income. The problem of ownership and loyalty has to do with the way the state was constituted and I have already discussed direct solutions to that problem. In the previous chapter, I also discussed the problem of ethnicity and its reduction. While these issues are being addressed, it is widely agreed in the policy community that African countries could also build institutions and organizational frameworks that directly reduce the level of corruption at any given level of income; that is, induce downward shifts in the corruption-per capita income relationship. The institutions and organizations—the rules and agencies—could, as I have argued, occur both outside government and inside government. Discussion and education within African countries to agree on the definition of corrupt behavior and on anti-corruption norms would go a long way to accelerate the process. Such discussion and education would benefit from a clear understanding of the economic welfare costs of corruption, an issue to which I shall now turn.

Economic Welfare Costs of High-Level Corruption

The basic argument is that, other things being equal, weak institutions (including the legal framework) in the African countries facilitate the extraction of what can be termed "corruption revenue," the magnitude of which the political leadership has some control over and thus is a variable (scc Johnson, 1975a). I shall discuss the nature of this corruption revenue and the empirical, allocative and welfare implications of it.

High-level corruption is practiced by the political leadership team (comprising cabinet ministers and their party members in parliament) that governs the country—the government in control of the state. The political leader (typically the President) is the head of this political leadership team. At the end of the contract term, that team would be reconsidered for reappointment (i.e. reelection) for another term (subject to term limit if such exists in the Constitution). At the same time, other persons would also compete for the right to be political leader and to form the political leadership team. I shall, for simplicity sake, treat the political leadership team as a group of individuals with common interests and goals. Thus, I treat the team as if it were one person. The important point now is that the attempts of the governing team to capture corruption revenue magnify distortions and misallocation of resources in the economy, with adverse effects on economic efficiency and investment and hence economic growth [see Johnson (1975a) for an early elaboration of this theme].

Corrupt government behavior[9]

A political leadership team (the government) has at its disposal the private resources of its members, comprising value of labor time, bank accounts, etc., that could be utilized in corrupt activities or in other, non-corrupt, activities. The government's basic corrupt activities are of two types. The first type is a direct diversion of state funds into the private coffers of the government members. The second type of corrupt activity involves the imposition of *corruption tax*. The latter is the amount of private individuals' and organizations' incomes that the government is able to capture through inducing and accepting bribes.

The government is faced with a set of constraints, which could be divided into self-imposed and externally imposed constraints. The self-imposed constraint is the government's own standard of morality: that is, its aversion to corruption or loyalty to the state. This morality can remain unchanged for a substantial length of time, although loyalty to the state could quickly surge with institutional reforms using stable equilibrium determination processes. As stated before, the initial moves in constituting the state soon after independence left little loyalty to the state among the citizens at large in the bulk of the African countries.

---

[9] This and the following sub-section heavily utilize the analysis contained in Johnson (1975a).

The externally imposed constraints are of two kinds. First, there is the legal constraint. This gives rise to a *legal cost* of corruption. The legal cost is the product of the probability of being caught by the legal system and the anticipated cost if caught. The cost if caught is itself an expected cost since one can escape punishment by bribery, legal maneuvering and the like. In addition, the punishment meted out is never unambiguously known in advance. Thus the legal cost is an expected cost. For simplicity one can assume that expectations regarding the probabilities associated with this cost are always held with certainty.

The other externally imposed constraint is competition. The current political leadership only has temporary authority to manage the state and there are other groups of people who are ready to compete for the authority (hence the right) to reap the benefit from being the government. This competitive constraint gives rise to a *competitive cost* of corruption. This cost is simply the (weighted) average reduction in the probabilities of being the government in future years as a result of a given corrupt act. In a democracy, for example, most forms of competition not involving violence are permitted, one political team replaces another one by elections held at stated intervals, and the right to bid for control of the state is considered to be due everyone subject to legal regulations that do not arbitrarily discriminate against any individual or team.

If a government spends one dollar of its own private members' resources on corrupt activities, the net gain or benefit from this expenditure would be the funds raised via direct diversion of state funds plus the funds raised via corruption tax minus the legal and competitive costs. These benefits and costs are expectations over time; hence, strictly speaking, they involve probabilities and discounting to their present values. The one dollar of expenditure is also a discounted value. A simple algebraic presentation is found in Johnson (1975a).

In this sort of analytical framework, one can think of the government as maximizing the net gain from corruption by selecting: (i) the fraction of state funds it would directly divert, (ii) a set of economic activities on which to impose corruption tax, and (iii) the levels of the corruption tax rates on the different activities. The government is, in turn, constrained by the fact that the more it tries to tax the greater the probability that it would not be allowed to remain in office in any future year and the greater will tend to be the legal cost that would be brought to bear on it. In short, one can legitimately assume that competitors and the legal system would try harder to punish the government as the diversion of state funds and the 'corruption tax' rates on private economic activities increase.

Of importance, in the above perspective, is that not all economic activities are equally profitable for the imposition of corruption tax. Activities will differ in especially two important respects: first, with respect to the level of the income streams that they generate and, second, with respect to the competitive and legal costs of realizing any given tax rate. It is, in other words, less costly for voters, the legal system and competitors to police the behavior of the government in some activities than in others. Similarly, it is less costly for the political leadership to conceal its corruption or to force a bribe in some activities than in others. The implication is that effective corruption tax rates will differ among economic activities; this alters the relative profitability to private entrepreneurs of engaging in the different activities.

With a democratic constitutional system and an independent judiciary, the maximum net gain attainable from any "dollar" of resource spent on corruption will be affected by the information possessed by the legal system and by the voters about the wealth consequences of the government's activities. The greater the information available to the legal system, the higher would be the probability of the government being caught for any corrupt act and the larger would be the legal costs associated with any corrupt act. Similarly the more complete the information in the hands of the voters and competitors, the lower would be the probability that a corrupt government remains in power in any given year, or would be renewed at the end of its current term (after controlling for term limits).

The amount and quality of the information that the legal system and the voters have depend on the information made available to them by competitors, the information directly sought and obtained by them (using means such as newspapers, radio, television, and their own labor), and on the information offered to them by the government. Hence a corrupt government could employ some of its own resources in activities that raise the cost to the legal system and the voters of generating and transmitting information on the government's activities.

Thus, in addition to direct diversion of state funds and the imposition of corruption taxes on chosen economic activities, a corrupt government could engage in several kinds of information activities, namely, actions and measures that increase the cost to competitors of supplying correct information to the voters and the legal system, that raise the cost to voters and the legal system of finding out the truth themselves, or that increase the ability of the government to supply favorable or wrong information to the legal system and to others. For example, a corrupt government could control access to television and radio or constrain the content of newspapers and other information-generating organs.

A system with a democratic constitution and an independent judiciary imposes constraints which any rational corrupt government would have an incentive to eliminate or weaken. Preventing or limiting open competition (e.g. by banning some or all political parties or by imposing special entry requirements limiting potential entrants into politics) would weaken the competitive constraint. Similarly, a corrupt government could take steps to diminish the independence of the judiciary and hence the latter's ability to prevent arbitrary actions of the government. The benefit for the government of all such actions is, again, an increase in corruption revenue.

As seen in the African continent since independence, there is a serious potential cost to a government of being corrupt, while limiting open competition and the independence of the judiciary. This cost is the probability of violent overthrow by non-democratic means (or else persistent protest until the government resigns even before its current term expires) multiplied by the expected penalties to a government thus overthrown (or forced to resign). The probability of violent overthrow depends on the resources at the disposal of competitors and the voters and their willingness to risk pain, injury or even death, as well as the willingness and ability of the government to resist (by force) any attempt at its overthrow. The existence of this cost of possible revolt serves to reduce, but not typically to completely wipe out, the net expected benefits to corrupt African governments of limiting open competition and the independence of the judiciary.

Allocative and welfare effects

So far, I have argued that corrupt activities of the government involve direct diversion of state funds; imposition of corruption taxes; influencing the costs of acquiring and supplying information to voters, competitors and the legal system; and influencing the openness of competition for control of the state as well as the independence of the judiciary to inflict legal cost for corrupt acts. The *corruption revenue* of the government is the total net income obtained from corrupt government activities, when the political team in power efficiently allocates its resources between corrupt and non-corrupt activities. The weaker (in a technological and constitutional sense) are the institutions that impose the competitive and legal constraints on corruption, other things such as the loyalty of public officials to the state being equal, the greater will be the corruption revenue expected and realizable, by political teams in the country, from gaining control of the state. Where in consequence of weak institutions, as in many African countries at the dawn of independence, the expected and realizable corruption revenue is significant relative to national income the consequent allocative, distributional and growth effects could be very substantial. In addition, as evident from this and previous chapters, the implications for the evolution of institutions controlling government and for the democratization process are calamitous.

A major point, then, to be emphasized in the education of the populace at large, becomes that the existence of substantial expected and realizable corruption revenue has behavioral consequences that cause aggregate output loss to the rest of the society to be of greater magnitude than the real revenue realized by those who share in this corruption revenue. Widespread corruption in government not only has distributional effects it also has economic growth and aggregate income effects, which make its reduction desirable to the country and the population as a whole. The corruption distorts productive activity in ways that are detrimental to economic growth.

If the government members belong to an entrepreneurial class and (i) invest a significant fraction of the corruption revenue in (ii) highly productive activities with (iii) significant positive effects on the rest of the economy, the adverse growth effects of government corruption would be mitigated, even if not eliminated. In the vast majority of African countries, whether as a result of conspicuous consumption, or a consequence of low incomes, or social loyalty bonds (e.g. ethnic, extended family), the consumption-income ratios tend to be rather high. In addition, in a situation of uncertainty as to what happens to one's wealth attained through corruption if there should be a change of government, there is an incentive to invest one's corruptibly acquired wealth where it would be difficult to confiscate. Thus, the incentive to invest these funds abroad is very strong. The effect of high propensities to consume or of investment in foreign assets is to prevent the corruption revenue from contributing significantly to domestic output growth. Here again, a major point to be emphasized in the education of the populace at large is that getting foreign authorities and organizations to help in recovering stolen funds will not reduce the distortions discussed above. In addition, it may trigger an incentive to find new ways of hiding stolen funds, and encourage even more conspicuous consumption among the corrupt officials.

The attempts to capture the corruption revenue have other significant harmful consequences for economic growth, which should be pointed out to the African public at large. One consequence of the existence of realizable corruption revenue is that it induces excessive resource flow into political activity, which in turn has effects harmful to the economy. By political activity is meant participation in the work of political parties and other groups, which aim, inter alia, at capturing control of the state, and in particular, of becoming the government. In a number of African countries this political activity includes participation in armed private militia maintained by political parties/leaders (Congo is a notorious example of this). This effect (excessive political activity) occurs because in a world of corruption capturing control of the state can greatly augment the rate of return to one's endowed (initial) resources. Control of the state allows one to extract corruption revenue from the rest of the society. Thus a relatively large number of teams will be formed to capture control of the state, and each team will employ more factors of production in its political activity (including hiring and equipping thugs and militia) than if there were no corruption revenue expected from being the government. The additional resources attracted into political activity produce services with lower social marginal valuations than the services that they performed (or would have performed) in the sectors from which they were drawn (or distracted from entering). This shift of resources is inefficient from the perspective of economic growth.

But this is not all. If a team has low standard of morality—that is, little or no aversion to corruption or loyalty to the state—the augmented rate of return to its own resources from having control of the state is due to (a) the corruption revenue and (b) the income it would have lost due to the corrupt government activity of another team. If a team has a high standard of morality—that is, its aversion to corruption or loyalty to the state is high (and therefore will be honest as the government)—then its augmented rate of return to own resources from having control of the state is due only to (b) above, i.e. the income loss it avoids. Since (b) is less than (a) + (b), the gain to political activity is greater to a team the lower its aversion to corruption and its loyalty to the state. The implication is clear. The presence of political teams with low morality induces not only excessive resource flow into political activity, but also political activity comes to be dominated by (i.e. most competing teams tend to be) teams with low morality. A deadweight loss is caused because of the lower social productivity of some of the resources diverted into political activity as compared to their social productivity in their best alternatives. A deadweight loss also arises if the individuals with the lowest morality, vis-à-vis the state, who get more heavily attracted into political activity, are also not the most efficient as managers of the state. For these and other reasons discussed below corruption tends to lead to decline in efficiency of the state.

A further deadweight loss ensues from the distortions in relative prices caused by the excess resource flow into political activity. The remuneration to specific cooperating factors demanded by political teams increase relative to those received by other factors of production. Also, the fall in output in the sectors from which resources flow into political activity induces obvious relative price changes since all sectors will not be equally affected. In so far as these relative price changes are not due to changes in the social marginal valuations or opportunity costs of different commodities, they are inefficient. In the typical African country, rural activities, including agricultural farming, especially suffer from these distortions, since the thugs, militia, and political advisers and activists tend to base themselves disproportionately in urban areas.

In its attempt to capture corruption revenue the corrupt government typically is, in the African setting, able to increase the productivity of its own resources by employing intermediaries to help in the collection of the corruption revenue. Such behavior also has consequences adverse to the economy. Indeed, there are usually segments in the society with comparative advantage in the collection of the corruption revenue, which have an incentive to aid the corrupt government (i.e., they will supply their services to the government for a fee) in collecting this revenue.

An important segment of society with such an incentive and ability is that containing private commercial firms. Private firms will offer to help the government in collecting this revenue in return for a share in the proceeds. Thus techniques are devised to effectuate a coalition of the government and private firms with the objective of taxing the rest of society. A particularly potent way in which this coalition can work is this: private firms would collect the corruption tax by obtaining monopoly rights with special concessions from the government and would share in the tax proceeds by not handing over (as bribes, gifts, etc.) all the monopoly rents realized. The implication is that monopoly franchises and special concessions will emerge as conspicuous features in systems with corrupt government.

A deadweight loss from the coalition arises from two sources. The first source is the well-known inefficiency of monopoly in closed-market situations. The second source is the possibility that monopoly rights and concessions are not granted to the most productive enterprises of all the potential competitors. This may be due to inefficiency of the processes used to decide who gets what rights or concessions; or it may be due to the possibility that some of the most efficient firms, whether for moral reasons or because of high risk aversion, will not associate with corrupt governments. Thus, putting pressure on foreign governments to pass laws prohibiting companies originating from their countries from engaging in corrupt practices when doing or bidding to do business in the African countries will not necessarily improve growth and efficiency in the African countries with corrupt governments. Such laws will help only if they are adopted in all countries of the world and are resolutely enforced by all countries. Otherwise, we run the risk that only the most efficient companies are likely to obey the laws or follow norms to that effect. The first line of attack on the problem should be addressing directly the corruption in the African countries.

Another set of persons in the country with incentive and ability to aid the corrupt politicians of the government in the collection of the corruption revenue in return for a share of the proceeds is the state bureaucracy, i.e. the civil servants. Being employees of the state, they not only are in position to influence tremendously the efficiency with which the corruption revenue is collected but also have easier (i.e. lower cost) access to information, as compared with the rest of the population, on the wealth consequences of the governing team's activities. Thus they can affect both the gross yield of corrupt activities and the legal and competitive costs to the government. The government, therefore, also has an incentive to co-opt them in corruption activities.

An example of a fairly effective way in which this government-civil service cooperation can work is this: the government will augment the power of the civil servants over cash income-producing activities in return for the civil servants helping to hide the wealth consequences of the government's actions. The bureaucracy will use its power to augment its wealth in corrupt ways. An implication is that the existence of a corrupt government will encourage corruption within the bureaucracy of the state. This tendency of a corrupt government to give rise to a corrupt bureaucracy is made more certain by competition outside the state for positions within it, and by competition among the state bureaucrats for top positions in the state bureaucracy. In deciding whom to employ and whom to promote in the state bureaucracy, expected and past efficiency in helping to collect the corruption revenue will become an important criterion of the government.

The welfare implications are again clear. Since efficiency in corruption-revenue collection affects employment and promotion in the state bureaucracy, the most efficient persons for the state may not be employed, and the allocation of positions may not be socially efficient. Also, some highly productive potential employees will not compete for state positions because of moral reasons or because of high risk aversion. Moreover, the incentive system has been altered. The state's employees will find it advantageous to divert some of their energies to improving their efficiency in corruption-revenue collection and less on traditional (and socially valuable) activities. In short, there is a deadweight loss in wealth associated with the government-civil service cooperation (or coalition). Corruption at the highest political levels of the state reduces efficiency of the state bureaucracy.

When the government-business coalition is grafted on to that of the government and the civil service, one has in essence a government-civil service-business coalition to extract corruption revenue from the rest of the population.

Unfortunately, the activities of this coalition do more than simply transfer income to the coalition from the rest of the citizens. The activities result in deadweight economic losses and hence reduce national income and economic growth.

Added to the welfare loss due to excessive political activity and the consequences of the government-civil service-business coalition is the social cost due to differential corruption tax rates mentioned before. The existence of differential corruption tax rates means that the relative profitability of different economic activities is altered. This alteration does not reflect changes in social opportunity costs or benefits of different economic activities and is, therefore, suboptimal. Resources are made to flow into various economic activities in response to suboptimal signals.

Government corruption, in addition, leads to exit of labor and capital from the economy, as well as discouragement of capital inflow, even when in many cases they are more productive in the country with corrupt government than in the alternative country to which they go. The exit is simply to avoid the corruption tax, by going to places where such a tax either does not exist or at worst is substantially lower. Any loss of income of the exiting labor and capital due to reduced earnings in the alternative country is more than made up by the corruption tax avoided. Such exit is another avenue via which corruption has adverse effects on output. The obverse of this consideration is that a country with corrupt government would tend to attract labor and capital which are efficient at corruption activities and not so efficient at production; they flow in to participate in the government-civil service-business coalition. Corruption at the highest political levels of the state thus reduces the average level of efficiency of the factors of production that remain in the country or that get attracted from abroad.

The effect of (a) the excessive resource flow into political activity, (b) the inefficiencies consequent upon the government-civil service-business coalition, (c) the misallocation consequent upon the differential corruption tax rates, and (d) the exit of labor and capital and reduction in average factor productivity, is to cause the economy to operate and to grow at levels of production below its potential. The loss to the rest of the society consequent upon behavior to capture the corruption revenue causes the loss to the economy from corruption to be much greater than the amount of the corruption revenue received by the government, civil service, and relevant private firms. The effect of the corruption is not simply distributional; there is also an adverse effect on economic growth and real income per capita.

Directly unproductive profit-seeking activities

In addition to the above approach, it may also be useful to look at the issue from another perspective and to point out to the African population that corrupt government is the root cause of much visible socially unproductive profit-seeking behavior of individual Africans. The behavior, of course, typically consists merely of exploiting opportunities created by government regulation, controls, and sub-optimal taxation. State regulation and controls not efficiently formulated and enforced—for instance, in the context of selective intervention of the state—could give rise to incentives for rent-seeking activity widely discussed in the economics literature (see, e.g., Krueger, 1974, and Tullock, 1993). Rent seeking is an aspect of what has been termed directly unproductive profit-seeking (DUP) activity that has also attracted much academic interest (see Bhagwati, 1982).

Rent seeking takes place when individuals and firms expend scarce resources "to capture an artificially created transfer" [Tollison (1982), p. 578]. African governments have created many opportunities for rent seeking, and economic agents in the countries have vigorously sought these artificially created rents. African governments have provided numerous opportunities for rent seeking through controls, protection, monopoly rights and special privileges, and government contracts and jobs. As regards controls, prices of certain commodities—basic foodstuffs and petroleum in particular—are often controlled or regulated, as are certain house rents. Governments also often specify minimum wages, and the wages of several categories of employees are regulated via tripartite arrangements involving government, labor unions and employers. In certain countries there are controls and limits on, or regulations governing, the employment of foreign persons by enterprises. Until recently, in a number of countries, selective credit controls were being administered as well (see Johnson, 1975b). Furthermore, many African countries have allowed their currencies to be officially maintained at overvalued exchange rates, and then exchange controls and import-licensing schemes are implemented to help ration the official stock of foreign currency in the light of the excess demand situation that normally exists in such circumstances. Due to pressures from the International Monetary Fund, especially, such currency regimes have virtually vanished from the continent.

Controls and regulations are designed to fix prices below what they would be under free market situation, and/or they seek to use criteria other than those (prices, rentals, collateral/security, creditworthiness) that open markets would normally use in allocating resources. In the process, shortages arise at the established market prices, and incentives to disobey, avoid, or weakly enforce the laws or regulations are engendered. Whosoever is able to obtain a commodity the price of which is set at a level below the market-clearing price is being granted a rent equivalent to the difference between the market-clearing price and the price paid to obtain the commodity. Hence, individuals and firms are willing to spend resources campaigning, lobbying, or bribing to obtain some of the quantities of a commodity subject to price control. Similarly, anyone who is forced to sell his or her commodity or service at a price lower than what he or she could obtain under open-market conditions realizes that he or she would be granting an economic rent to anyone to whom the good is sold. Hence, he or she has an incentive to extract additional side payments from the purchaser thereby effectively reducing (in his or her favor) the effective economic rent created by the law. Moreover, those who oversee the enforcement of the laws and regulations are aware of the existence of the rents and of the incentives of market participants to capture or diminish the artificial transfers. The law-enforcement officials, therefore, have an incentive to relax enforcement of the laws and regulations and rather to act as intermediaries and mediators in the distribution of the artificial rents created—all for some fee (bribes and tips) of course.

Protection and monopoly rights and special privileges are also common in African countries and often operate together. In trade policy, rather loose and often arbitrary criteria (as opposed to say the principle of equal effective protection) are typically invoked to determine tariffs and quantitative controls on imports. Here, much of the motivation is revenue as imports are one of the most important sources of government revenue. As regards privileges, special fiscal incentives are often granted to enterprises on the basis of criteria that are generally imprecise enough to permit ad hoc, arbitrary, and capricious application. Once again, artificial rents result and those with the chance of sharing in the rents—firms and government officials—are often willing to spend resources, or induce side offers, to obtain or grant, respectively, the protection and the privileges in question.

Also, with respect to monopoly rights and special privileges, there is a particular problem in the area of minerals and petroleum, the rights to which can be extremely valuable. Many governments in Africa deliberately keep tight control over the rents created in this area—except in connection with artisanal mining rights granted by the issue of licenses sold to individual miners and small companies (as in Sierra Leone) for fees that are usually below market-clearing prices. Part of these become elements of the corruption revenue discussed above; the political teams in power (the governments) capture directly—through inducing and accepting bribes—some of the value of the mineral and petroleum rights. Indeed, in the case of monopoly rights, special privileges, and public sector contracting, the real big rents can usually be obtained by winning contracts and deals that are under the direct control of the political team in power (the president/head of government and cabinet ministers) rather than the bureaucracy (civil servants and state enterprise employees). In December 2001, the High Court of the Republic of Congo sentenced (in abstentia) former President Pascal Lissouba (at the time exiled in Britain) to 30 years imprisonment with hard labor plus a fine of 25,000 million CFA francs for deals signed in April 1993 between the Congolese government under Lissouba and an American oil company, OXY, in which Congo was to sell 50 million barrels of crude oil for US$150 million. At the time of the deal, oil was selling at US$14 a barrel in world markets (as compared with the US$3 a barrel of the deal). Four of Lissouba's cabinet ministers were also tried and convicted in absentia (each got a 20-year sentence plus a fine of CFA11, 000 million).

The government and the civil service bureaucracy typically hand out a substantial number of contracts every year for a wide array of services—supplies of spare parts, food to employees, transportation, repair and maintenance, cleaning, security, purchases of uniforms for the military, etc. States in Africa are also the biggest single employers, clearly dominating the wage and salary employment in the labor force of the formal sector. Contracts to provide certain commodities and services to the public sector, and access to government jobs, often yield economic rents to the favored recipients. Anyone who has lived in Africa knows that it often costs money—in bribes and gifts—to obtain a good job at the middle and lower levels. At the higher (senior) levels, corruption enters via the government-business-civil service coalition that we discussed earlier. It is the senior civil servants that are typically inner members of that coalition.

The ultimate challenge for agents of good economic policies is how to push for elimination of most of the above rents, by reforming the government regulations, controls, and sub-optimal taxation, while arguing for rents created in the context of selective intervention for the purpose of accelerating economic development (see Chapter 8). An appropriate approach would be to have all rents decided utilizing deliberative councils that ensure that the rents are created in light of their positive economic effects and that access to them is based on merit defined in turn using criteria that are clear, transparent, fair and legitimated by the population at large.

Designing Government Reforms

From the discussion so far in the chapter, it must by now be evident that in discussing control of corruption, it is important to distinguish the case in which the corruption to be controlled is at the middle and lower levels of government from the case in which the corruption to be controlled is at the highest levels of government. I deal later in the section with the latter case. First, I shall focus on the case in which corruption is a serious problem at the middle and lower levels of government but it is not significant at the highest levels. In such a case, where the institutions are weak, the political leaders have the incentive to change the rules and to put in place the organizational arrangements to enforce them. In that context, in the design and implementation of a *government* program to control corruption, credibility and legitimacy would be the two most important fundamental criteria to be applied in assessing the quality of a reform program. The substantive reform measures should also have clear objectives, and be effective, enforceable, and sustainable.

Credibility and legitimacy

It seems logical that, for a corruption reform program to be successful, it must have credible commitment from both the state and the elites of society and be supported (and hence legitimated) by the population at large. Credibility and legitimacy of a program should lower its implementation costs and enhance the prospects for its sustainability. In the African context, this is a major challenge. Even if the rules are strengthened, their enforcement are made difficult by strong societal loyalty bonds (ethnic and familial) in the face of an absence of a feeling of ownership of (and hence loyalty to) the state. The cooperation required for enforcement (e.g., via whistle blowing) may be lacking. In this sort of environment, credibility and legitimacy would be advanced by: a fairly open and inclusive process of deliberation in drawing up the program (rules, procedures, and organizational aspects); transparent implementation; and clear signals from the elites in state and society that they are committed to the program.

As mentioned before, a major difficulty in addressing corruption in Africa is that it is often tolerated at the highest levels of the state. The role of a government-business-civil service coalition in high-level corruption was also discussed. When the government in power is committed to reducing corruption and wants to put in place a program at the middle and lower levels it must demonstrate its true commitment via appropriate signals. The behavior and actions of the political leader, his or her family members, close political associates and cabinet ministers would constitute strong signals of commitment on the side of the ruling elite (the government). Permitting the press freely to investigate and report possible acts of corruption would be another important signal. Moreover, speedy and heavy punishment—dismissal, prosecution, conviction, etc. — of important state officials for corrupt acts would be pertinent signaling of commitment to implementation of the program. Transparent implementation would be crucial in assuring ethnic groups that there is no discrimination among them in applying rules.

In Uganda, for example, in the early years of the Yoweri Museveni regime, apart from determined attempts to build a sound legal basis to fight corruption, including better attempts at enforcement of anti-corruption laws in the books for a number of decades (such as the Prevention of Corruption Act of 1970), freedom of the press in this area was promoted, and scores of civil servants dismissed. A leadership code was also promulgated, among other things calling for annual declaration of income, assets, and liabilities by leaders; standards of behavior with respect to gifts and other benefits in kind; avoiding conflicts of interest; and limits for use of public property by public officials. Most interestingly, perhaps, the political leadership in Uganda worked on building broad support for the anti-corruption campaign, by encouraging formation of associational groups in civil society, including youth and women's organizations (see Ruzindana, 1997).

In Nigeria, which has received the Berlin-based Transparency International label of being close to (and sometimes) the most corrupt country in the world, President Olusegun Obasanjo declared a "war" against state corruption, and insisted that there would be "no sacred cow." Given the long involvement of the army in politics, he found it useful to start there (among other measures by retiring several officers who had held political office). He succeeded in having legislation he deemed appropriate enacted (including an anti-corruption bill in 2000), to facilitate, for instance, probing financial excesses of state officials and removing corrupt government officials promptly. He organized an anti-graft panel, which among other things recommended cancellation or modification of several approved contracts agreed by previous government(s). General Obasanjo also showed determination to recover a substantial amount of funds stolen by previous governments (especially the Abacha government and family). During his years in office he worked to enhance transparency in state contracting (and hence bidding processes) and other state operations. He also directed all ministries and parastatals to establish anti-corruption units, to help give teeth to his program. General Obasanjo's problem remained, nevertheless, enormous and his achievement in reducing corruption in that complex environment remains for future investigators to assess. At the core of his difficulties was that it remained unclear that he had succeeded in getting a critical minimum of committed domestic support for several elements of his program.[10]

Objectives and instruments

A program to fight corruption should no doubt be part of a larger governance agenda to improve efficiency and accountability of the state. To

---

[10] See, also, the discussion in Kallon (2004) of the history of attempts to control corruption in Sierra Leone and some of the reasons why there has not been much success.

advance credibility and legitimacy and ensure effectiveness and sustainability, the governance agenda would benefit from clear objectives and instruments. In this light, it may be useful to have instruments that are easy to understand and transparent in their use and application. As regards the anti-corruption campaign, useful would be quantifiable indicators of success in fighting corruption. The whole program would also be made public.

For example, objectives of the governance program could be stated as promoting: (1) efficiency in the allocation of government resources, including reducing corruption and waste; (2) efficiency and fairness in government revenue operations; and (3) objectivity in government employment and promotions. It should be possible, then, to have clear elaboration as well as public disclosure of the substantive content of these objectives and the instruments to be used to achieve them. The instruments would include, for example: personnel selection committees and processes that are objective with respective to membership and standards; open competitive bidding for contracts; proper and timely auditing of government accounts; sound legal basis for fighting corruption; penalties for corrupt acts; steps taken to clean up (from corruption) the legal system, including the police; measures to ensure the autonomy of the judicial system; cost-benefit analysis in making government investment decisions; increasing pay in government; and objectivity (examinations, performance criteria, seniority) in determining personnel action (such as promotions) in government. Indicators of success in fighting corruption would perhaps be of two basic types. One would be testament to convince outside observers that the instruments to enhance efficiency were being consistently applied. The other would be a listing of corrupt acts actually discovered and the punishments meted out. These objectives and many of the instruments and indicators are widely known and accepted in principle. African civil society leaders and the international community can help African governments do better in their design and implementation of programs in this general area.

Sustainability

Once a program begins to be implemented, all sorts of difficulties could emerge to threaten its sustainability. To reduce the risk of reversal one would suggest paying particular attention to the deliberative process in putting the program together, the legal framework for the program, and to civil service reform.

Of major importance would be getting the deliberative process rationalized, to ensure credibility and accountability at a national level. The deliberative process would involve broad scale consultation of various segments of the state and civil society to ensure that diverse viewpoints are considered in designing the program and planning its implementation. A formal deliberative or consultative council seems most advisable. This council could be in place for several years with varying intensity of work depending on the circumstances. The council could advise on issues like legal framework, appropriate signals to indicate commitment of state and society, public education about the costs of corruption, and general publicity campaigns.

It would be essential at the very start of the program to take measures to solidify the legal framework. This would involve ensuring that all the necessary laws exist, authority to make regulations are clearly delegated, and that all the required agencies are in place with appropriate authority to perform their assigned tasks. The process of cleaning up a corrupt legal system—the police, the courts, etc.—would also be pursued in earnest.

Finally, it would be advisable to address, comprehensively, certain fundamentals affecting civil service performance, namely, pay, and the transparency, fairness and objectivity of public sector employment and promotion. Most Africans do not believe it realistic to fight hard-core and widespread corruption without addressing personnel remuneration, recruitment and development issues in the public sector. This, inter alia, means that measures to address corruption via monitoring and punishment will not have widespread support in the absence of salary changes. It would be tantamount to promulgating a norm that is not generally supported by the community concerned; there will be no enforcers of the norm in the population at large. Hence the measures will not be implemented effectively. It follows, therefore, that civil service reform must be vigorously pursued; for it would be difficult to raise, substantially, public sector salaries in many of the African countries without such a reform, coupled with fiscal reforms and more rational economic policies to boost general economic development. Once again, agency to increase demand for good economic policies will play an essential role here as well.

The case of high-level government corruption

When the problem is the control of corruption at the highest levels of government (the political leadership), it is necessary to strengthen the institutions and organizations (the press, electoral system, legal system) that impose competitive and legal costs on corruption. Yet those who should strengthen these institutions and organizations have an interest (appropriation of corruption revenue) in perpetuating the weak institutions and organizations. One approach to this dilemma would be to simply wait for political mutation/innovation to occur. For instance, by sheer chance, some political team might emerge with such a high degree of aversion to corruption that it voluntarily chooses to begin the process of strengthening the institutions and organizations that can effectively control corrupt practices of governments. Until such political mutation/innovation takes place, the governments of African countries—in the face of weak constitutional and other legal constraints as well as nondemocratic political regimes—could remain merely sets of economic men maximizing the corruption revenue (net of collection costs) they receive from gaining control of the state.

To wait for the eventuality of political mutation to bring about noncorrupt leadership is not really a good alternative, because such mutation is not predictable and, worse still, may never happen. At the same time, since the powerful political forces benefit from corruption they might never support institutional changes to deal with the corruption. I have already stated above, in this chapter, that, in the face of high-level government corruption, spontaneous-order agency organizations may be unavoidable, if a substantial reduction in corruption is to occur. But I also stated that this may not be enough because low incomes and ethnicity will tend to hamper the willingness and ability of African societies to cooperate and facilitate such an approach. Even the education about the economic costs of corruption, as suggested earlier, may not suffice to elicit the appropriate cooperation to dent the problem. But the education may have one salutary effect. The fact that corruption adversely affects economic growth might strengthen agency for good economic policies as discussed in Chapter 2. This raises a possibility in the fight against corruption. Namely, rather than focus heavily and directly on high-level corruption, societal agency could focus mainly on economic growth. Increasing the demand for good policies via the mechanisms discussed in Chapter 2 should force governments to introduce sound policies that in turn reduce corruption at the highest levels. In general, finding a way to hold the political leadership accountable for the economic performance of the country seems, therefore, a feasible short-term to medium-term approach to reducing government corruption at the highest levels. Such an indirect approach is likely to succeed as it is far less confrontational vis-à-vis the political leadership. In addition, mobilization of popular support for the approach should be far easier. As incomes increase, other factors engendering reduction in high level corruption will begin to emerge, as discussed at the beginning of the chapter. In the meantime, a political leadership which has the incentive to reduce its own corrupt practices to promote economic growth will also have the incentive to introduce and enforce reform measures to reduce corruption at the middle and lower levels of government.

Concluding Remarks

The analysis of the chapter suggests that African countries that succeed in addressing the problem of government corruption, especially at its highest levels, would be ones where the citizens cooperate to (i) bring about a state towards which citizens have a sense of ownership and hence loyalty; (ii) agree anti-corruption norms; and (iii) give autonomy to the state from society and demand accountability in return. This would all benefit from constitutional reforms utilizing stable equilibrium determination processes. Civil society, supported by the international community perhaps, can also find a way to convince the political leadership that the latter has a self-interest in reducing government corruption, because of the adverse effects of corruption on economic growth. An indirect way to achieve this is to mobilize society to demand good economic policy environments and make the government in power accountable for the economic performance of the country. There is, once again, a need for agency. Finally, a campaign by the political leadership to reduce government corruption in the state bureaucracy would be most successful if it is an element of a comprehensive and legitimated economic program that stresses economic growth and government efficiency—in short, in the context of instituting a good economic policy environment.

7

Political Leadership

It is remarkable how often one hears people, especially Africans, when talking about the continent as a whole or about a given country, will say that the main cause ultimately for the poor economic performance of the sub-Saharan African countries is a failure of leadership.[1] They might go on to indicate how this poor leadership manifests itself, e.g., corruption, poor economic policies.[2] Yet one would wait in vain for explanations as to why good political leadership can be so hard to find in a whole continent (with the possible exceptions, some would say, of Mauritius, Botswana, and South Africa). The institutions of the modern state, after all, are the outcome of political and social forces within a country. Therefore, it is difficult to avoid the conclusion that to explain the failure of political leadership in the modern African state one must look beyond the state

---

[1] See, for example, Achebe (1983) and Museveni (2000). Ayittey (1992) is also all about the failure of leadership in the continent—a kind of betrayal of the trust put in leaders to guide the ships of their states to great heights. Gyimah-Boadi and Van de Walle (1996) also see the emergence of a developmental state in the typical African country unlikely without effective political leadership.

[2] Many authors simply point out that Africa's poor economic performance is the result of poor "policy environment"—evidenced mainly by poor delivery of public services and weak macroeconomic policies—without much discussion of the socio-political context that produces these policies [see, e.g., Collier and Gunning (1999)].

itself to the whole national community at large that instituted (by default or design) the state and its institutions.

I believe that, fundamentally, there are two sources of failure of political leadership in economic governance in the modern African state. First, consistent with the argument in Chapter 2, in their first moves following independence, African societies focused on political power sharing among social groups and regions and neglected economic governance, in disputations over the institutions of their modern national states. One consequence was a general failure of citizens of African countries to cooperate to establish a clear institutional framework (including ways to ensure implementation) for broad and sacrosanct rights of citizens (vis-à-vis the government) to be consulted on economic policy matters, including through their elected representatives in parliament. This institutional framework would have included clear understandings on the autonomy and accountability of the government—the political leadership in power—in economic policy and management. The omission has been particularly costly in the sub-Saharan African context. The typical modern African state was effectively a new political community established at independence—even before shared ethical values and norms had been agreed and internalized to help regulate behavior and complex interactions within the new national state. Until such shared values and norms emerged, the modern African state was bound to find indispensable formal legal and bureaucratic rules to constrain behavior and guide expectations in interactions among persons domiciled within it.

Second, in addition to the absence of broad consultation rights agreed at independence, there has been little cooperation among citizens since, either to ensure the efficient and effective management of the state or to decide the rules and norms governing the distribution of benefits flowing from the state. This has resulted in free riding in monitoring the efficiency of the state and tragedy of the commons ('free pasture for all') in exploiting state benefits. Citizens in the African countries use one or more of three strategies in the commons exploitation game. The first is participation in a government-civil service-business coalition to tax everyone else and share the proceeds (see Chapter 6). The second strategy is use of some appropriate loyalty bond of solidarity either to capture government itself or to claim special benefits from some particular leadership group in power. Such bonds tend particularly to be grounded in ethnicity (see Chapter 5). The third strategy involves use of familialism—the ability of one to convince the political leader of the sincere depth of one's reverence for him or her as father or mother of the nation, thereby establishing a connection to use to extract some special perk from the leader, a perk ultimately paid for from state resources. [3]

Compounding this second factor—little cooperation among ordinary citizens (including societal elites)—in many if not most African countries is the absence, since independence, of any sizable group of persons with independent economic base and with sufficient incentive (economic or political) and ability (especially organizational) to emerge with a coherent and credible agenda for improved economic governance by the state. Such an agenda would entail putting in place an adequate institutional and organizational framework for better accountability of the government to society at large.[4] One consequence is that the role of the government (or the state in general) in distribution has come to completely overshadow its role in production (that is, output).

Recent discussions at the global level of leadership failure in Africa, and governance in general, often quickly turn to a discussion of democracy and democratization in Africa. One is then left with the implication that to improve political leadership and economic governance of the state one must press for democratization. I would argue that the democratization problem should be kept separate from the leadership problem, at least from an economic perspective. They are both elements of a socio-political equilibrium, but democratization is

[3] In an interesting book, Schatzberg (2001) gives his perspective on how familial and other metaphors reflect Africans' perspectives on aspects of power, legitimacy and other political factors in their world.

[4] For example, many authors have emphasized the role of what Moore (1966) calls "men of commerce in both the countryside and towns" in the constitutional reforms of England, which included especially the Glorious Revolution of 1688. See also North and Weingast (1989, 1996).

neither necessary nor sufficient for improving political leadership for prosperity. Indeed, the relationship between political leadership and economic development is far more straightforward and easier to observe than the relationship between democracy and development. In this chapter, the interest is in an analysis of the factors in the socio-political equilibrium of the sub-Saharan African continent as they relate to political leadership. In this author's view, good political leadership will occur in a socio-political equilibrium where demand pressures or exogenous constraints impel the government to have self-interest in improving economic policy and management. In such equilibrium, the socio-political environment contains structural factors that ensure effective government autonomy and accountability.

From a positive perspective, other things being equal, the prospect for improving political leadership in African countries will vary positively with citizens' ability to reach understandings to bring about such a socio-political environment. From a normative perspective, the challenge would be to work out the nature and content of understandings that could realistically be reached—understandings that are self-enforcing in the sense that everyone would willingly obey them. In many of these countries, it will be difficult to reach such understandings, because the political leaders will be hard to convince about accepting voluntarily the required government accountability while societal leaders will be difficult to convince about granting the necessary autonomy of government from the society.

Political Leadership and Economic Development

Political leadership is a very important factor in the economic performance of national states. Hence a political leader (or the political leadership in power) with certain qualities could make a substantial contribution to the economic development process (see Johnson, 1986, for an earlier treatment of themes developed in this section).

Transactional and transforming leadership

One useful view of *leadership* is that of James MacGregor Burns. He defines leadership as "the reciprocal process of mobilizing, by persons with certain motives and values, various economic, political, and other resources, in a context of competition and conflict, in order to realize goals independently or mutually held by both leaders and followers"(Burns, 1978, p. 425). John W. Gardner, somewhat similarly, defines leadership as "the process of persuasion or example by which an individual (or leadership team) induces a group to pursue objectives held by the leader or shared by the leader and his or her followers" (Gardner, 1990, p. 1).

Burns, in discussing the crucial role of goals, distinguishes two aspects of leadership—*transactional* leadership and *transforming* leadership. In the former case, the object of the relationship between leader and follower is to complete a bargain, which furthers the individual interests of the persons, or groups involved, each as it were "going their separate ways." Thus the trader who contacts another person to engage in an exchange transaction would have assumed transactional leadership.

A more important form of leadership is what Burns calls *transforming* leadership. Of this, he writes [Burns, p. 425]:

> "The premise of this leadership is that, whatever the separate interests persons might hold, they are presently or potentially united in the pursuit of 'higher' goals, the realization of which is tested by the achievement of significant change that represents the collective or pooled interests of leaders and followers."

Important in Burns' analysis is that true leaders are power holders but they are not power wielders. Leaders, rather than manipulating followers to act solely in the interest of the leaders, induce "followers to act for certain goals that represent the values and the motivations . . . of both leaders and followers"

[Burns, p. 19]. The "genius of leadership lies in the manner in which leaders see and act on their own and their followers' values and motivations" (Burns, p.19).

An implication is that a *government* (that is, a governing team of politicians) when it is exercising transforming political leadership is in a relationship with its followers that does not involve naked power wielding. The motive for the actions of the government exercising transforming political leadership cannot be simply the enhancement of the private wealth of the government. For where this is the case the government would be generally corrupt. We have seen in an earlier chapter that an economy with corrupt government would operate below its capacity to produce goods and services—that is, inside its social production possibility frontier.

This last point also serves to bring out a difference between transforming political leaders and entrepreneurs (of private and state-owned enterprises). The driving motive of the private entrepreneur is profit; his or her profit-making activity directly enhances own private wealth. But the government, even though its activity might increase the general wealth of the nation, by creating a favorable environment, should not act mainly in light of the private wealth implication for itself (i.e., its members) when it is exercising transforming political leadership.

Innovation, opportunity, and ability

A leader can effect *institutional innovations*, i.e., he or she can induce radical changes in the institutions of the country. The scope for institutional innovations will vary among societies—for some societies have deeply embedded institutions that are difficult for any leader to drastically modify.

A leader may accept a set of relevant basic or fundamental institutions, but make *methodological innovations* to change the effectiveness of institutions, including the introduction of lower level bodies and organizations that help determine the effectiveness of the fundamental institutions. In short, the leader can engender marginal changes to the set of institutions of the country.

One can call the *opportunity for leadership* the chance to motivate institutional and/or methodological innovations in the pursuit of certain goals (ends). For this, the leadership (the government) will have certain tools at its command. Borrowing from Arndt (1984), these tools could be classified within three functional groupings, viz., authority, inspiration, and management. In the pursuit of the goal of economic development, in the African context, the institutional and methodological innovations could work via intermediate targets or goals, namely, the risk to private entrepreneurship and the incentives for efficient allocation of private resources.

One can also speak of the *ability for leadership*—that is, the capacity for transforming leadership. This would comprise four general elements. Failure of a particular leader can therefore be due to deficiencies with respect to one or more of these abilities.

The first element in the ability for leadership is general *moral character*—i.e., honesty, integrity, and discipline. The greater the degree to which these characteristics inhere in an individual, the greater, other things being equal, would be his or her ability for leadership. The leader with low moral character will exhibit tendency to corruption, lack of integrity, or capriciousness in behavior. As a result, general uncertainty is increased and economic incentives become distorted. Efficiency in corrupt practices that enrich the leader would be rewarded over social efficiency in resource use. Moreover, there would be a tendency by the leader to reward sycophants, and to manifest nepotism, prejudice, and arbitrary discrimination in his or her economic decisionmaking. An important consequence is that the most efficient private producers may not be awarded property rights and contracts, and some of the more able individuals and firms in the society may be induced to leave or close down, respectively.

The second element of leadership ability is basic *societal understanding.* The deeper the understanding of the people—namely, their basic aspirations and how to motivate them to act in a particular way—the greater is the ability for leadership. Also, the greater the understanding of the nature of the political and resource constraints faced by the country both in its domestic policy and in its international relations, the greater is societal understanding, and thus the ability for leadership. Lack of societal understanding will reveal itself in lack of realism in policies, techniques and aspirations of the leader, which will cause him or her to fail to provide appropriate incentives. He or she would, therefore, be generally unsuccessful in attempts to motivate followers to cooperate and participate actively to produce results desired by the leader. Such a leader might even provoke passive resistance or active opposition to his or her policies. As in the case of low moral character, the leader with limited societal understanding could induce capital flight and brain drain by citizens, and suboptimal direct investment by foreigners.

Related to the second element of leadership ability is a third, namely, *persuasive communicative skills*. This is the capacity to communicate effectively with others in the society to persuade them about the merits of adopting certain ideas and practices. This communication could be effected via speeches, writings, and meetings, in public, formal or informal settings (Oliver, 1989, gives life stories of leaders in Asia who were very effective in this regard.) A leader without strong persuasive communication skills would not be able to inspire powerful persons in the community to make major institutional and structural changes in the society. In desperation, a leader with political power might then resort to coercion to implement his or her policies, which could lead to serious human cost and unpredictable consequences for the future, particularly in the area of constitutionalism and the sustainability of the policies themselves.

The fourth element of the ability for leadership is what could be simply termed the *innovative ability* of a person. This skill would tend to be greater the deeper the general conceptual understanding of institutions and their possibilities in the particular social setting of the country concerned; the less the aversion toward risk-taking; and the greater the willingness to bear uncertainty. Lack of innovative ability shows up as dearth of imaginative ideas—institutional and methodological—and trepidation to be avant-garde. A leader without innovative skills but with societal understanding would invariably know what doesn't work but can hardly devise policies and techniques that work in his or her society. He or she copies and fumbles without serious analysis. By trial and error he or she might succeed but could fail too.

Leadership and development

In sum, transforming political leadership helps create the conditions or the environment for the efficient organization of society's resources, for investment, and for sustained economic growth. No doubt, the leader or the leadership team makes this contribution by performing the *tasks* that Gardner (1990) elaborates so clearly in his book. That is, following Gardner, the leader's tasks can be seen as: (1) goal setting; (2) affirming and regenerating values; (3) motivating followers; (4) managing programs and people as necessary; (5) achieving workable unity and diminishing and resolving conflicts among followers; (6) explaining—tasks, problems, and rationale for action; (7) serving as a symbol for the group; (8) representing the group in its dealings with others; and (9) fostering the process of renewal to maintain the vitality of the group and its ability to cope in a changing world.

The success of leadership could be measured by the degree to which it clearly contributes to raising the potential rate of economic growth and the extent to which it helps ensure that the actual growth rate of the economy is normally (i.e., barring adverse impact of forces external to the economy) kept equal to the potential of the country. In short, the contribution of the leadership is the marginal increase in growth that can be attributed to the improved conditions that it creates. Political leadership makes this contribution by (a) reducing the risk of entrepreneurship and private investment, and (b) erecting appropriate signals for inducing efficient allocation of resources in the economy, thereby augmenting the marginal productivity of all resources available to the economy. In broad terms, using expressions employed by Arndt in discussing the three major "functions" of political leadership mentioned before, which also encapsulate Gardner's tasks of leadership, the means of political leadership involve (1) the exercise of authority, (2) inspiration and (3) management.

Political Leadership Failures in Africa

Listening to Africans leaves one with a feeling of consensus that political leadership failures have resulted from low moral character, limited societal understanding, and lack of innovative ability. This is consistent with the fact that, in their illustrations of leadership failures, corruption and inappropriate economic policies have loomed large.

Societal complicity

If Africans hold this view, the obvious question is how come African societies have allowed the situation of poor leadership to continue? Surely this would indicate systemic failures. These, in turn, could reflect structural weaknesses in the political systems such that there is no logical tendency for those with the greatest ability for leadership to also be given the opportunity for leadership. Namely, in the existing political systems it would be only a matter of chance that persons among the most capable in the societies become leaders, as the methods and systemic processes by which leaders get chosen do not have a natural tendency to produce good leaders. A search for poor leadership in Africa must therefore look closely at the socio-political systems that produce the leaders.

Indeed, those who have studied leadership have never ceased to reiterate that the context (historical or social setting, etc.) is extremely important in determining leadership; that leadership is a team effort; and that where there is effective leadership in a society, leadership is dispersed throughout that society (on this see, especially, Gardner, 1990, chapters 1-4). Poor leadership at the top cannot be blamed on one man or woman alone. As evidenced from the two definitions given earlier, followers are important in the process. For the leadership team is in principle helping to achieve shared goals founded on shared values of the community comprising leaders and followers. The role of the leader in giving shape to the goals is not always clear and may or may not be substantial. The role of the leadership team in forming values is often even minor, as cultural and social constraints and history may be very important. In dynamic settings, of course, when the environment is changing rapidly, the role of the leader could be quite substantial. Yet, even in such dynamic situations, the society matters a great deal. In general, the two-way relationship between followers and leaders, despite the very important role that leaders might play in this interaction, is behind the statement: "*good constituents tend to produce good leaders*" (see Gardner, 1990, p. 24).

The political leadership problem in sub-Saharan Africa is traceable to the mistakes made at independence, discussed in Chapter 2. As a result of the processes used to establish institutions, Africans were left with weak institutions controlling the state, an absence of loyalty of citizens to the state, and low cooperation among citizens in establishing standards and norms for institution building and for selecting their leaders. In this environment, African politics have come to be dominated by ethnicity and the attraction of corruption revenue. Hence, those who have a comparative advantage in playing the ethnic game and in mobilizing resources for the high stake battle to obtain the right to capture corruption revenue by controlling government are able to dominate the political leadership. There is, thus, a serious social dilemma problem here. The median African voter, in deciding whom to vote for, inter alia by calculating the net benefits to him or her of voting for a team competing for leadership, looks mainly at ethnic ties, the possibility of sharing in any corruption revenue, and the ability of a political team to raise corruption revenue; only marginally does the median voter look at whether the leadership team will introduce good economic policies that will benefit the whole country. Reducing ethnicity and strengthening the institutions to control corruption at the highest levels are, therefore, two ways to remove this distortion in the playing field for political leadership. Mobilizing citizens to focus on the ability of the political teams to introduce good economic policy environment will also contribute. Cooperation is required for these solutions to the social dilemma. Until such cooperation comes about, and the relevant constitutional and other changes are put into effect, the winning political teams for leadership in most of the countries will not typically be ones with the greatest ability to bring about good economic policy environments.

Cooperation and shared understandings

Citizens, to be effective in their demand for transforming political leadership in economic governance, would benefit from having shared understandings within civil society in three areas. The first is the role of the state in economic development. The second area is the role of the political leader and his or her team (that is, the government comprising the cabinet and the government bureaucracy) in ensuring that the state perform its assigned role well. This role of the government (the executive) would be vis-à-vis those played by Parliament (or some other representative body), autonomous public bodies (such as a central bank and state enterprises), and private bodies (such as institutes and interest groups in the public sphere). The third area where shared understandings help would be the nature of institutional and organizational arrangements to ensure that the most appropriate persons contend for leadership, get chosen, and then be held accountable for their performance. Citizen groups and bodies (societal agents) could develop strategies of cooperation with the extant government. Such cooperation would include finding ways to convince the leader that it is in his or her self-interest to reform the processes involved in selection of the political leadership of the state. This approach could require enormous leadership within civil society itself.

Role of Democratization

It is sometimes felt that good leadership would emerge with democratization. One can think of democracy, in the same way as Tilly (1997a), as consisting of (1) broad citizenship, (2) relatively equal citizenship, (3) binding consultation of citizens with respect to state policies and personnel, and (4) protection of citizens, especially minorities, from arbitrary state action. This approach seems comprehensive enough to be consistent with other approaches. For instance, in discussing democracy in Southeast Asian countries, Neher and Marlay (1995) use three broad characteristics in grouping regimes, namely, citizen participation, electoral competition, and civil liberties. Electoral competition is assessed according to "regularity of elections, diversity of candidates and platforms, impact of the elected national legislative body, impact of the elected chief authority, and absence of election fraud and control" (p. 195). *Competition* and *participation* are generally thought to be the two most essential requirements for the *democratic process* (see, Dahl, 1989). *Competition* is the degree to which elections are contested; hence an indicator could be "the percentage of the smaller parties' total share of the votes cast" in an election. "*Participation* is the percentage of the total population that actually vote[s] in [an] election" [Dahl (1989), p. 240].

Tilly argues that there is no a priori reason to believe that only one set of circumstances produces and sustains democracy. The "militaristic itinerary" of Europe, he concedes, is only one road to democracy. "Others pass through the federation of small-scale democracies, the defeat or self-destruction of authoritarian regimes, and the imposition of constitutions by outside powers." He does feel, though, that in all cases social construction matters. It matters through its impact on shared understandings, especially with respect to expectations "that agents of the state will in the future honor the relatively equal rights of a broad citizenry, that they will yield to citizens' collective decisions, that they will protect citizens from arbitrary state action"(pp. 212-3).

Political leadership and democracy

One knows from experience that the following proposition is not true. *Proposition 1: Good political leadership in economic governance if and only if democracy.* One only needs to point to the recent history of some East Asian countries. But the case for democracy would still be strong (that is, democracy still wins) if the following two propositions hold true. *Proposition 2: Poor political leadership is more likely in nondemocratic regimes than in democratic regimes. Proposition 3: Poor political leadership survives longer on average in nondemocratic than in democratic regimes.* I would contend that propositions 2 and 3 are both supported by experience. Hence, the following proposition holds true. *Proposition 4: A country with a nondemocratic regime and poor political leadership will very likely benefit economically from having a regime change that brings about democracy.* This, no doubt, is why so many external agents—governments and international organizations—with leverage over African countries push for democratization as part of the process of improving political leadership and economic policymaking and governance in general.

Still the line of causation between economic growth and the political regime is unclear (see Barro, 1996, for instance) and it appears that it is legitimate and good political leadership that really matters for economic growth in the end. There would, indeed, seem to be a problem in trying to approach leadership and good governance indirectly by striving or waiting for democracy. Both democracy and leadership are socio-political constructs and the one does not necessarily imply the other. This is why Proposition 1 does not hold in general. In particular, for sustainability, democracy requires legitimation, via broad acceptance and consent from the population at large and from different cohesive groups.

Democratic transition

For more than one generation, various social scientists have wrestled with the question of how to bring about democracy (the issue of transition to democracy) and, even more importantly, with how to sustain democracy (the consolidation issue). After all that discussion, the view seems to be that factors such as national unity (all citizens agree they belong to the same political community), literacy, urbanization, per capita income, international pressures (especially from donors and lenders during a country's serious economic crisis), and the existence of a strong middle class (especially if committed to capitalism), all appear to contribute to make transition possible and to ensure consolidation (and hence sustainability).

There is virtually always struggle and bargaining among elites involved. Thus, the transition is more difficult without support from those in power (political leaders) and sustainability is virtually impossible without broad social acceptability [see, e.g., Rustow (1970), the papers by Haggard and Kaufman, Joseph, and Waterbury in Anderson (1999), and Przeworski (1988)]. As Przeworski (1988, p. 64) puts it: "Democracy is possible when the relevant political forces can find institutions that would provide a reasonable guarantee that their interests would not be affected in a highly adverse manner in the course of democratic competition. Democracy cannot be a result of substantive compromise, but it can be a result of an institutional compromise" [see, also, Rueschemeyer, Stephens, and Stephens (1992)]. As Huber, Rueschemeyer, and Stephens (1993) put it in reporting on their extensive comparative research: "the economically dominant classes accepted democracy only where their political interests were effectively protected by large parties of a conservative or non-ideological character" (p. 75). In addition, "the bourgeoisie often comes around to support democracy once it turns out that its interests can be protected within the system."

On the evolution of democratization in Africa

I would posit that, in Africa, in the evolution of democratization, there has been a convergence towards a particular institutional and organizational model that, once achieved by a country, would tend to last for some time as a temporary equilibrium before the next leap forward in the process.[5] I shall call this—for identification purposes—*transitional African democratic model (TADM)*. The model is emerging in light of several forces. First, there is some genuine fear that democracy in the western sense (multi-party majoritarian democracy) could aggravate ethnic tensions. Of course, there are those who see this (with some justification) as really a leadership ploy, namely, that the ruling elites use ethnicity for political advantage and the political leaders use the argument of trying to prevent disruptive ethnic conflict (including violence) as an excuse to defend their authoritarianism and effective one-party rule (see, e.g., Ake, 1993). Second, to many, both Westminster-type parliamentary systems and one-party regimes have failed in Africa.[6] Museveni, who came to power in 1986, until recently for example, pushed, via his National Resistance Movement, the idea of a no-party state, as an inclusive approach to democracy in the interest of national unity (see the discussion in Mugaju and Oloka-Onyango, 2000). Third, authoritarian regimes, whether military or civilian, have tended to degenerate and end up being corrupt, inefficient, and repressive of basic civil rights. Fourth, under regimes without term limits, it has been difficult to get rid of ineffective leaders in a peaceful manner. The protests in Zambia, which forced Chiluba to change his mind from trying to alter the Constitution so that when his second term ended in 2001 he could run for a third term, was a clear message that the people were determined to insist on term limits. A similar determination of the populace in Malawi discouraged Muluzi from tampering with constitutional limit on presidential terms. Fifth, from an economics perspective, ideological or class cleavages are not very important (although not unimportant) in African countries.

[5] See, also, the very interesting case studies in Villalón and VonDoepp (2005) of the democratization experience since 1990 in Benin, Central African Republic, Congo, Guinea-Bissau, Madagascar, Malawi, Mali, Mozambique, Niger, and Zambia, especially highlighting the interactions of institutions and elite behavior in shaping this experience.

[6] For an analysis of the "dismantling of the multi-party competitive regimes introduced in the period of decolonization", see, e.g., Ruth Collier (1982). The discussion of factors in the emergence of one party states in West Africa by Zolberg (1966) is also of value in this context.

Finally, thanks to Africa's poor economic and financial situation, the leverage of western democracies and international financial organizations (notably the IMF and the World Bank) have increased tremendously in the majority of African countries, and these donors and lenders have sometimes used their leverage to press for what are essentially democratic reforms in exchange for financial support.

The TADM includes, especially, from a constitutional point of view, the following: (1) guarantee of basic civil liberties (freedom of expression and association) and open competitive elections with universal suffrage; (2) presidential systems (in contrast to parliamentary systems)[7]; (3) a strong executive, relative to parliament, in economic decisionmaking; (4) term limits for presidents; and (5) substantial local autonomy (by region, chieftaincy, town, district, etc). An essential part of the TADM compromise is that (6) government (comprising the executive and the civil service) is expected, in its economic and political management, to practice co-optation.

It is not clear yet whether there will be convergence, in the continent, to any particular electoral system, in particular majoritarian (or so-called plurality) system versus proportional representation system. In addition, the nature and degree of political devolution (local government) systems are likely to vary enormously, resulting in a large number of effective political organizational structures in the continent.

The TADM will have to address a number of basic and troublesome issues that will arise along the way. The first is how to guarantee the fairness and independence of the judicial system. The second is how to guard against the risk that the co-optation strategy, if managed effectively, would lead inevitably to one-party hegemony, even without coercion. While these are real dangers, especially the first, I do believe that the tendency toward term limits will help in this regard. Once a dominant leader is no longer running for office, his or her party will not necessarily have an advantage. Indeed, persons who have accumulated grievances

[7] Presidential systems here also include systems with both a president and prime minister.

against the ruling party but have been reluctant to alter their votes because of a feeling of loyalty to the leader will now feel released from that burden once the particular leader concerned is no longer in the running.

The third problem that TADM will face is how to prevent co-optation from degenerating into a policy of simply ensuring tribal or ethnic balance, thereby fueling ethnic consciousness and frustrating efforts to reduce such consciousness over time. Again, there is reason to worry here. In line with the argument in Chapter 5, it is the hope that the authorities would strive for reducing ethnicity over time; indeed, in the current context, they should rather accelerate policies to ensure that other interests (e.g., professional) come to influence the corporate identity of persons far more than does ethnic origin.

The fourth problem for TADM is the devolution question. Apart from the details, which need to be worked out in each country, serious attempt would need to be made to ensure that such devolution does indeed improve governance of the country at large and increase local participation in national decisionmaking and monitoring of the state. Ake (1993), for example, states that the attempts of African states to institute more local governments may be simply to "separate [the local peoples] from meaningful participation at the national level; the granting of local authority is not a liberty but a constraint" (p. 75). Of importance would be the twin issues of citizenship and citizenship rights at the local level, inter alia, to prevent social and political exclusion of certain individuals and to ensure equality of basic rights at the local level. Given the history of local government structure and administration in many countries, as well as the traditional structure of political and property rights, modernization will prove to be challenging exercises in many cases. Fanthorpe (2001) notes that holding on to "traditions" that allocate basic "rights to land, living space and legal protection" according to certain criteria of "native" status—criteria that promote attenuated rights among citizens and frustrate certain "independent initiatives in wealth creation"—risk enlarging the numbers of persons who feel excluded, in the rural areas (Mamdani, 1996, should be interesting reading in this regard).

Fifth, the issue of autonomy and accountability of the executive (and of the government in general) in the economic sphere still will need serious attention. A strong executive vis-à-vis parliament is not necessarily autonomous from certain groups in society, due especially to the factor of ethnic and family loyalty that was mentioned before. In addition, given the relative weakness of the parliaments, it is not clear that these TADM systems will include adequate arrangements for accountability of government to the citizens as a whole. Only at election time will citizens be able to exercise some control, and even then their ability to change a poor leader will be limited by the ability of the current government to rig elections. Ethnicity and potential share in corruption revenue also mainly determine voters' choice as mentioned before. Barring the intervention of nature, leadership seems often to be changeable only under serious protest or with term limits, both rather inefficient (that is second-best) ways of handling the accountability question. African countries will certainly benefit from strengthening their parliaments vis-à-vis the executive branch of government as regards economic policy and management. Steps will, of course, then need to be taken to ensure that societal cleavages—notably ethnicity—do not somehow come to disturb the efficient functioning of the parliaments themselves. Again, cooperation—especially within civil society—to work out shared understandings, and the implied institutional and organizational arrangements, appear unavoidable for success.

From a normative perspective, external (foreign) agents and others (civil society activists within the countries, for example) can continue to try to persuade African leaders and citizens to carry on with progress toward democracy. The challenge will be finding the right approach to persuade all concerned of the virtues of democracy as a device for ensuring that citizens have an input into the policymaking of the state; as an effective process for peacefully resolving conflicts; and as a method of peacefully ridding the country of poor leadership. This author's view is that, in light of the underlying socio-political (structural) conditions, the evolution to full democratization will be slow, but that it is still possible to have a much faster transition to an environment that supports sound and effective political leadership for economic governance and prosperity.

Concluding Remarks

Many African citizens need to be educated and convinced that political leadership matters for economic growth and that it is not merely a distributional issue. Currently, the median African voter in the typical country estimates the benefits of voting for a political leader or team by taking into account mainly ethnic ties and the potential of sharing in corruption revenue. Societal agents can help in the educational process. Institutional changes and agency activities with success in reducing ethnicity and corruption at the highest political levels will also help by reducing the weight of ethnicity and corruption revenue in the median voter's benefit calculation. At the same time, success in convincing the median voter of the effect of political leadership on output and economic growth will cause the weight of credible and sound economic policies by a political leader or team to become heavily weighted in the median voter's benefit calculation. In debating the problem of leadership, societal leaders could also encourage citizens to address some broader fundamental issues in this whole area, with a view to reaching shared understandings. Namely, community values and norms regarding standards for political leadership, efficiency of the state, and the role of the state are still only emerging in the typical African country.

It is easy to say that political leaders and state employees should be nationalistic and ought to know that it is good to have the interest of the country at heart. First of all, this would also require that society at large—citizens outside the governing bodies of the state—cooperate, by also having such nationalistic fervor and refraining from pressuring individuals inside the governing bodies to sacrifice the state's interests in the face of other loyalties. Over and above that, state building and enhanced efficiency of the state governing bodies are, historically, traceable to an organized group of citizens who see it in their self-interest to pursue those goals and then to coerce or persuade others within the geographic area concerned to go along. Broad nationalism from the get go has been confined to very small communities with sufficient group solidarity for each person to have an encompassing interest in the community as a whole.

When President John Kufuor of Ghana (flanked by his cabinet members) held what was billed as a "People's Assembly" meeting, on January 8, 2002, on the first anniversary of his coming into office, it was good to see that citizens were preoccupied with economic policy and economic welfare and thus had questions in their minds of the sort that triggers national debates on fundamental as well as immediately practical issues. This was an unprecedented meeting—the President answering questions from ordinary Ghanaians, as opposed to lecturing or addressing them; it is the sort of meeting that could be useful across the continent if held frequently and openly, with wide publicity and with no intimidation of citizens before or after the meeting.

8

Facing the Globalization Challenge

It would be an understatement to say that African countries have done a poor job of facing up to the globalization challenge. Over the last thirty years African countries have lost markets for their non-mineral and non-oil exports. Apart from Mauritius and South Africa, they have failed to diversify their exports, and non-oil and non-mineral foreign investors have found African countries increasingly unattractive. This evolution has contributed to the decline of the per capita incomes of African countries relative to that of other regions.

African countries need to develop coherent strategies to face the globalization challenge. The most basic way to benefit from the opportunities opened up by globalization and to reduce the associated cost, so as to achieve attainably high benefit-cost ratios in exploiting the opportunities, is by putting in place sound macroeconomic and structural economic policies. For this, crucial is country ownership in policymaking. Chapter 4 has already explained the difficulties many Africans find with the structural policy recommendations under the structural adjustment and other programs associated with the World Bank and the IMF. When these policies are rammed down the throats of leaders desperate for money, the leaders simply fail to implement the policies. The really awkward situation is in the sphere of macroeconomic policies. After all these years of dealing with the IMF, it is often surrealist to observe the substantive differences African governments have with that organization on policies in the areas of inflation, exchange rates, budget deficits, debt, subsidies, and tax structures and incentives. Much of it is because the Africans themselves do not have serious domestic debates on the policy issues, even among their own economists in think tanks, universities, and the government. So the Africans hardly ever really work out coherent home-grown policies to bring to the table of discussions with the IMF. The African governments, who are usually to blame for this predicament of their countries, are then left only with having to react to proposals and views of the IMF and sometimes of the World Bank as well. Luckily, a few African countries are beginning to see that there is a problem with this state of affairs and are beginning to organize themselves to change the status quo. This trend would need to continue, made routine and institutionalized. That would constitute a welcome element of a trend toward country ownership. The IMF and the World Bank have themselves begun to appreciate that they would also benefit from encouraging such a development.

As African countries make progress toward tackling corruption at all levels, reducing ethnicity and improving political leadership, they will be creating the conditions for the emergence of good economic policy environments, as discussed earlier especially in Chapters 2 and 5-7, thereby strengthening the ability to succeed in the global economic community. Obtaining country ownership in economic policymaking and getting rid of policy-based conditionality (see Chapter 4) will also help. Moreover, success in regional economic integration (see Chapter 9 below) will make a great contribution to the ability of African countries to benefit from globalization.

The rest of the chapter is organized as follows. The next section discusses two responses to globalization that still have some adherents in the African countries but which are played down by the political leaders in discussion of globalization and its impact on African countries. Indeed, these leaders have begun to recognize that there are certain complaints that very few outside the continent will help them address or even heed, and that they will have to come up with domestic policies to tackle the problems themselves. One of the historical responses to globalization to which I am alluding is dependency theory. The other is the proposition that African countries that mainly export agricultural commodities and raw materials face adverse long-run trends and excessive cyclical fluctuations in their commodity terms of trade. The section following after that looks at three approaches widely discussed in meeting the challenge as regards exports, namely, participating in commodity agreements; pushing for market access, with or without special preferences; and structuring domestic policies to focus on diversification of exports at a rapid pace. Although these approaches are not mutually exclusive, African countries have focused on the first two and as element of their poor policy environment have not made resolute attempts at the third approach. Then the chapter, in the last section, addresses another major challenge the African countries need to meet, namely, attracting private capital, especially in the form of foreign direct investment. Once again, creating a good policy environment is emphasized in trying to meet the challenges in attracting private capital.

Worn-Out Responses to Globalization

Of importance for Africans in preparing themselves to benefit from globalization is to stop blaming external forces for their problems and underestimating their own abilities to compete in a level playing field. This would shift the African countries' focus in globalization discussions and in global organizations' debates to that of ensuring that the playing field is indeed level and to getting agreement that some forms of "affirmative action" may be fair in order to control for any long-term adverse effects of past unfairness on the ability of Africans to compete in a level playing field. In this context, it is of relief to sense that certain past arguments of neocolonialism and unfair commodity markets no longer feature prominently in political statements of African leaders. Yet, the arguments still influence attitudes of African politicians and other elites towards international markets, multinational firms, joint-ventures, and multilateral organizations. Where this is true, the African countries would benefit from internal public debates, sometimes even involving international experts as well, with a view to reaching better understanding of the forces at play and developing some consensus on national strategies towards these international forces. Of particular importance here are any lingering influence of dependency theory, and the related fear of exploitation of African countries by multinational corporations, as well as of the hypothesis of an inherent tendency of the terms of trade of primary producers to decline relative to producers of manufactures and services. Unfortunately, such lingering influences, in addition to distrust of the IMF and the World Bank, do affect current attitudes of Africans towards globalization. In developing their strategies, African countries need to take note of the fact that countries in other continents are increasing their participation in world markets, not shying away, and are developing expertise in reaping gains from such participation.

Dependency theory[1]

Dependency theory, in its heyday in the 1960s through the 1980s, did raise important issues in the theory of development policy in Africa that still resonate in some circles in the African continent. Namely, does the nature of economic relations between the African countries and the industrial countries impose constraints on the ability of the African countries to attain rapid and sustained economic growth and reduce the income gap between the two sets of countries? If so, what are the institutional and historical sources of these constraints? In addition, how effective are all the barrage of liberal neoclassical, neo-Keynesian or monetarist policy instruments (of traditional mainstream economics) to achieve

---

[1] An earlier treatment of the material in this sub-section can be found in Johnson (1977b).

employment, growth, balance of payments, and price level targets in African countries given the nature of relations between organizations of the industrial countries and those of African countries? Furthermore, what changes need to be made to reduce the tightness of any constraints imposed by this relationship? In particular, what kind of new international economic order will remove or mitigate any constraints? Economic dependency theory although being applied to African countries was developed by writers on the Latin American experience. Frank, for instance, argued that countries like Argentina, Brazil, Chile and Mexico experienced their most important industrial development during the two world wars and the great depression when trade and investment ties with the center (i.e. the West) was loosened (see especially Frank, 1969a, 1969b).

One approach to the issues raised by dependency theorists was dictated by the proposition that the advanced countries were a positive factor in the development of less developed countries (LDCs) and that any widening gap between the two groups of countries must have been the result of bad economic policies in the LDCs or simply their citizens attitude to work or native institutions that were not conducive to growth and development. Dependency theory rejected this approach because it was considered ahistorical and argued instead that the extant state of underdevelopment of the LDCs could not be understood without historical analysis of their relationship with the current industrialized market economies.

Dependency theory was built from quite a diverse set of approaches to development issues and problems. It was influenced by the "cumulative causation" and disharmony of interest ideas of Myrdal (1953, 1957); by the idea of a center and a periphery in international economic relations of economists like Prebisch (1962); by the imperialist models of colonial policy by Balogh (1962) and others; as well as by the Marxian notion of unequal exchange (Emanuel, 1972) and a distribution of gains from international investment and trade (Singer, 1950) that was adverse to the LDCs. Dependency theory also exploited the application of the demonstration effect in international economic relations by

Nurkse (1953) as well as the central ideas of Baran in his analysis of the nature of the economic surplus, the distinction between potential and actual surplus, and the diverse ways in which surplus absorption occurred (see especially Baran, 1957, Chapter 2). To all of this dependency theorists added a historical perspective.

A basic thesis of dependency theory was that the nature of the historical relationship between the less developed countries and the industrial countries was such that, over time, the per capita *wealth* (or income) gap between the two sets of countries tended to widen. In fact, it was hypothesized that the nature of the historical relationship *caused* the widening gap over time by retarding the rate of growth of the LDCs relative to their potential. The implication was that this trend would continue unless the nature of the relationship changed. In analytical terms, the argument in support of this view was, basically, that the trade and exchange relationships between the two sets of countries had harmful effects on the development potential of the LDCs. Most important here was that the exchange and trade relationship resulted in a significant replacement of traditional activities in which local entrepreneurs and capitalists were dominant by activities in which foreign entrepreneurs and capitalists from the industrial countries predominated. Techniques that had become available to producers in the industrial countries allowed them to produce, at relatively low cost, commodities that were technically and physically very close substitutes for the traditional commodities of the LDCs. In addition, the associated elasticities of supply were relatively high. On the demand side it also turned out that not only were those industrial substitutes in fact considered good enough to cause a shift of demand away from traditional activities, but also their relatively low cost, and hence supply prices, considerably increased the amount demanded of the foreign commodities.

The obvious effect of this development was, presumably, that many local citizens of the LDCs that would otherwise have been members of the entrepreneurial and capitalist class were transformed into laborers or members of the "working class." But more than that dependency analysis implied that the nature of the cost functions of the producers from the industrial countries in conjunction with (1) pure competitive labor markets in the LDCs, (2) oligopsonistic behavior of the foreign capitalists, in their demand for labor services, and (3) oligopolistic behavior of these same capitalists in the markets for their outputs, created the roots for differential wealth accumulation over time. That is, the above four conditions enabled the foreign capitalists from the industrial countries in their operations in the LDCs to (1) pay the laborers only the latter's reservation wages, (2) charge a low enough price to substantially weed out traditional activities in the LDCs and (3) earn returns on their capital that were well above their own opportunity costs.

As a result of the above factors, the argument then was that domestic incomes of nationals did not increase as rapidly as would have been the case if factor shares were closely associated with marginal value productivity. This in turn meant that the domestic markets could not expand rapidly enough to encourage profit-reinvestment ratios in the LDCs to be high enough to lead to a reduction in the per capita income gap, over time, between the LDCs and the industrial countries. The limited size and rate of expansion of domestic markets in the LDCs were of course not sufficient conditions to discourage significant reinvestment of profits. Dependency theorists would accept that in some LDCs domestic cost conditions did not make such reinvestment profitable. This was especially so in the African countries where the potential industrial labor force was very limited and the cost of training was rather high. But dependency analysis tended to the conclusion that in many LDCs the limited size and rate of growth of domestic markets became an effective obstacle to profit reinvestment because of tariff and other barriers in the industrial countries that precluded the production, for exportation especially to the industrial countries, of many commodities benefiting from economies of scale. Such high tariffs and other barriers to trade, which, by hypothesis, were inefficient from an economic point of view, were maintained for political reasons.

In dependency theory the *multinational corporation* played an important role. In analytical terms the dependency theorist's argument was that unless controls were instituted the multinationals would participate in the local African economy in ways and at levels such that their social net contribution would be less than their private profitability, in a static sense; and that in a long-run (present value) sense this social net contribution could in fact be negative. The multinationals, it was argued, were highly instrumental in the perpetuation of certain types of international division of labor. The dependency theorists would have supported Stephen Hymer who suggested that the multinationals would tend to produce "a hierarchical division of labor between geographical regions corresponding to the vertical division of labor within the firm" (Hymer, p. 114). Thus, for example, top management—those who determine goals and plans—would be in the world's major cities like New York, London, Paris, Bonn, and Tokyo (Hymer, 1972, p. 124). But this problem of intra-firm division of labor was considered a relatively minor one as compared to the problem that really concerned dependency theorists. This latter problem was that certain kinds of activities and industries, directly or indirectly, would be preserved for the industrial countries. Thus there would be underinvestment in the capital goods sector in the typical African country, as argued, especially by Arrighi and Saul (see, e.g., Arrighi, 1973). Development of the capital goods industry was considered important for the dependency theorist because it would have enormous advantages for augmenting the size of the market, encouraging technologies suitable to the factor endowment in the country, and stimulating local technological innovation.

Apart from the adverse effects for the African country of the division of labor that would be engendered by multinational firms, such enterprises, as with the early foreign firms that participated in these LDCs' economies, were accused of being able to reap monopoly rents, as well as replacing much local entrepreneurs and businesses. The monopoly rents were thought of as akin to taxes on local citizens to subsidize the multinational enterprises; since those taxes (and subsidies) would be transferred abroad they would create a classical transfer problem for the African country. In addition, the adverse effects on local businesses would increase the cost of creating a local entrepreneurial class in an open-market situation leading to dependence on the multinationals for the stock of entrepreneurship in the country—a situation supposedly detrimental to long-run development. Whatever the merits of the above argument it should perhaps be noted that several authors [see, e.g., Alejandro (1970)] pointed out that multinationals and other foreign capitalists were often able to earn monopoly rents because of government policies in the LDCs themselves in the form of inflation, "overvalued" exchange rates, controlled interest rates, and special investment bonuses and subsidies.

Dependency theorists believed that some reduction of "dependence" would lead to an increase in the rate of development of the typical LDC, even if a certain period of costly adjustment was required. Dependency theorists believed that this proposition was correct because certain strategies and policies which, in the light of long-run benefits and costs, needed to be pursued, and certain institutions which needed to be developed by the LDC, could not be pursued or developed because the state of "dependence" hindered their efficiency or simply precluded them. Hence, the "reduction of dependence" (RD) was, essentially, a real capital good yielding pecuniary returns, in which some investment would be profitable. That is, the typical African country should be willing to accept, in the short run and medium run, some trade-off of real income for increased RD because the long-run benefits would be such that, in a present (discounted) value sense, the real (pecuniary) income of the country would be greater than if no such investment were made. Supposedly, increased RD would imply some (deliberate) disengagement from the international economic system "dominated" by the industrial countries. Sometimes this call for increased RD was put simply in the form a call for increased self-reliance (SR) associated particularly with Nyerere the former President of Tanzania (see Nyerere, 1968).

Still amazing is the fraction of Africans that still believe that the industrial countries—their governments and their big enterprises—are doing something, in collaboration with the IMF and the World Bank, that's not good for the development of Africa. The evidence cited most frequently is that African countries have been sliding backwards during a period of time when so many African countries are highly aid dependent, the mineral and oil companies in the continent are dominated by Western companies, African countries have been subjected to structural adjusted programs of the IMF and the World Bank with their policy-based conditionalities, and privatization typically means selling to foreign enterprises, including from industrial countries. It is a real intellectual challenge to come up with convincing arguments to Africans that they have more than marginal responsibility for the debacle in the continent since independence. Even ethnicity, corruption and poor political leadership are all blamed on Western countries' machinations and manipulations of Africans. Many Africans do not stop to ask why Africans have no control over their fate but rather allow others to control them so easily for the others' own benefit. There is a real agency challenge here.

Adverse or large fluctuations in terms of trade

African leaders increasingly do not complain about the terms of trade of primary producers having an inherent tendency to decline relative to the terms of trade of producers of manufactured goods and services, or that the prices of raw materials and agricultural commodities fluctuate far more than those of manufactured goods. But they still insist that, on average, in world commodity markets the producers in African countries have less influence over the prices of their exports than do producers of industrial countries. For much of the second half of the twentieth century, one of the burning economic issues in the relations between the so-called industrial countries and the developing world was the terms of trade question. At least from the time when Prebisch advanced the thesis (see Prebisch, 1950, and Macbean, 1966) that there was a long-run tendency for the commodity terms of trade—namely the price of exports relative to the price of imports—to move against raw-material producers, many low-income country leaders somehow believed that there must be much truth to that.

The basic frustration was that developing countries, particularly those in Africa, saw that, individually, they did not have any perceptible influence over the world prices of their commodities, whether imports or exports; hence their (external) commodity terms of trade seemed given to them by "outsiders." The countries, it was argued, found themselves, for the most part, to be price takers in world markets with the risk that all technical progress and productivity increases in the production of their commodities would be passed on to industrial country consumers in the form of lower prices. This was supposed to contrast sharply with the circumstance of the industrial country producers who, by some degree of monopolistic control over their individual markets, were purportedly able to appropriate much of the gains of technical progress and productivity increases in the form of higher factor incomes (wages and profits) in the producing enterprises concerned. In addition, African countries appeared to be producing goods for which, with only a few exceptions, the income elasticity of demand seemed low so that, over time, even with growth in world incomes, increased world supply only led to price declines. This predicament seemed aggravated by the fact that entry into the activities concerned was relatively easy—particularly for agricultural commodities—so that price rises due to increases in demand got quickly eroded by supply increases from new entrants. Again this situation was contrasted with that of industrial commodities the demand for which was thought to benefit from reasonably high income elasticity while the price elasticity of supply was limited by technological barriers to entry. Furthermore, technological advances, resulting in the introduction of substitutes or in material-saving innovations in production, have been a constant threat to producers of raw materials as the experience of rubber and copper have so clearly demonstrated. To cap it all, cyclical disturbances in the industrial countries have played an important role in the demand for, and prices of, developing-country products, whereas the reverse has not been as strong.

It should, of course, be obvious that the concern here is especially for the countries whose exports are not dominated by oil. It is also understandable that for the African countries, export price instability makes planning and budgeting challenging. It also supposedly increases economic uncertainty, particularly where small-scale farmers are involved, with adverse effects on incentives for acreage expansion, investment, and increasing labor productivity. But before looking at appropriate responses, it should be noted that there are substantial differences in the individual circumstances of the African countries that reflect, especially, the commodity composition of their exports.

For instance, where world demand forces have been important, the circumstances of different crops have varied substantially. First, the demand for certain commodities have been affected by taste and health concerns. Hence meat, tobacco, groundnut and palm products have been adversely affected by health considerations, while cotton has been helped by some tendency to shift to natural fibers. Second, some commodities like wood, hides and skins, wool, mohair and vanilla have tended to experience favorable income elasticities of demand as world income has grown. Third, there are commodities demands for which are particularly affected by protection or price support policies in the industrial countries. In this regard sugar was, until recently, an important example in the African setting (particularly for Mauritius). Fourth, despite conservation policies around the world, demand for petroleum has been kept high and increasing because of rapid economic expansion in countries like China and India. Fifth, some commodities—especially the metals and certain minerals (copper and iron ore for example)—have depended heavily on industrial production, housing construction, and capital investment activity in the industrial and newly-industrializing countries. Sixth, some mineral commodities (gold, gem diamonds) have been good stores of value, and commonly held as hedges against inflation; hence their prices have often responded to the general state of uncertainty with respect to exchange rates, inflation and interest rates.

Given that price fluctuations are unavoidable, under the best of circumstances, it would seem desirable for African countries to design and implement fiscal, monetary, foreign exchange reserve management and other domestic policies to minimize the consumption and/or output effects of terms of trade fluctuations. Policies regarding saving could be designed to help smoothen out the effect of cyclical price and income fluctuations on disposable income, and/or on real consumption, of individual households. An optimal saving strategy could contain three elements. One of these elements would be the management of the foreign exchange reserves of the country so as to compensate for cyclical movements in export earnings—by accumulating "excess" (over trend) reserves in times when prices and demand conditions are abnormally good to be drawn down when conditions are adverse and export earnings are relatively poor. The second element of the optimal saving strategy would be part of budgetary policy; a smaller-than-normal budgetary deficit (or larger-than-normal budgetary surplus) would be generated during periods when exports are booming, and budgetary revenue larger than normal, while the reverse budgetary policy would be pursued when exports are experiencing a downswing that has an adverse effect on budgetary revenue.

The third element of an optimal saving strategy would be to encourage higher-than-normal private domestic saving rate when incomes are benefiting from a cyclical upswing and the reverse during a downswing. An important instrument in pursuit of this policy would be the deposit interest rates in financial institutions. A regime that promotes interest rate flexibility and, for a growing economy, positive interest rates—the latter defined to be approximately equal to the nominal rate of interest on some representative financial instrument minus the rate of inflation—would enhance the prospects for attaining an optimal saving rate for the economy at large. In addition, policies that promote development of the capital market, build confidence in financial institutions, and facilitate the introduction of a wide variety of savings instruments—differing in liquidity, risks, and maturity—will also encourage optimal saving behavior.

Monetary and exchange rate policies can also be used to address fluctuating terms of trade, by helping to insulate output from terms of trade fluctuations, via flexible exchange rates and interest rates. A fall in the terms of trade tends to tighten money and credit markets while improvements in the terms of trade tend to relax money and credit markets. Thus, when terms of trade decline, the domestic currency should be allowed to depreciate in foreign exchange markets and interest rates to decline. The opposite should be allowed to happen when the terms of trade improve: the domestic currency should be allowed to appreciate and interest rates to increase. Normally, this strategy calls for appropriate intervention in foreign exchange and money markets by the authorities or changes in central bank (discount) rate(s) or exchange rates. The choice of policies would, thus, depend on the exchange regime and the monetary policy instruments at the disposal of the authorities. But the fundamentals of the approach will not change. It should be noted that the exchange rate and interest rate variations have output effects that will influence the nature of the optimal policy response. In general it is good to see that African countries are increasingly able to implement such monetary and fiscal polices to help them deal adequately with external terms of trade variations.

Facing the Challenge—African Exports

Believing that external forces are at work in causing price and demand fluctuations for their exports, popular view in many African countries has been that direct attempts should be made by multilateral or other action to attack the forces responsible for short-term instability and for the price declines of their export commodities. In addition, African countries want the industrial countries to remove the subsidies they tack on to many of their agricultural commodities and lift or drastically lower tariffs and non-tariff barriers they impose on some manufacturing commodities in ways that hurt developing countries. In fact, barriers to trade in agriculture are much higher than protection in general. It has been argued, by some economists, that part of the reason why OECD barriers to trade in products in which developing countries have a comparative advantage remain higher than other products is that small, poor countries "have little to offer in the mercantilist WTO exchange of concessions to induce large countries to remove policies that harm them" (Evenett and Hoekman, 2005, p. xxv).

Commodity agreements

To improve their external terms of trade and/or reduce price fluctuations for their exports, African countries have historically been active in commodity agreements and vocal in their support of various proposals for commodity stabilization funds. Hence African countries are prominent members of the Organization of Petroleum Exporting Countries (OPEC), the International Cocoa Organization, the International Coffee Organization, and the Common Fund for Commodities (CFC).[2] In addition, African countries have been participating in the EEC – African Caribbean Pacific (ACP) conventions with their commodity stabilization elements (Stabex and Sysmin), providing aid to countries badly hit by fluctuations in world prices.

Unfortunately, there are serious limitations, problems, and development costs, of commodity agreements in general. First of all, apart from OPEC, such agreements usually require the cooperation of consuming countries, which is bound to make their scope rather limited. Consuming nations will usually be unwilling to support arrangements that would encourage prices to remain on average above market equilibrium prices or that would set up artificial barriers to entry of new producers.

More importantly, commodity agreements, to the extent that they result in the establishment of cartels, are difficult to sustain so that any benefits in terms of high prices are likely to be ephemeral. Such cartels encourage cheating, since

[2] Among other things the CFC supports buffer stock operations undertaken in the context of international commodity agreements.

those who break the price and quantity agreements by secret arrangements can end up with total receipts much greater than they would have received by obeying the cartel agreements. Constant as a threat to success of a cartel are free-riders who stay out of the cartel and benefit from the high prices without the concomitant obligation to restrain quantities. When entry into an industry is easy, as is the case for most agricultural commodities, the attraction to producers to free-ride can be irresistible.

Furthermore, commodity agreements can retard the economic progress of a country by reducing the incentive to diversify or to make needed productivity improvements. If a commodity agreement finally collapses or if underlying demand and supply factors force a sudden drop in an artificially-maintained price, the loss in economic welfare can outweigh the short-term benefits accrued during the period of unsustainable high prices. Economic progress can also be hampered by discouraging the development of institutions and tools to deal with uncertainty and price and income fluctuations. Hence, the development of domestic buffer stocks, forecasting agencies, forward foreign exchange markets, commodity exchanges, financial instruments for saving, and government fiscal stabilization instruments, can all be retarded by attempts to shield domestic residents from the reality of international price and demand fluctuations.

Market access

Now, in the arena of the World Trade Organization (WTO), it makes sense for African countries to continue the fight for removal of agricultural subsidies in industrial countries and for lowering of tariff and non-tariff barriers to trade in manufacturing and services, when the Africans deem such reductions in their own self-interest. This puts added pressure on African countries, which may want to preserve some right of protection of their own producers on infant-industry grounds. But I also would suggest that African countries use protection wisely, so as not to foster infants that never grow up, and rather provide incentives to accelerate export-led industrialization and tradable services expansion. In this regard, there may be cases where it makes far more sense to selectively intervene to assist domestic "infants" penetrate foreign markets than to pursue protection of "infants" in domestic markets. There may, of course, be a need to obtain agreement in the international community (particularly multilaterally), if objections are raised to the domestic policy interventions.

Indeed, more and more African countries may come to see their quest for ownership over their domestic policies threatened not only by policy-based conditionality related to aid but also by other countries' concerns about the relationship between domestic policies and the fairness of the playing field in international trade relations, because of adverse spillovers on trading partners. In the WTO framework, there is already much concern about domestic policies with respect to procurement, competition, investment incentives, and trade facilitation.[3] I suspect that many countries will be watching African countries, especially in their regional integration moves, although not too closely for some time. African countries will need to think ahead about how they want to react to complaints about their domestic regulatory policies and the bargaining power they would need to muster to hold their own in the global world of international economic cooperation.

Diversification

On the whole, African countries need to take resolute steps to diversify their economies in general and their exports as well. I do not believe that serious and appropriate diversification of production and exports will come soon in the majority of these countries without more active and efficient selective intervention of the state in markets—that is, close cooperation between private

[3] Trade facilitation has to do with certain types of domestic policies that affect the transaction costs of transporting goods across national borders, such as customs procedures and various cross-border regulations, including activities, practices, and formalities connected with collecting, presenting, communicating, and processing data required for moving goods in international trade.

entrepreneurs and enterprises on the one hand and government on the other. In this regard, one approach could be the following. The authorities of an African country could: (1) establish clear benchmarks, indicators, and targets for diversification; (2) conduct periodic analyses of the areas where the country's comparative advantage was emerging and could emerge with appropriate assistance, and specify what needs to be done to speed up the processes; (3) design economically efficient criteria for selective intervention by the public sector, including direct incentives to entrepreneurs (tax relief, subsidies, entrepreneurial and other types of training, market research, assistance in market penetration, fostering of joint ventures, etc); and (4) make continuous formal assessment of the effects of indirect policies on diversification—indirect policies such as education and training of young people, labour and manpower policies, health policies, infrastructure policies, financial sector policies, policies to address corruption, and monetary and fiscal policies—with a view to restructuring and fine-tuning those policies, as necessary, to promote diversification.

For the countries with small populations, like The Gambia, Gabon, Botswana, Central African Republic, Lesotho, Swaziland, Liberia, Guinea-Bissau, or even Sierra Leone, the limits to beneficial diversification will come much sooner than for the more heavily populated countries like Nigeria, Kenya, Democratic Republic of Congo, Sudan or Ethiopia. But countries like Luxembourg and Singapore have found optimal ways to diversify. In the specialization-diversification spectrum, countries benefit by finding ways to produce commodities and services with sufficiently rapid growth in world demand. Countries must also establish sufficient flexibility and spontaneous dynamism to cope with the effects of free entry and competition. What all this means is that the countries—large, medium, or small—must develop sufficient technological, organizational, and scientific sophistication to enable them to adapt to the changing demand and supply conditions of the world economy.

Facing the Challenge—Private Capital

The more African countries can depend on private foreign direct investment and borrowing in foreign capital markets, to supplement saving and investment by their own nationals, the less they need to worry about policy-based conditionality, and the greater the freedom they will have in designing and implementing their domestic policies. The countries will then face other challenges, some of which are mentioned below. Still, if African countries take appropriate actions to create good policy environments, they will increase their ability both to attract foreign private capital and to develop and use optimal policy instruments to ensure that such capital make substantial contribution to their development efforts.

Market credibility

African countries face enormous credibility problems in attracting foreign direct investment, because the African environment has not appeared hospitable—both the economic policy and socio-political environment adversely affect expected returns from investing in the typical African country. Among the environmental factors (the importance of each varying from country to country in the region) are the security situation; the availability and quality of basic infrastructure; the efficiency and honesty of government; the state of development and efficiency of labor and financial markets; violent ethnic conflicts; and the political and social attitudes toward private foreign capital. All of these make for a higher-than-world-average risky and uncertain environment for which foreign direct investment (FDI) demands a premium.[4] Africa as a region is considered

---

[4] An extensive theoretical and empirical literature exists on the determinants of foreign direct investment. See, for example, Agarwal (1980), Jeon (1992), Wheeler and Mody (1992), Moore (1993), Barrell and Pain (1996), Belderbos and Sleuwaegen (1996), Okeahalam and Bah (1998) and S. Davidson (1999). Despite the difficulties [see Johnson (2004, 2005b)], various studies also

high risk and the credit ratings of the countries are adversely affected simply by their being there [see Haque *et al* (2000)].

Addressing some of the above problems would require public investment. In addition, specific action would be needed to alleviate doubts about the credibility and sustainability of policies. Certain well-known strategies of the state could be effective in helping to build the requisite credibility. For instance, active support of joint ventures could be made an integral part of a 'business activity and private sector coordination' element of development strategy. This could be combined with direct information to foreign investors on potential investment opportunities in the country.

Indeed, joint ventures between local and foreign investors have a number of well-known advantages for countries with low credibility among foreign investors, two of which could be mentioned. First, and foremost, they demonstrate that local investors are willing to take a bet on the policy environment. Given the factors about which foreign investors are typically ill informed, and given the informational advantage of local investors, information on the investment activity of local investors becomes a powerful signal to foreigners in assessing the future performance of the economy, an important consideration given the fixity of much physical investment and the high adjustment costs of relocation of capital once the investment is made.[5] Second, such ventures could greatly help expand the private sector in the country; for many African countries, it could be an effective way to begin substantive export-oriented industrialization. Foreign investors could bring with their investments certain levels of technology and organizational skills, and could open up invaluable contacts with international markets.

---

try to capture the adverse effects of Africa's ethnic conflicts on the environment for investors; see, e.g., Easterly and Levine (1997).

[5] Adjustment costs affecting supply response and/or reallocation of capital would include: (1) quasi-fixed factor costs (such as waiting time to order and set up new machinery and facilities); (2) the loss from discarding obsolete machinery; (3) costs of training old and new workers in using new equipment or in adapting to new unfamiliar work practices and production lines; and (4) costs (most notably redundancy pay) of firing unwanted employees (e.g., with outdated skills). On these and their economic significance, see for example, Lucas (1967), Pindyck (1982), Dixit (1989), and Dixit and Pindyck (1994).

Mkandawire and Soludo (1999) discuss examples—Mauritius and other countries—of where there has been successful cooperation between domestic and foreign capitalists in the African continent. As they put it: "Outsiders (foreign firms in some form of partnership with local firms or nonindigenous entrepreneurs) have sometimes been instrumental in initiating the process of building up the capabilities needed to improve competitiveness. This has occurred when these outsiders were incorporated into the national accumulation process, and their capital and know-how were transferred to others..." Mauritius is a star in this area, and in fact, "local private capital has been progressively buying out foreign capital" [Mkandawire and Soludo (1999), p. 110]. The Mauritius example, underscores the importance of having a significant entrepreneurial class, sound macroeconomic policies, and a climate favorable to investment (both local and foreign investors) [see the valuable collection of papers in Dabee and Greenaway (2001)]. If they could somehow guarantee sound macroeconomic and infrastructure policies, as well as much greater government efficiency and/or lower corruption, other African countries, such as Ghana, Kenya and Nigeria also have entrepreneurial capacity and experience adequate enough for becoming real global stars in the exploitation of joint venture opportunities [see, e.g., Forrest (1994) and Himbara (1994)].

Challenges

Policymakers would be faced with certain challenges to fully benefit from private capital inflows. These are well-known and include; (1) guarding against corruption of domestic residents in joint venture arrangements; (2) ensuring social optimality in the trade-off between efficiency and building local African capability; and (3) developing policy instruments to address financial and GDP instability in connection with capital mobility.

Domestic residents could dupe both foreign investors and the government, in the joint venture policy area. Duping foreign capitalists hurts the reputation of the country while duping the government has adverse budgetary effects. For example, it is not uncommon for domestic residents to invite small and medium business people and take money, promising services to effect a joint venture arrangement that never materializes. Or the local person may entice the foreign businessperson to invest in a venture that the domestic person knew was never going to be profitable or at least not as profitable as he or she made the foreigner to believe. These kinds of deception are usually for relatively small sums of money, but they contribute to damaging the reputation of the country. As regards duping the government, domestic persons—typically with the connivance of the foreign joint venture partner—would obtain special incentives and monopoly rights for some business venture that turns out to be far less profitable than contained in the business plan of the enterprise. The government may then end up protecting the enterprise for an extended period on top of tax holidays and other special incentives that may have been granted. Transparency in decisionmaking and a properly designed business coordination program that includes measures to foster efficiency could go a long way in preventing these kinds of malpractices. So also would a coherent program to reduce government corruption, which typically provides the enabling environment for the above kinds of activities.

An issue highlighted by Lall and Stewart (1996), among others, is that industrialization should be efficient but at the same time there is need to build up African technical and managerial capabilities so that the Africans can graduate into running efficient industrial enterprises. As Lall and Stewart see it: "Efficiency calls for strong external competitive pressures, whereas the nurturing of capabilities may require protection from those pressures, at least for a time." Because of the need for general education and training as well as "enterprise-specific investments in capability acquisition," they suggest that there would be "the need for coordinated interventions in product and factor markets."

A third challenge would come if FDI opens a country to capital movements that may be destabilizing. This, of course, tends to be less of a problem for long-term capital, which FDI tends to be mainly, than for short-term capital. Still, uncertainty could lead to capital flight and lower reinvestment of profits than would otherwise take place. This challenge should not be unwelcome because it, after all, only demands sound macroeconomic management and favorable investment climate—political, security, infrastructure, taxation—a climate that the authorities should in any event want to create. A more difficult situation arises when the uncertainty results from factors beyond the control of the country. For example, many foreign businesses may decide to exploit the opportunities created by the Africa Growth Opportunity Act (AGOA) passed by the US in 2000, to give producers in the vast majority of African countries certain preferential access rights to the US market. If foreign businesses decide to establish or expand their production of certain goods within African countries—independently or in partnership with African producers—for export to the US, it is unclear what would happen if the preferential access evaporates, for instance, because of generalized liberalization in the US. Moreover, the AGOA is due to expire in 2008 and would need to be renewed, which can never be taken for granted in the real world of politics.

Economic policymaking, which would involve state-civil society cooperation and government-business cooperation with perhaps special emphasis on government coordination (see Chapter 3), should enable the African country to meet the above challenges, employing strategies and policies that are fully legitimated by the citizens of the country. In such a good policy environment, corruption would be controlled and government macroeconomic and structural policies would be growth-enhancing and domestically owned.

9

Regional Economic Integration

Since the early years of their independence, African countries have been discussing and coming up with treaties, protocols and various arrangements to bring about regional economic integration among neighbors, with the hope of one day having economic integration that incorporates the whole continent or the vast majority of the countries. The most enduring idea has been to move towards regional common market type arrangements because that would substantially augment the effective economic might of the African economies. With common markets, they expect better prospects for industrialization, higher average factor productivity, and greater ability to spearhead research and technological innovations appropriate to the African environment. These in turn would make the countries more attractive to foreign direct investment and enable them to obtain a bigger share of world trade and payments, and hence to benefit from greater bargaining power in international economic relations. In this chapter, therefore, the focus will be on economic integration initiatives with common market and/or economic union goals. Hence, I do not discuss initiatives restricted to monetary union and clearing-house arrangements.[1] Monetary union, of course, is expected

[1] These are, nevertheless, discussed in Johnson (1991, 1995), where most of the ideas contained in this chapter had been previously explored.

to accompany full economic union and may even precede such a union.[2]

The Integration Landscape

It is the common market and economic union arrangements that the Economic Commission for Africa (ECA) and the Organization of African Unity (OAU) have most vigorously promoted. The African Union (AU) was launched in July 2002 to replace the OAU. The Lagos Plan of Action adopted in April 1980 at an extraordinary session of the heads of states and governments of the OAU made the creation of regional unions (of the common-market type) a centerpiece in the grand strategy for Africa in the pursuit of development.

As part of the Lagos Plan of Action, the ECA has been encouraging three main arrangements in sub-Saharan Africa. These are: (i) the Economic Community of West African States (ECOWAS), created in May 1975 by treaty (revised in 1993);[3] (ii) the Economic Community of the Central African States (ECCAS), with treaty approved in 1983,[4] which began operations in 1985 but was inactive for a number of years beginning in 1992, mainly due to non-payment of membership fees by the countries and the conflict in the Great Lakes area;[5] and (iii) the Preferential Trading Area for Eastern and Southern Africa (PTA), whose treaty came into effect in 1981 and which was established in 1982. The PTA was

---

[2] See Johnson (1995). Also of interest with regard to the chapter as a whole are Aly (1994), Lavergne (1997), Aryeetey (1998), and Mistry (2000).

[3] The current members of ECOWAS are Benin, Burkina Faso, Cape Verde, Côte d'Ivoire, The Gambia, Ghana, Guinea, Guinea-Bissau, Liberia, Mali, Niger, Nigeria, Senegal, Sierra Leone, and Togo. The treaties of ECOWAS, ECCAS, and PTA are available from the organization's headquarters or secretariat or the ECA.

[4] The signatories to the treaty were Burundi, Cameroon, Central African Republic, Chad, Congo, Democratic Republic of Congo (then Zaïre), Equatorial Guinea, Gabon, Rwanda, and Sao Tome and Principe. Angola has since joined, bringing the current membership to 11.

[5] At the 2nd Extra-Ordinary Summit of ECCAS held in Libreville on 6 February 1998, the Heads of State/Government present, nevertheless, committed themselves to resurrecting the organization. The Conference of Heads of State and Government (the highest authority of the Community) has been meeting on a regular basis since then, to set priorities and agree on activities and initiatives, despite the continued poor security situation in the region.

transformed in 1994 into the Community of Eastern and Southern Africa (COMESA).[6]

In West Africa, there is also the Mano River Union (MRU), established in 1973 between Liberia and Sierra Leone; since 1980 Guinea has been a third member. Political turmoil in the sub-region left the organization essentially dormant for many years. At a one-day summit on 20 May 2004, in Conakry, Guinea, the leaders of the three countries committed themselves to reactivating the MRU. This would include especially support for initiatives promoting security in the sub-region, building confidence to get back to cooperative efforts in trade and development. Also, in West Africa, there is the West African Economic and Monetary Union (WAEMU), established in early 1994, with the explicit aim of broadening the goals of the West African Monetary Union to include economic integration.[7]

In Southern Africa, there is the Southern African Development Community (SADC), which came into being in August 1992 following a treaty signed in Windhoek in the same year. It was formerly the Southern African Development Coordination Conference (SADCC), set up in 1979 (operations began in 1980) to strengthen the economies and reduce their collective dependence on then apartheid South Africa. In August 1994, South Africa itself joined SADC, which has now changed its focus to that of promoting economic development, including through greater trade among the member states and harmonization of policies [8] In Southern Africa there is also the Southern African Customs Union (SACU), established back in 1910.[9]

In Central Africa, there is the Central African Customs and Economic

---

[6] There are currently 20 members: Angola, Burundi, Comoros, Democratic Republic of Congo, Djibouti, Egypt, Eritrea, Ethiopia, Kenya, Libya, Madagascar, Malawi, Mauritius, Rwanda, Seychelles, Sudan, Swaziland, Uganda, Zambia, and Zimbabwe.

[7] WAEMU comprises Benin, Burkina Faso, Côte d'Ivoire, Mali, Niger, Senegal and Togo.

[8] The current member states of SADC are Angola, Botswana, Democratic Republic of Congo, Lesotho, Madagascar, Malawi, Mauritius, Mozambique, Namibia, South Africa, Swaziland, Tanzania, Zambia, and Zimbabwe.

[9] The current members of SACU are Botswana, Lesotho, Namibia, South Africa, and Swaziland.

Union (CACEU), better known by its French acronym UDEAC (for Union Douanière et Economique de l'Afrique Centrale).[10] In March 1994, its members agreed to create, by treaty, the Central African Economic and Monetary Community (CAEMC). ECCAS contains all the members of CAEMC.

In Eastern Africa, the East African Community (EAC), comprising Kenya, Tanzania, and Uganda, survived between June 1967 and 1977 as the most successful economic integration effort in sub-Saharan Africa.[11] The three countries recently agreed to revive the Community, and the Heads of state signed the Treaty for the Establishment of the East African Community in Arusha on 30th November 1999. The treaty entered into force on July 7, 2000, and the East African Community was formally launched on January 15, 2001. The Community aims to establish a customs union, a common market, then a monetary union, "and ultimately a Political Federation in order to strengthen and regulate the industrial, commercial, infrastructural, cultural, social, political and other relations of the Partner States to the end that there shall be accelerated, harmonious and balanced development and sustained expansion of economic activities, the benefit of which shall be equitably shared" (EAC, 1999).

The three main regional economic communities (RECs), namely, COMESA, ECOWAS, and ECCAS, have basically the same general goals, although they vary with regards to rhetoric on the ultimate common market or economic union, and the scale and breadth of activities. They all formally stress cooperation and coordination (especially through joint projects): in infrastructure development (mainly transport and telecommunications); in industrial projects to diversity their economies; in framing policies relating to energy, natural

---

[10] The member states are Cameroon, Central African Republic, Chad, Congo, Equatorial Guinea, and Gabon.

[11] For a discussion of the first EAC and its breakup, see Eken (1979), Hazlewood (1979), and Johnson (1991). In December 1993, the heads of state of the three countries signed an Accord in Arusha, Tanzania, to revive regional cooperation. Apart from agreeing to cooperate in several areas such as agriculture, aviation, and meteorology, the Accord allowed for free movement of goods and persons among the three states. A Tripartite Commission for Cooperation was established to promote economic, social, cultural, and security cooperation.

resources, the environment, tourism, agriculture, food security, etc.; and in liberalizing trade and payments among member countries. Where they have not, they also want to establish a common external tariff; promote free mobility of labor and capital among the member countries; and harmonize most aspects of their macroeconomic and economic governance policies. Harmonization is especially intended in the areas of monetary, fiscal, and exchange rate policies, investment strategy, and various standards and codes promoting best practices in, for example, payment systems, banking supervision, securities market regulations, anti-money laundering, debt management, transparency in monetary and financial policies, corporate governance, gender policies, and treatment of the marginalized. Each REC has an authority comprising the Heads of State and Government as its highest body; a Council of Ministers; a full-time Secretariat; and specialized Technical Committees.

The ECOWAS Treaty provides for a Court of Justice. Justices were sworn-in in January 2001. The ECOWAS Treaty also provides for a West African Parliament, which was inaugurated in Mali in November 2000. Its membership is currently 115, distributed according to population but with each member country guaranteed a minimum number of five seats.[12] The Parliament is intended as a forum for consultation and consensus building on integration issues. ECOWAS also has a number of financial institutions, technical commissions, and specialized agencies (e.g., regional development fund, bank for investment and development, a monetary institute, and health organization). The West African Monetary Institute was established in January 2001 as a forerunner to a West African Central Bank. The issue of the best way to achieve monetary union appears problematic for ECOWAS. Six non-CFA countries (The Gambia, Ghana, Guinea, Liberia, Nigeria, and Sierra Leone) agreed in Accra, in April 2000, to proceed to achieve monetary union, as a first step toward an ECOWAS-wide monetary

[12] Of the 115 seats, Nigeria has thirty-five, Ghana eight, Côte d'Ivoire seven, Burkina Faso, Guinea, Mali, Niger, and Senegal have six each, and Benin, Cape Verde, the Gambia, Guinea Bissau, Liberia, Sierra Leone and Togo each have five.

union. Initially, they hoped to achieve that objective by January 2003. But the date has been pushed back due mainly to macroeconomic problems that the countries need to address. In addition, ECOWAS is encouraging private sector initiatives with a community focus. Thus it encouraged the establishment of a privately owned regional commercial bank—ECOBANK—the Federation of West African Manufacturers Association, Federation of West African Chambers of Commerce, West African Journalists Association, West African Youth Union, West African Women's Association, and West African Road Transporters Association.

COMESA achieved a free trade area (FTA) on 31 October 2000, when nine of the members (Djibouti, Egypt, Kenya, Madagascar, Malawi, Mauritius, Sudan, Zambia, and Zimbabwe) eliminated tariffs on products originating within COMESA. Burundi and Rwanda joined the FTA on 1 January 2004. The hope is to have every member state join the FTA by May 2007. If that happens, then COMESA may achieve its goal of attaining customs union status by 2008; if not it seems likely to do so soon after. COMESA has also been particularly active in developing organizations and institutions to promote sub-regional cooperation and development in general. The achievements include: the COMESA Trade and Development Bank in Nairobi; the COMESA Clearing House in Harare; the COMESA Association of Commercial Banks in Harare; the COMESA Leather and Leather Products Institute in Ethiopia; and the COMESA Re-Insurance Company (ZEP-RE) in Nairobi. An African Trade Insurance Agency (ATI) was launched in 2001 and seven countries had signed the agreement by August 20, 2001 when the ATI was officially launched in Kampala; the offices of ATI are in Nairobi. All members of the African Union are eligible to be members. COMESA has also established a Court of Justice, which will adjudicate matters brought by states, companies, or even private individuals.

In June 1991 a treaty establishing an African Economic Community (AEC) was signed in Abuja, Nigeria. Among several organizational units, a Pan-African Parliament and a Court of Justice are envisaged. The AEC Treaty has been operational since May 1994. AEC plans to come into fruition in six stages, involving activities of the regional economic communities; that is, the RECs are regarded as the "building blocs" of the AEC. In fact, the first stage, originally expected to last for five years, involves strengthening existing RECs and creating new ones as needed. The existing RECs are: The Arab Maghreb Union (AMU),[13] ECCAS, COMESA, SADC, and ECOWAS. The hope at the start was that the transitional period to full fruition of the AEC would last for no more that forty years from the date of entry into force of the Treaty (see OAU, 1991).

The Rationalization Issue

There is clear need for rationalization of the integration groupings to eliminate overlap and reverse the tendency to proliferation of groups. The overlapping membership of ECOWAS, Mano River Union and WAEMU in West Africa, of COMESA and SADC in Southern Africa, and of COMESA, SADC and EAC in Eastern Africa, engender policy dilemmas; these groupings are outcomes not only of history but also of ambivalence of the countries that straddle the various arrangements. The coexistence of UDEAC/CAEMC and ECCAS seems to have attracted less debate, no doubt because all the members of the former are in the latter organization. Having overlapping groups seeking economic integration appears disorderly. Countries, for example, may not be able to follow different rules and practices of two separate groupings (for instance, for external tariff structures).

Eastern and Southern Africa

In Southern Africa, the political foundations of SADCC were quite strong, namely, anti-apartheid sentiments and the desire for economic independence from

[13] The AMU comprises Algeria, Libya, Mauritania, Morocco, and Tunisia.

South Africa. COMESA, in contrast, was started with the more clear-cut objective of bolstering intraregional trade and economic integration. Now, SADC has become much more focused on economic development and integration, and South Africa itself has joined it instead of COMESA. In addition, as compared with COMESA, it appears that SADC has within it countries that are much more culturally homogeneous and share political experiences and fundamental economic interests of great relevance to cementing relationships.[14] In fact, SADC has as one of its stated objectives: "to strengthen and consolidate the long standing historical, social and cultural affinities and links among the people of the Region."[15] These factors, from the perspective of economic integration, should work in favor of SADC, if South Africa is enthusiastic on economic integration of the common-market type involving all (or even most) of the countries of SADC.

Despite the structural advantages of SADC, it is COMESA that seems clearly committed to integration of the common-market type. In that context, the evolutionary process is likely not to favor the survival of EAC over the long haul, despite the progress of its member states in regenerating that former union, if one or both of the two larger groupings (SADC and COMESA) progress to full common market(s). My prognosis would be that, as a minimum, in that eventuality, rationalization would entail Tanzania leaving SADC and rejoining COMESA, thereby bringing all the EAC members into COMESA; Swaziland will end up with SADC for historical reasons; and Burundi, Democratic Republic of Congo (DRC), and Rwanda will most likely be all together either in COMESA or ECCAS, and I suspect they will end up in ECCAS, once that organization is fully resurrected with the emergence of greater peace and security in the region. Thus, the struggle will end up being between COMESA and SADC for Angola, Malawi, Mauritius, Zambia and Zimbabwe. In this scenario SACU will become assimilated into SADC.

---

[14]See also, for example, Arnold (1993) and Southern African Economist (1994) for discussion of some of these issues.

[15] See www.sadc.int.

Meanwhile, SADC and COMESA set up a Task Force in 2001 to harmonize the programs of the two organizations and foster collaboration in a number of activities and areas. Harmonization discussions which have been progressing earnestly, since at least early 2003, cover areas including customs procedures and trade policy and programs in transport and communications that they hope will reduce the cost of intra-regional trade. Other possible areas of collaboration on which the Task Force have had, or plan to have, substantial discussions include sharing of trade statistics and statistical training, development of a regional customs bond guarantee scheme and third party vehicle insurance, non-tariff barriers, and the development of a common program in air traffic liberalization. COMESA and SADC are also working closely together in a number of other ways (Press release by COMESA and SADC, 6th February 2003).

Western Africa

In Western Africa, ECOWAS contains the countries of WAEMU and the Mano River Union, the Lusophone countries (Cape Verde and Guinea-Bissau), Guinea, and two other Anglophone countries, namely, Nigeria and The Gambia. For cultural, historical, and political reasons, WAEMU is likely to stay stable and fairly cohesive as an economic and monetary union for some time to come—that is, until at least ECOWAS is ready to become a more complete union. From the standpoint of cooperation in various infrastructure projects, ECOWAS has had major successes. Many of these projects have been financed via the ECOWAS Fund for Cooperation, Compensation, and Development (see the ECOWAS Fund Protocol, 1976).

But there are serious issues in the monetary area. ECOWAS has come to grips with the reality of the BCEAO and the CFA franc,[16] while the CFA Franc

[16] One of the benefits that monetary integration of the BEAC and BCEAO type has yielded is low inflation in the member states (see, e.g., Johnson and Nascimento, 1993).

Zone countries appreciate that the non-CFA franc countries are not going to accept the CFA franc as the common currency for ECOWAS. The plan being pursued now is to make orderly progress toward a common currency and central bank in the region. The West African Monetary Institute was established in January 2001 to steer The Gambia, Ghana, Guinea, Liberia, Nigeria, and Sierra Leone toward achievement of a second monetary zone, the West African Monetary Zone (WAMZ). WAMZ, once achieved, will have a single currency and central bank, the West African Central Bank (WACB). At that point, negotiations can begin for a common ECOWAS currency for the BCEAO countries and WAMZ countries.

Central Africa

In central Africa, I have noted the rationalization that would be needed among ECCAS, SADC, and COMESA. All the members of the CAEMC are members of ECCAS. But, as in West Africa, the monetary union arrangement of CAEMC can be considered solid for the time being, while at the same time it is not likely that all the other ECCAS members would want to give up their currencies in favor of simply joining the CFA Franc Zone of BEAC (as did, for example, Equatorial Guinea in 1984). Rationalization with ECCAS emerging as the sole union has a good chance of success if, for example, an exchange regime is crafted such that the non-BEAC members of ECCAS establish fixed parities vis-à-vis the CFA franc and all the countries then conduct their macroeconomic policies consistently with the requirements of such an exchange regime, with periodic realignments kept rather infrequent. If such a program were resolutely implemented, not only would convergence of inflation rates occur, but also the low inflation benefit of the BEAC countries would redound on the others. Over time, a single currency, different from the CFA, could be agreed. An alternative transition scenario could be one similar to that chosen by the non-CFA ECOWAS countries. Namely, the non-BEAC countries could decide to achieve an arrangement with a single currency and common central bank, and once that was achieved they would then discuss with the BEAC countries the evolution of a single ECCAS currency and central bank.

Addressing the Purported "Problems" of Attaining Integration

Progress toward regional economic integration in Africa has been slowed down by factors considered "difficulties" and "obstacles." The classic example cited continues to be the breakup of the EAC (see, for example, Eken, 1979, and Hazlewood, 1979). Similar and other reasons are being adduced to explain, for instance, why ECOWAS, SADC, and COMESA have not made more rapid progress toward becoming full common markets. I shall discuss these problems briefly and argue that none of them is really insoluble if the commitment to integration is strong.[17] Then I shall address the issue of commitment to economic integration. As in Johnson (1991), the purported problems can be grouped into three main types: (i) loss of sovereignty over macroeconomic policy to some union authority or body; (ii) consumption costs from protection; and (iii) unequal distribution of gains and losses.

Loss of sovereignty

Outside of the BCEAO/WAEMU and BEAC/CAEMC arrangements, African countries in economic community and preferential trading arrangements have only a fair record of following through, in their domestic policies, on important decisions taken at the community/union level. No doubt this is partly due to the fact that the community decisionmaking processes do not fully take into account the domestic realities of member countries. But more importantly, the lack of full implementation of community decisions and the failure to

[17] See the discussion in Johnson (1991) for elaboration of some of the points that will be made below. See also Adejugbe (1984), Lukács (1987), Brown (1989) Arijo (1992), Nomvete (1991/2), and Arnold (1993).

coordinate and harmonize according to initial timetables seem to be due to an underlying fear of countries of losing control over certain economic policies that directly affect their own nationals, or inability to persuade their nationals to go along with the agreements. Clearly, the willingness of countries to lose sovereignty over some aspects of their economic policy is related to the degree of their commitment to integration, which I shall discuss later. Fortunately, as evident from the discussion so far, COMESA seems to be showing the way in making resolute progress.

Common external tariff

In the major RECs supported by the African Union, African Economic Community and Economic Commission for Africa (ECOWAS, ECCAS, SADC and COMESA), a common external tariff is an important objective.[18] Hence, the levels of various tariffs must be decided. But the structure of a tariff system has important implications for the effective protection bestowed on different commodities. If a simple rule were established, such as that all commodities should, to the extent possible, be granted equal effective protection, then the determination of tariff rates would be left to technical experts to decide. Another simple rule that could be agreed, instead, is to have the same rate of nominal protection for different commodities.

But African countries, in the light of considerations related, inter alia, to infant industry assistance and industrial development policy, want differential nominal tariffs and effective protection. Given their economic structures and the state of development of the various countries concerned, different schedules of tariff rates have dissimilar implications for comparative advantage of countries in a community/union. Once member countries begin to deviate from simple rules, such as those mentioned above, political-economic considerations come to

[18] This discussion is based on that contained in Johnson (1991), pp. 4–11. See Kakoza (1972) for a discussion of the common external tariff in the former East African Community.

dominate discussions of the detailed tariff schedules to be put into effect.

Consumption cost

The preferential trading arrangements that the proposed unions want to create might entail short-run to medium-term consumption costs as relatively high-cost industries within a union are made to keep out some cheaper imports. An obvious solution to this problem would be to have a common external tariff no higher than what prevailed in the member country with the lowest pre-integration tariff. But, in practice, countries find this solution not totally acceptable in terms of goals with respect to industrialization and diversification. Even where the countries agree in principle that indeed some positive consumption cost is inevitable as a price in the transition to a higher degree of industrialization and diversification of their economies, differences arise with respect to the specific policies that should be pursued in order to minimize the short-term real consumption cost per unit of additional output achieved, within some specific time horizon, and the distribution of the burden involved.

An important aspect of the argument boils down to whether specific industries should be targeted for preferential treatment and, if so, which ones. This can involve making an assessment of the industries with the greatest potential for rapid increases in total factor productivity; the nature of the intervention package—in particular, the role of tariffs, lump-sum subsidies, in-kind and less direct cash subsidies (notably tax relief and preferential treatment in the areas of credit and interest rates); and who pays for these costs.

The principles involved in addressing these issues are no different from those that would be considered if an African country were designing its own policy independently (see Chapter 8). But in the context of economic union the coordination of industrial development strategy in the light of domestic resource constraints and the determination of the tolerable consumption costs are much more formidable tasks. General economic theory would lead one to the conclusion that the optimal approach would involve a combination of lump sum, indirect cash, and in-kind subsidies, as well as tariffs. The attempt would be to limit distortions in relative prices, avoid quantitative controls, take due account of administrative and efficiency costs of taxation, have consumption costs made as explicit as possible, and limit such costs by allowing market forces to play a major role in the choice of any industries or activities for selective intervention by states.

Distribution of gains and losses

Many in the continent fear that gains to countries from economic unions will be positively related to the degree of their economic development and/or the size of their domestic economies. [19] The allegedly "unfair" distribution of gains and losses is widely believed to have been at the root of the breakup of the first EAC, where it was felt that Kenya's industrialization was greatly helped but that, in the process, Tanzania's might have been adversely affected. An attempt to use differential intra-union tariffs—designated transfer taxes—could not alleviate the problems, at least not to the satisfaction of Tanzania.[20]

Many supporters of integration in the continent want to see a coordinated approach to industrial development. In that case, leaders will struggle for the location in their countries of those industries considered the most advanced technologically. If national politicians and/or officials cannot get what they prefer by negotiation, then they are likely to ignore the integration agreement, which they may have signed, and rather proceed to set up their own national facilities. Alternatively, as in the earlier EAC, they will seek some kind of internal (intra-union) tariff structure that protects some national domestic production activities from direct competition within the union. In contrast, if the principle is accepted

[19] This sub-section is based on the discussion in Johnson (1991).

[20] Of relevance and interest, see Djah (1990) and Rosenberg (1995).

(and applied) that the location of industries among countries should be determined in a world of open competition and free mobility of factors, rather than in an arena of negotiated industrial planning buttressed by restricted mobility of factors, especially labor, this problem would disappear.

A challenge would still remain as to how to balance such a market-oriented approach to the location of industries with permitting selective intervention, which I have argued may be necessary for many countries to achieve optimal dynamic evolution of diversification of production and exports. Clearly the answer would involve placing macroeconomic constraint(s) on what countries can do. In other words, selective intervention policies cannot have negative externalities on other countries in the union/common market. Hence, they must be pursued while continuing to observe certain macroeconomic constraints set by the union as a whole. This could be as simple as imposing limits to the government budget deficit and government debt in relation to gross domestic product.

Differences in taxation systems and structures also engender issues of unequal gains and losses. In particular, countries have different reliance on import taxes as sources of government revenue. This fact, for example, has slowed down reduction of intra-union tariffs, since a formula to compensate those who will lose tax revenue from large intra-union tariff reductions has, in general, proved difficult to find.[21] Thus, countries realize they need to reform their tax systems to lessen their dependence on import taxes if substantial and rapid intra-union tariff reductions are to occur in practice. The success of countries to effect reforms of tax systems and to move toward greater reliance on income, profits, and value-added taxes should be of help in this regard.

Leaving aside the issue of the problems arising from differential dependence on import tariffs, which could be addressed by tax reform, supplemented perhaps by some compensation system, the question of unequal net

[21] Article 39 of the ECCAS Treaty establishes a Fund for Compensation for Loss of Revenue, in this context, and further elaboration is contained in Annex VI to the Treaty: Protocol Relating to the Compensation Fund for Loss of Revenue. But that is still a far cry from an actual workable (that is, sustainable) formula.

benefit from economic union has remained a sticky one because African countries have not recognized fully some obvious solutions to the two underlying sources of the problem: (i) that differential benefits to countries from integration in terms of the relative impact on their gross domestic product (GDP) are probably unavoidable, and (ii) that the occurrence of current account imbalances within common markets is inevitable and normal. For the first of these two underlying problems a sustainable solution is to take measures to ensure that the differential impact on GDP of countries does not aggravate disparities in productivity and in *per capita* real incomes among the populations of the different countries. This would call for genuinely free factor mobility (labor and capital) as an essential element of union arrangements from the outset. The right to be mobile would not, of course, totally eliminate the *personal* real income effects of divergent production gains among *countries*. Immobile assets would be unevenly affected (prices and rentals), and this would have personal income repercussions. But the bulk of the problem would have been resolved.

As regards the second underlying factor, if the exchange rate and reserve management policies of a country are such that its overall balance of payments situation is sustainable, then its current account imbalances with others in the union have no particular significance. In such a case, transfer taxes are not needed for balance of payments reasons. For a country with a weak current account vis-à-vis the union as a whole would have a strong current account with the rest of the world; thus the necessary settlement of accounts within the union would not create balance of payments problems. Only if a country has its surpluses with nonmember countries accrue in nonconvertible currencies (for instance, if the country is involved in certain kinds of bilateral payments arrangements) would there be a problem of intra-union settlement. But, in that situation, the direct solution is to move away from settlement in nonconvertible currencies in its extra-union trade. In addition, free capital movements within the union would facilitate the adjustment process and hence, once again, should form an important element of the integration process from its early stages.

The Commitment Question

One of the more complex (some would say sensitive) themes in the integration debate in the African continent is the degree to which African leaders by and large are committed to full economic integration in the foreseeable future. As Percy Mistry (2000), for example, puts it: "Seen from an objective, impartial perspective, Africa's commitment to integration appears to have been visceral rather than rational, more rhetorical than real." From my perspective, there are three interrelated aspects to this debate: (i) the global benefits to the group and the optimal pace of integration; (ii) the domestic political authority and hence support for integration; and (iii) the ideological compatibility of the political leaders.

The global benefits and pace of integration

Because, for many of the countries, intraregional trade is very small in relation to extraregional trade, and because many of the countries in each of the regions tend to produce similar goods, the urgency for a common market is not sometimes felt. In this context, it is not a fear of trade diversion from integration as such, especially since that could be easily avoided by lowering effective protection rates, but rather a belief that integration would yield only minor benefits for a long time.

Perhaps every single leader of the countries would willingly concede that, in time, the benefits of integration will be substantial, as the effective size of the domestic market is greatly enlarged, so that technological economies of scale can be exploited and the marginal efficiency of investment enhanced. Indeed, many productive activities should benefit from the combination of common external tariff and large internal market. Hence, it is along these lines that the most ardent integrationists have argued their case. In contrast, those who prefer a slower pace—partly in the light of the other two aspects of the debate, to be discussed below—are content to push now for: (i) promotion of greater intraregional trade, employing the instrument of common external tariff, probably supplemented by some form of transfer tax or *taxe de coopération régionale*, until full labor mobility becomes socially and politically feasible; (ii) cooperation in infrastructure and industrial "regional" projects; and (iii) some harmonization of policies (especially macroeconomic) as feasible. This could be followed, in the eyes of the gradualists, by some form of monetary union.[22] Only later, when mass support for integration is strong and ideological obstacles are minor, according to this view, should full integration be pursued.

Domestic political authority for integration

Economic integration efforts are unavoidably sustained by an interaction of economic and political forces, whatever might have been the motive for the initial drive.[23] It is doubtful that, without legitimate political authority to pursue integration, political leaders would be able to sustain any degree of commitment to the integration effort. The evidence that African leaders have clear (that is, legitimate) political authority from their populations to pursue, vigorously, regional economic integration is not very clear.[24] For instance, in the case of ECOWAS, ECCAS, COMESA, or SADC, one does not see discussions in the national political debates of the countries focusing on important integration issues (pace, timing, and content) as happened, for instance, over the years, in European countries on their integration issues. Also, there is no particular deference to

---

[22] The economic analysis does support the view that the net benefits of monetary union tend to increase with the degree to which the economies are truly integrated—for instance, as measured by the ratio of intraregional trade to GDP (see, e.g., Krugman [1990] and De Grauwe [1994]).

[23] Mahant and De Vanssay (1994) have, for example, recently visited this issue of the interaction of political and economic motives in integration.

[24] Legitimate political authority is being used here in the same sense as in Johnson (1994). This authority is an *asset*, which gives the government/leaders the *right* to rule, lead, control, and take certain decisions. This right is acknowledged by the population because it has been acquired by methods that, in the light of history or tradition, are considered appropriate (that is, legitimate).

protocols and treaty programs signed by representatives of the countries, including heads of states, when the countries design their domestic macroeconomic and public policies, to ensure that there is no conflict with union agreements. Moreover, there has been no consistent and resolute organizational effort within member countries to follow through on formal integration commitments (see, for example, Agyemang, 1990, for an early but still relevant illustration of the point).

It is possible to speculate about the reasons for the lack of clear evidence of legitimate political authority to seek full integration—and hence an assurance of mass popular support for particular measures fostering integration. One obvious hypothesis is that regional group identity is not strong, particularly since even within individual African countries the struggle to build national states is still not over. Another hypothesis is that the benefits of integration are not sufficiently known within the populations. A third, related, hypothesis is that the people are not fully aware of the integration agenda as set out by their political leaders. A fourth hypothesis is that there are competing interest groups (e.g., labor versus big business in South Africa, see Hentz, 2005) with different attitudes toward alternative approaches to regional cooperation and that political leaders are finding it difficult to reconcile those interests and, moreover, to have all groups agree that the regional integration approach of the African Union is the optimal one for them.

ECOWAS political leaders seem to have decided to face the issue not by asking country leaders to obtain the authority from their people directly, but rather by proposing to launch an action program involving informing the populations of the member states about ECOWAS activities (e.g., through radio and television programs, newspapers, and educational institutions); establishing highly visible ECOWAS symbols (ECOWAS Day, ECOWAS press card, ECOWAS flag, a meritorious award to be called ECOWAS Order of Merit, and an ECOWAS anthem); and organizing regional fora so that ECOWAS persons of different background, education, and occupations can get to discuss matters of material interest and thereby build some common identity (see *West Africa*, 16–22 January 1995). This, of course, is the traditional mobilizing approach to obtaining support that has been used by many regimes in Africa. For this approach to work, not surprisingly, the political leaders must be committed enough to launch the action program and have the skills to ensure its success. Perhaps a more open debate (a democratic approach) to supplement the mobilizing approach should be tried. In sum, the suggestion is that ways be found to obtain clear authority from the citizens of the member countries to pursue certain kinds of regional economic integration.

Ideological compatibility of political leaders

Ideological differences and personal antagonism among political leaders are commonplace, and the African continent has had its share of these experiences. In the integration context, this has meant that leaders manifest reluctance to commit themselves to an organization with whose decisions they might disagree for ideological reasons, or to cooperate with certain countries, always, irrespective of the particular leadership of those countries at any particular point in time.

The first EAC provides an example of the harm that could result from personal antagonism in an integration environment. Cooperative arrangements among the three countries went back to the 1920s. Thus, when the community was established in June 1967, a high degree of political will was expected to prevail. Displeasure, nevertheless, set in over the belief that Kenya was benefiting disproportionately from the union. The personal dislike of Tanzania's President for Uganda's President at a particular juncture was probably the final straw that doomed the union. The three Heads of State formed the East African Authority, the supreme organ of the Community. The Authority did not meet from January 1971 when a new President of Uganda assumed power until the final breakup of the Community in 1977; the Tanzanian President, the Chairman at the time, would not convene a meeting (see the discussion in Tordoff, 1984, pp. 233–4 and Johnson, 1991).

There is substantial justification for the conjecture that ideological and personal differences will play less of a role in retarding integration efforts in sub-Saharan Africa in the future than in the past. The acceptance of open and representative democracy as an ideal to aim for and of market solutions to most economic problems is approaching universality among the leaders in the continent, despite difficulties in achieving successful democratic transitions. Perhaps even more important, there is evidence that those who argue and push for integration realize that institutions and organizations must be established that enable an economic union to function in spite of hostilities in high political circles. In other words, there is growing recognition of the need for supranational institutions such as a well-functioning bureaucracy of the union, a body of union laws that take precedence over national laws, and a community/union Parliament and Court of Justice. It is unlikely that full common market–type regional integration would be formalized in practice ahead of the establishment and smooth functioning of such institutions and organizations, with adequate safeguards to guarantee sustainability of whatever arrangements are agreed.

Contribution of State-Business-Civil Society Cooperation

I think it is a major mistake to have the promotion of intraregional trade as the driving force of economic integration in the continent. Rather, the main motivating force should be integration of small domestic markets into single regional markets. This also means that contribution to domestic market integration and not to promotion of intraregional trade should determine the sequencing of integration policies. In the African continent, I would posit that substantial growth in intraregional trade would follow effective and successful domestic market integration. In this respect, it is really unfortunate that recent discussions on economic integration in Africa have been dominated by those who want to put the emphasis on intraregional trade liberalization and expansion in contrast to a whole generation of African leaders who gave prominence to escaping the limitations of small domestic markets, promoting industrialization, and attracting foreign direct investment.

Integration of national markets into single regional markets would require policies that are very similar to those used when trying to integrate regions within countries. Thus one would be trying to integrate physical infrastructure; financial market infrastructure; labor, capital, and commodity markets; and various standards and codes regulating markets. The harmonization of macroeconomic policies—in particular, monetary, fiscal, and exchange rate policies—would, of course, also contribute to achieving the objective of market integration. Intraregional trade liberalization would be part of the integration measures taken; but when seen in the light of market integration as the main objective, the short-term importance of intra-community trade liberalization fades in comparison with the other integration measures just mentioned. Once again, substantial intra-regional trade expansion will follow once market integration has attained some high level.

In this context, substantial state-business-civil society cooperation in designing and implementing specific economic reforms and development programs would greatly accelerate the economic integration in the continent. First, a country's approach to regional integration would be discussed and legitimated by the citizens at large. Second, it is not only governments that would be discussing economic integration details. Civil society leaders and private business sectors across countries within the region would get involved too—discussing among themselves, coordinating their views, and engaging and pressuring their governments. The African countries would then be able to move away from the current situation in which their leaders in government, civil society and private business extol the virtues of economic integration and then governments go ahead and agree plans and protocols without substantial inputs from their civil societies and business sectors. Once civil society leaders and the business sectors get involved in the details, and policies get legitimated, governments would have the requisite authority to implement agreements to harmonize and coordinate policies, thereby enhancing implementation prospects.

For market integration to be fully legitimated as the ultimate driving force behind regional integration efforts, it would be essential that policies be coordinated. As I have argued, African countries need to have intra-regional mobility of labor and capital at an early stage of the process. Such mobility should encourage the less-developed countries to accept intra-regional free trade without elaborate compensation arrangements. Unavoidably, the mobility would push wages toward equality within the region—that is, across the countries wanting to integrate. For the more advanced and well-run countries to accept such mobility, they must therefore be assured that they would not end up with politically unsustainable immigration—especially of low-skilled labor. Thus, they would want to see economic policies maintained in all countries such that even the weakest or least developed countries are fairly attractive to labor and capital, thereby ensuring that wage equalization does not mean reduced wages for the citizens of the most advanced countries of the region. On top of this, for the market integration approach to be sustainable politically in all countries, any trade diversion vis-à-vis the rest of the world must be short-lived. Hence, policies must be instituted to ensure that production costs decline and total factor productivity increase rapidly enough to prevent unbearable consumption costs of citizens of the region as a consequence of integration policies.

Concluding Remarks

At least since the mid-1960s, sub-Saharan African political leaders have demonstrated great interest in pursuing regional economic integration. Significant strides have been made in the form of cooperation in infrastructure and other specific projects; intraregional clearing and settlement arrangements; and harmonization of certain policies, procedures and standards, as well as in intra-community trade liberalization especially in COMESA. But much remains to be done to accelerate the integration process. A good number of the African countries are implementing economic programs that are expected, inter alia, to lower inflation rates, enhance economic efficiency in government, increase the reliance of central banks on market instruments in the conduct of monetary operations, and promote an institutional framework that fosters market mechanisms in the allocation of resources. These programs, if resolutely implemented, will contribute to convergence of national inflation rates, ensuring market-determined exchange rates of all currencies of the countries, and to greater coherence in policy approaches to similar economic problems among the different states. These developments would facilitate the economic integration process.

I have argued that overcoming the traditional obstacles slowing down regional economic integration in sub-Saharan Africa would involve, among other things, taking steps in the different countries to obtain domestically the legitimate political authority for integration efforts. Also important, at a more technical level, would be opting for a simple rule for the determination of the common external tariff; reforming tax systems to lessen the budgetary dependence of countries on import taxation; and agreeing to use the market as the allocation mechanism for the location of industries among member states, rather than to rely on a political or administrative process.

In my view, arguably the three most important underlying issues that need to be addressed urgently to accelerate the integration process are: (i) the legitimation of the authority of governments to pursue regional integration, including the form, pace, and sequencing of integration steps; (ii) the rationalization of the regional groupings with a view to reduce overlapping membership; and (iii) shifting decidedly the primary focus of integration policies from trying to promote intraregional trade to that of fostering the integration of small domestic markets into single regional markets. Once these issues are addressed and appropriate decisions and actions taken, African countries will make great forward strides towards successful and sustainable regional economic integration arrangements. Effective developmental states, with substantial state-business-civil society cooperation in designing and implementing economic reform and development programs, would greatly accelerate the whole process.

Once legitimate political authority for integration is obtained domestically, the political commitment for integration would be enhanced, since economic ideological differences among African political leaders are small and diminishing and institutions are likely to emerge that enable economic union arrangements to be sustained independently of the personal attitudes of political leaders towards each other. Of course, differences will continue to exist over the exact form, pace, and sequencing of integration, affecting the achievement of timetables often set out in protocols.

10

Conclusion

There is a lot of justifiable criticism about the economic failures of Africa. But too many make it appear as if it all has to do with the nature and the culture of Africans. I do not think that the ultimate cause of Africa's economic problems is the nature or the culture of Africans. Neither of these is inimical to rapid economic development and transformation. The typical African is no less *homo economicus* than typical humans of other continents. The rational self-interest behavior of Africans can stand up to competition from anywhere. Africans also can save, invest, and work hard in response to appropriate economic incentives. Indeed, all economic advice to those countries have assumed that it is the information and incentives that are faulty not the nature and culture of the people, and there is no evidence that this assumption is wrong. Collective action is complex and the fact that certain institutions have not emerged in certain settings has something to do with power, self-interest, information, mistakes, and inertia. Culture is evolving, and agency and cooperation are important in this evolution as is collective self-interest.

The dearth of certain institutions and organizations in Africa, at this stage of their development, cause Africans to behave in ways that some ascribe to culture or nature rather than to economic optimization. Lack of financial institutions with variety of assets in which to save adversely affect saving rates. The absence of formal organizations collecting and distributing charity means that charity has to be given on a personal basis; many of the relations and friends that ask for charity despise the fact that they need to, since everyone prefers to be at the other end, namely, the 'big person' that is doing the giving. In fact, some observers fail to notice the reciprocal relationships in extended family transactions and the fact that opportunity cost does affect gift-giving and the nature and extent of reciprocal relationships. The power of ostracism has its limits too; economic tradeoffs do matter. Also, parents do not count on their kids for financial assistance as a matter of culture but rather of economics and sometimes the dependence is reversed. The old may be revered, but in traditional societies leaders lose their legitimacy once they cease to evince wisdom, good judgment, and integrity. The old must continue to earn their respect or lose it. It is the modern leaders, with guns and state funds to bribe, who are able to stay in power even after they have lost their legitimacy and ability to govern well. Weaknesses in property rights and enforcement of contracts, as well as the informal or incomplete nature of many contracts, explain much of the corruption in business relationships; such behavior is not condoned in any African culture. This is why generalized trust, if anything, keeps declining and there are increasing calls for improvements in the legal framework.

This book has discussed the role of institutions, loyalty to the state, lack of country ownership in economic policymaking and political leadership in contributing to Africa's backwardness and underdevelopment. But I believe that ultimately one must start with cooperation. There is, in this author's view, *cooperation deficit* among African citizens and the biggest contributing factor is the way the states were instituted at the dawn of independence. To solve Africa's problem one must remove this cooperation deficit. For it is via cooperation that Africans can demand country ownership over policymaking, create the institutions that will build loyalty to the state, ensure good political leadership, and put in place economic polices to transform their economies for sustained and rapid economic growth and development.

So how will or should the process for the elimination of the cooperation deficit begin? Throughout, this book has stressed the role of agency and of constitutional reform via processes that mimic the stable equilibrium determination process described in Chapter 2, the occurrence of the latter itself being affected by agency. Ultimately, then, African countries must wait for a critical mass of agents with self-interest and/or altruism to begin the process of eliminating the cooperation deficit. That wait does not need to be long. Still, the emergence of the initial agents will have to occur somewhat spontaneously. Those initial agents will do well if they then begin the process of eliminating the cooperation deficit by mobilizing support for constitutional reform, promoting generalized trust in the population, and getting Africans to cease blaming external forces and agents for their problems. In some countries it may be possible for outsiders to "plant" the initial agents. Whether the initial agents emerge spontaneously or via plantation, they would then proceed to mobilize additional local support and sensibly order their program of action as discussed above. Where such agents do not emerge, the African countries would have to wait for an evolutionary process that can hardly be mapped in advance.

Individuals in the typical African country are playing a collective game, which one could call a *prosperity game.* It is infinite in time. In the game, individuals interact with each other to produce goods and services, which they then share and/or appropriate via diverse mechanisms. At any given point in time individuals decide their strategies in such interactions based on their beliefs about the types of persons with whom they are playing. In other words, individuals act on the basis of their beliefs. The beliefs themselves are based on experience. What I have been arguing in this book is that the experience that people have had since independence have led them to believe that there is an extremely high probability that other persons they come across (that is, with whom they may or may not interact), are ethnically biased; will be corrupt and inefficient if chosen as political leaders or officials of the state bureaucracy; will dupe and cheat as partners in any cooperative venture; or will free ride, shirk responsibility, or steal as workers in enterprises.

One major implication is a general belief among individuals that there is only a very low probability that other individuals they come across will have a long-term commitment to cooperation in the context of any business venture; namely, such individuals are very likely to behave as if they have high discount rates and are prepared to defect anytime and stop playing the "game." No "stranger" is trusted to keep promises; so contracts cannot be signed based on trust, except with a few well-known persons. The adverse implication for general cooperation is magnified by official corruption. The fact of official corruption means that there is a very low probability of punishing anyone who breaks a contract or dupes partners in a business deal. This is particularly damaging when the potential capital loss from being duped during a given period can be a very substantial fraction of one's wealth.

The experiences, which engendered the beliefs that individuals now hold, have been greatly influenced by the collective actions of nationals at the dawn of independence and the path dependent actions that followed those initial actions. In general, the actions at independence did not result in institutions—rules of the game that everyone was expected to obey—that were legitimated by the population at large. In fact, the typical case was an absence of transparent, objective, and sacrosanct rules agreed via broad participation and deliberation. A state of the world thereby emerged tantamount to absence of legitimated rules of order. In consequence, African citizens have turned the prosperity game into another Prisoners' Dilemma game in which the dominant strategy is "Don't Cooperate," and for the classic reasons, namely, lack of communication and credible commitment to build and maintain legitimate institutions that are by and large incentive compatible (that is, in the self-interest of persons to support). In other words, individuals lack a feeling of loyalty to the institutions and an interest in obeying and monitoring them. Worse still, the "hemmed-in" perspective is not far-fetched,[1] because Africans have been observing their payoffs from the lack of cooperation, and have seen that on average the payoffs have been low and declining for many years; and yet, the Africans seem unable or unwilling to act to change the institutional and organizational order. I have spent time in the book elaborating on this thesis and do not want to repeat the arguments here.

For African countries in such predicament (beliefs and environment), one feasible way out is instituting a process that provides citizens with the opportunity to have experiences of the kind that would enable them to revise their beliefs in ways that promote cooperation. The solution must also address the highly limited ability to punish contract violators in a context in which individuals are too poor to afford capital losses from duping by others. The solution envisaged should lead individuals along a path where they would realize equilibrium strategies that facilitate prosperity of citizens and their countries. I believe that the leadership that starts the process and proposes equilibrium strategies could come from self-interested, altruistic and/or reciprocal persons.

As an example, some such leadership group could, via education, preaching, and organizational activity:

(1) foster a national 'culture' of rule-making (institution-building) via deliberative processes that ensure broad participation and consensus among the relevant persons—inter alia by encouraging explicit, transparent, and legitimated institutions (rules) everywhere (in government, business, and voluntary associations); and

(2) propose strategies (rational rules chosen by individuals to determine how they would act in their self-interest, in interaction with other "players" in the game) that pre-empt free riding and cheating of others while based on a belief that a majority of individuals are willing to

---

[1] See Callaghy and Ravenhill (1993).

> cooperate without cheating or free riding as long as they expect others to behave in a similar manner.

The societal leadership types must suggest strategies that are appealing to all especially the pure self-interested. Note, again, that *institutions* are rules that everyone is expected to obey but *strategies* are plans that could differ among persons.

With respect to strategies, I would propose what one could call *deterrence,* as one that could be an equilibrium strategy, at least initially. The persons employing this strategy would be operating under the assumption that everyone really wants to cooperate but that without preemptive constraints a significant fraction of the population would not keep promises or respect long-term commitments because of a belief that other persons could not be trusted to do the same. Thus, persons playing deterrence would be willing to impose mutual constraints on each other—internal or mutual control mechanisms—that are adequate to deter duping and shirking. The objective would not be to *punish* wrongdoing (free riding or duping) but rather to *prevent* wrongdoing. In an environment in which individuals can escape punishment (e.g., by leaving the country or escaping into tribal protection) institutional and organizational arrangements that prevent free riding and cheating are superior to those that punish. In this scenario, altruistic persons, when they can identify each other, can still play *reciprocal altruism* in their interaction with each other; but in their interaction with others they are better off playing deterrence or reciprocity. Both altruists and reciprocal persons are better off playing deterrence with the pure self-interested, where the pure self-interested care only about the expected material benefits (present and discounted future) to them and, in the African context, one can assume that they have high discount rates.

Simultaneous with the above process, transforming leadership (which includes the initial agents) in civil society and the business community would work to put in train particular processes to address collectively the basic problems of ethnicity, political leadership, government corruption, spontaneous order, authoritarian order, national ownership in policymaking, and regional integration, as I have been discussing in the book. More specifically, in those contexts, the leadership types would be interested in promoting certain specific collective actions. These would include: (1) rewriting the constitution using processes that mimic the stable equilibrium determination process; (2) agreeing to deliberative processes, using focal points embedded in their cultures and traditions, for arriving at rules, laws, and norms to promote societal civility and other ways to reduce rather that simply manage ethnicity; and (3) agreeing to a framework for guaranteeing citizens' rights of consultation in economic decisionmaking.

A real difficulty for the leadership types as discussed earlier in the book is how to identify each other. As stated before, a rational approach is to deduce a person's type from his or her action (behavior). Technically speaking, one tries to guesstimate the probability that for a person to behave in some observed way he or she must be of a certain type. As a start, therefore, one may logically arrive at some conclusions by observing people and their actions. For instance, take the case of altruistic types. First, one could look at membership in voluntary associations. Persons who are members of truly ethnically diverse voluntary associations that are not profit oriented could prima facie be seen as, potentially, persons that are not only self-interested. Second, of importance is the willingness of a person to stay in the country, rather than emigrate, even when he or she is fully qualified to be profitably mobile. For instance, in a poor country with very corrupt political leadership, one could argue that any self-interested person who has not exited after some substantial period of time is either able to share in the corruption revenue, is immobile, or able to shield herself from the "system." For it could be shown that, for conceivable expected payoff structures, if the government is corrupt and inefficient, it pays a mobile person (someone with excellent economic opportunities abroad), who is also self-interested, to exit. Thus, it is reasonable to hold as a prior belief that, with a high probability, anyone who is mobile in our sense and does not share in the corruption revenue and yet has not exited is a pure or reciprocal altruist.

Note, also, that in any game that could last well into the future the first move at an "initial" point in time is important. Path dependence can greatly influence developments after that. Sometimes one might recover from a suboptimal (less than wealth or utility maximizing) first move and arrive at some position (node) that one would have reached even with the optimal first move. But typically this would come at a cost—money, time, energy, health, damage to third parties, etc. In an infinite game, the loss could be substantial, because the incentive to correct the first move may be daunted by the feeling of having time in the future to compensate or by a willingness to simply wait for 'something good' to turn the tide. This is a fear that one has for many countries in Africa—an absence of potential agents manifesting any sense of urgency to correct the early mistakes; for what one sees is a willingness to just keep trudging along and waiting for 'something' to happen naturally, or by chance, to reverse the trend. And yet what I have intimated, for example, is that amending the initial mistakes, via some stable equilibrium determination process, is inescapable. The choice that the Africans have is whether they do so through purposive and resolute collective action or through a long and painful evolutionary process of fumbling and ad hoc experimentation.

Africans tend to blame others or forces they cannot control for their problems. They blame colonialism, neocolonialism, the global markets, the IMF and the World Bank, and the multinational corporations. My experience is that the political leaders encourage this. Today's leaders have the knowledge that the strategy worked in mobilizing support for the leadership in the early days of independence. So now they use it to conceal the fact that their poor policies are mainly to blame for the continent's problems. Unfortunately, it is even worse than that. All the members of the government-civil service-business coalition have an interest in blaming outside forces and participating in this deception. This makes addressing this issue very challenging.

The strategy of agents for good policies must be to educate the population at large. They should let the African populations outside of the government-civil service-business coalition engaged in extracting corruption revenue know that other developing countries have faced the same challenges of globalization and have succeeded. They should then reinforce the education on the growth effects of poor leadership and corruption. Moreover, they should indicate the importance of country ownership of policymaking and the importance of the developmental state in the development process, citing the examples of East Asia. They would have to address the propaganda of many African leaders that it was American aid that was really behind the growth of some of those East Asian countries rather than the cooperation between state and business and the legitimated policies of the countries themselves with regard to saving, investment, equity, human capital development, industrialization, infrastructure development, etc.

Given the corruption and poor leadership in the continent and the suffering of many of the citizens, many casual but sympathetic observers wonder why the people outside the government-civil service-business coalition imposing corruption tax do not rise up and why protests are not more frequent and persistent in the continent. I believe that the answer is clear from the pages of the book, especially Chapters 2 and 5. The main reasons are: limited information of the poor on what good policies can accomplish; the ability of many in the middle class to shield themselves from much of the effects of poor policies which make the cost (including risk of being hurt) of protesting not worth taking except in extreme circumstances; the high cost of organizing, partly related to ethnicity and low generalized trust; and the low per capita incomes which reduce the ability to financially support agencies fighting for good government. This all means that agents that spontaneously emerge to begin the mobilization process will not have an easy time. But none of their difficulties will have anything to do with the culture or the nature of the Africans. These are systemic issues which can be addressed. The international community can therefore continue to be of great value if it continues its pressures for democratic change in the continent and its financial support for NGOs and for other activities, mentioned in Chapter 2, to build a knowledgeable public in the African countries that can demand good government and good policies.

Major structural aspects of aid—content and donor-recipient relationship—should change, so that aid donors are not directly trying to impose certain policies but rather to remove domestic obstacles to the emergence of good policies, engage in some capacity building to enable good policies to be effective, and support domestic agents working to raise the domestic demand for good policies and create incentives for governments to introduce good policies. It would seem that donors can usefully focus especially on projects for expanding the public (libraries, think tanks, etc.); on education (equipment, library materials, and teachers and trainers, especially in science and mathematics); and on technical assistance (in all areas of economic management, financial sector development, and institution building). Apart from these, other aid could stress physical infrastructure. Outcomes of policies should be closely monitored and reports on policy design and implementation detailed and regular. Ex ante selectivity should be resolutely applied. Humanitarian aid can also continue, via international agencies.

References

Achebe, Chinua, 1983, *The Trouble with Nigeria* (London: Heinemann).

Addis, Adeno, 1997, "On Human Diversity and the Limits of Toleration," in *Ethnicity and Group Rights*, edited by Ian Shapiro & Will Kymlicka, Nomos 39 (New York: New York University Press), pp.112-153.

Adejugbe, M.O.A., 1984, "Cooperation, Conflicts and Contradictions in West African Economic Integration Schemes," African Studies Center (Boston University) Discussion Paper No. 3.

Agarwal, Jamuna P., 1980, "Determinants of Foreign Direct Investment: A Survey," *Weltwirtschaftliches Archiv*, Vol. 116, pp. 739-773.

Agyemang, Augustus Asante, 1990, "Trade Liberalization Under the Treaty of the Economic Community of West African States (ECOWAS): Some Preliminary Highlights of Legal and Economic Problems," *Journal of World Trade Law* (Geneva), Vol. 24, No. 6 (December), pp. 57–79.

Ahmed, Masood, Timothy Lane, and Marianne Schulze-Ghattas, 2001, "Refocusing IMF Conditionality," *Finance and Development*, Vol. 38 (December), pp. 40-43.

Aiyede, E. R., 2003, "The Dynamics of Civil Society and the Democratization Process in Nigeria." *Canadian Journal of African Studies* 37: 1-27.

Ake, Claude, 1993, "Rethinking African Democracy," in *The Global Resurgence of Democracy*, edited by Larry Diamond and Marc F. Plattner (Baltimore: The Johns Hopkins University Press), pp. 70-82.

Alchian, Armen, 1950, "Uncertainty, Evolution, and Economic Theory," *Journal of Political Economy*, Vol. 58 (June), pp. 211-21.

——, 1977, "Some Economics of Property Rights," *Economic Forces at Work* (Indianapolis: Liberty Press), Chapter 5, 127-149.

Alejandro, Carlos F. Diaz, 1970, "Direct Foreign Investment in Latin America," in Kindleberger (ed.), *The International Corporation: A Symposium* (Cambridge, Mass.: M. I. T. Press), pp. 319-344.

Alesina, Alberto, and David Dollar, 2000, "Who Gives Foreign Aid to Whom and Why?" *Journal of Economic Growth*, Vol. 5 (March), pp. 33-63.

Alesina, Alberto and Eliana La Ferrara, 2002, "Who Trusts Others?" *Journal of Public Economics*, 85 (2), 207-234.

Aly, Ahmad A. H. M., 1994, *Economic Cooperation in Africa: In Search of Direction* (Boulder: Lynne Rienner).

Anderson, Lisa, 1999, *Transitions to Democracy* (New York: Columbia University Press).

Andreoni, J. and J. H. Miller, 1993, "Rational Cooperation in the Finitely Repeated Prisoner's Dilemma: Experimental Evidence," *Economic Journal*, Vol. 103 (May), pp. 570-585.

Aoki, Masahiko, Hyung-Ki kim, and Masahjiro Okuno-Fujiwara, 1997, *The Role of Government in East Asian Economic Development* (Oxford: Oxford University Press).

Arijo, Ademola, 1992, "Tariff Harmonization, Government Revenue, and Economic Integration within ECOWAS: Some Reflections," *Development Policy Review* (London), Vol. 10 (June), pp. 155–174.

Arndt, Heinz W., 1984, "The Role of Political Leadership in Economic Development," *Canadian Journal of Development Studies*, Vol. 5, pp. 51-63.

Arnold, Guy, 1993, "Challenge Facing the SADC," *New African* (London), No. 306 (March), pp. 28–29.

Arrighi, G., 1973, "International Corporations, Labor Aristocracies, and Economic Development in Tropical Africa," in G. Arrighi and J. S. Saul, *Essays on the Political Economy of Africa* (New York: Monthly Review Press), pp. 105-151.

Arthur, Brian W., 1988, "Self-Reinforcing Mechanisms in Economics," in *The Economy as an Evolving Complex System*, edited by Philip W. Anderson, Kenneth J. Arrow, and David Pines (Reading, Massachusetts: Addison-Wesley), pp. 9-31.

Aryeetey, Ernest, 1998, "Sub-Saharan African Experiences with Regional Integration," in Zubair Iqbal and Mohsin S. Khan, *Trade Reform and Regional Integration in Africa*" (Washington: International Monetary Fund), pp. 395-431.

Awasom, N. F., 2002, "Politics and Constitution-Making in Francophone Cameroon, 1959-1960," *Africa Today*, 49 (4): 3-30.

Axelrod, Robert, 1981, "The Emergence of Cooperation among Egoists," *American Political Science Review*, Vol. 75, pp. 306-318.

——, 1984, *The Evolution of Cooperation* (New York: Basic Books).

——, 1986, "An Evolutionary Approach to Norms," *American Political Science Review,* Vol. 80 (December), pp.1095-1111.

Ayittey, George B. N., 1991, *Indigenous African Institutions* (New York: Transnational Publishers, Inc.).

——, 1992, Africa *Betrayed* (New York: St. Martin's Press).

Balogh, Thomas, 1962, "The Mechanism of Neo-Imperialism: The Economic Impact of Monetary and Commercial Institutions in Africa," *Bulletin*, Institute of Economics and Statistics, Oxford, Vol. 24 (August), pp. 331-46.

Baran, Paul A., 1957, *The Political Economy of Growth* (New York: Monthly Review Press).

Bardhan, Pranab, 2002, "Decentralization of Governance and Development." *Journal of Economic Perspectives* 16: 185-205.

Barr, Abigail, 2003, "Trust and Expected Trustworthiness: Experimental Evidence from Zimbabwean Villages," *Economic Journal*, 113, 614-630.

Barrell, Ray and Nigel Pain, 1996, "An Econometric Analysis of U.S. Foreign Direct Investment," *Review of Economics and Statistics*, Vol. 78, pp. 200-207.

Barro, Robert J., 1996, "Democracy and Growth," *Journal of Economic Growth*, Vol. 1 (March), pp. 1-27.

Belderbos, René and Leo Sleuwaegen, 1996, "Japanese Firms and the Decision to Invest Abroad: Business Groups and Regional Core Networks," *Review of Economics and Statistics*, Vol. 78, pp. 214-220.

Benson, Bruce L., 1997, "The Spontaneous Evolution of Commercial Law," in Daniel B. Klein (ed.) *Reputation: Studies in the Voluntary Elicitation of Good Conduct* (Ann Arbor: University of Michigan Press).

Berman, Bruce J. and Colin Leys (editors), 1994, *African Capitalists in African Development* (Boulder: Lynne Rienner Publishers, Inc.).

Bethlehem, Douglas W., 1975, "The Effect of Westernization on Cooperative Behaviour in Central Africa," *International Journal of Psychology*, Vol. 10 (No. 3), pp. 219-224.

Bhagwati, Jagdish N., 1982, "Directly Unproductive Profit-Seeking (DUP) Activities," *Journal of Political Economy*, Vol. 90 (October), pp. 988-1002.

Binmore, Ken and Larry Samuelson, 1994, "An Economist's Perspective on the Evolution of Norms," *Journal of Institutional and Theoretical Economics*, Vol. 151 (1994), pp. 45-63.

Bird, Graham, 1996, "Borrowing from the IMF: The Policy Implications of Recent Empirical Research," *World Development*, Vol. 24 (11), pp.1753-60.

——, 1998, "The Effectiveness of Conditionality and the Political Economy of Policy Reform: Is It Simply a Matter of Political Will?" *Journal of Policy Reform*, Vol. 2 (Issue 1), pp. 89-113.

Boahen, Adu, Jacob F. Ade Ajaye, and Michael Tidy, 1986, *Topics in West African History* (London: Longman Group).

Bourdieu, Pierre, 1986, "Forms of Capital," in John G. Richardson (editor), *Handbook of Theory and Research for the Sociology of Education* (Westport, CT: Greenwood Press), pp. 241-60.

Brennan, G., and Hamlin, A., 2000, "Nationalism and Federalism: The Political Constitution of Peace." In: Gianluigi, G., Salmon, P., and Wintrobe, R. (eds.) *Competition and Structure, The Political Economy of Collective Decisions: Essays in Honor of Albert Breton*, pp. 259-83. Cambridge: Cambridge University Press.

Brown, M. Leann, 1989, "Nigeria and the ECOWAS Protocol on Free Movement and Residence," *Journal of Modern African Studies*, Vol. 27 (June), pp. 251–73.

Burns, James MacGregor, 1978, *Leadership* (New York: Harper & Row).

Burnside, Craig, and David Dollar, 2000, "Aid, Policies, and Growth," *American Economic Review*, Vol. 90 (September), pp. 847-868.

Callaghy, Thomas M. and John Ravenhill (eds.), 1993, *Hemmed In: Responses to Africa's Economic Decline* (New York: Columbia University Press).

Campos, Jose Edgardo and Hilton L. Root, 1996, *The Key to the Asian Miracle: Making Shared Growth Credible* (Washington: The Brookings Institution).

Cho, Lee-Jay, 1994, "Culture, Institutions, and Economic Development in East Asia," in Lee-Jay Cho and Yoon Hyung Kim (eds.), *Korea's Political Economy: An Institutional Perspective* (Boulder: Westview Press).

Chung-yum Kim, 1994, *Policymaking on the Front Lines: Memoirs of a Korean Practitioner, 1945-79* (Washington, D. C.: The World Bank).

Claessens, S., 1996, Comment on 'Why Is There Multilateral Lending?' by Dani Rodrik, *Annual World Bank Conference on Development Economics 1995* (Washington: World Bank), 197-202.

Cohen, Mark A., 1994, "Norms versus Laws: Economic Theory and the Choice of Social Institutions," in Kenneth J. Koford, and Jeffrey B. Miller (eds.) *Social Norms and Economic Institutions* (Ann Arbor: University of Michigan Press).

Coleman, James S., 1990, *Foundations of Social Theory* (Cambridge, Massachusetts: Harvard University Press).

Collier, Paul, 1997, "The Failure of Conditionality," in *Perspectives on Aid and Development*, edited by Catherine Gwin and Joan M. Nelson (Washington: Overseas Development Council), pp. 51-77.

——, 2000a, "How to Reduce Corruption" *African Development Review* 12 (December), pp. 191-205.

——, 2000b, "Ethnicity, Politics and Economic Performance," *Economics and Politics*, 12 (November), pp. 225-245.

——, 2001, "Consensus Building, Knowledge, and Conditionality," *Annual World Bank Conference on Development Economics 2000* (Washington: World Bank), pp. 67-83.

Collier, Paul and Ashish Garg, 1999, "On Kin Groups and Wages in the Ghanaian Labour Market," *Oxford Bulletin of Economics and Statistics*, 61(2), pp. 133-151.

Collier, Paul, Patrick Guillaumont, Sylviane Guillaumont, and Jan Willem Gunning, 1997, "Redesigning Conditionality," *World Development*, Vol. 25 (September), pp. 1399-1407.

Collier, Paul and Jan Willem Gunning, 1999, "Why Has Africa Grown Slowly?" *Journal of Economic Perspectives*, Vol. 13, No. 3 (Summer), pp. 3-22.

Collier, Ruth Berins, 1982, *Regimes in Tropical Africa* (Berkeley and Los Angeles: University of California Press).

Dabee, Rajen and David Greenaway, 2001, *The Mauritian Economy: A Reader* (London: Palgrave).

Dahl, Robert A., 1989, *Democracy and its Critics* (New Haven: Yale University Press).

Davidson, Sinclair, 1999, "Okeahalam and Bah on Corruption: A Comment," *South African Journal of Economics*, Vol., 67, No. 1 (March), pp. 157-165.

Dawes, Robyn M. and Richard H. Thaler, 1988, "Anomalies: Cooperation," *Journal of Economic Perspectives*, Vol. 2 (Summer), pp 187-97.

Dawes, Robyn M., Alphons J.C. van de Kragt, and John M. Orbell, 1990, "Cooperation for the Benefit of Us--Not Me, or My Conscience," in Mansbridge, pp. 97-110.

Decalo, Samuel, 1997, "Benin: First of the New Democracies," in John F. Clark and David E. Gardinier (eds.) *Political Reform in Francophone Africa* (Boulder: Westview Press), pp. 43-61.

De Grauwe, Paul, 1994, *The Economics of Monetary Integration* (Oxford: Oxford University Press, 1994).

Deng, Francis M., Sadikiel Kimaro, Terrence Lyons, Donald Rothchild, and I. William Zartman, 1996, *Sovereignty as Responsibility: Conflict Management in Africa* (Washington: Brookings Institution).

Diamond, L., 1999, *Developing Democracy: Toward Consolidation* (Baltimore and London: Johns Hopkins University Press).

Dixit, Avinash, 1989, "Intersectoral Capital Reallocation under Price Uncertainty," *Journal of International Economics*, Vol. 26, pp. 309-325.

——, and Robert S. Pindyck, 1994, *Investment under Uncertainty* (Princeton, New Jersey: Princeton University Press).

Djah, Kouacou, 1990, "Coûts et avantages de la taxe de coopération régionale dans la Communauté Economique de l'Afrique d l'Ouest," *African Development Review*, Vol. 2 (June), pp. 31–51.

Dollar, David and Jakob Svensson, 2000, "What Explains the Success or Failure of Structural Adjustment Programmes," *Economic Journal*, Vol. 110 (October), pp. 894-917.

Doornbos, Martin, 1998, "Linking the Future to the Past," in Salih and Markakis (1998), pp. 17-29.

Dunbar, Robin, 1999, "Culture, Honesty, and the Freerider Problem," in *The Evolution of Culture*, edited by Robin Dunbar, Chris Knight, and Camilla Power (New Brunswick: Rutgers University Press), pp.194-213.

East African Community (EAC), 1999, *The Treaty for the Establishment of the East African Community* (Arusha, Tanzania).

Easterly, William, 2001a, *The Elusive Quest for Growth: Economists' Adventures and Misadventures in the Tropics* (Cambridge, Mass: MIT Press).

——, 2001b, "Can Institutions Resolve Ethnic Conflicts," *Economic Development and Cultural Change*, Vol. 49 (No. 4), pp. 687-706.

——, 2005, "What Did Structural Adjustment Adjust? The Association of Policies and Growth with Repeated IMF and World Bank Adjustment Loans," *Journal of Development Economics*, Vol. 76, pp. 1-22.

Easterly, William and Ross Levine, 1997, "Africa's Growth Tragedy: Policies and Ethnic Divisions," *Quarterly Journal of Economics*, Vol. 112 (November), pp. 1203-50.

ECOWAS Fund, 1976, *Protocol Relating to the Fund for Cooperation, Compensation, and Development of the Economic Community of West African States* (Lomé).

Eken, Sena, 1979, "Breakup of the East African Community," *Finance and Development*, Vol. 16 (December), pp. 36-40.

Eller, Jack David, 1999, *From Culture to Ethnicity to Conflict: An International Perspective on Ethnic Conflict* (Ann Arbor: University of Michigan Press).

Elster, Jon, 1986, "The Market and the Forum: Three Varieties of Political Theory," in *Foundations of Social Choice Theory* (Cambridge: Cambridge University Press), edited by Jon Elster and Aanund Hylland, pp. 103-132.

——, 1989, "Social Norms and Economic Theory," *Journal of Economic Perspectives*, Vol. 3 (Fall), pp. 99-117.

Emmanuel, Arghiri, 1972, *Unequal Exchange* (New York: Monthly Review Press).

England, Richard W., 1994, *Evolutionary Concepts in Contemporary Economics* (Ann Arbor, MI: University of Michigan Press).

Evans, Peter B., Dietrich Rueschemeyer, and Theda Skocpol, 1985, *Bringing the State Back In* (Cambridge: Cambridge University Press).

Evenett, Simon J. and Bernard M. Hoekman (eds.), 2006, *Economic Development & Multilateral Trade Cooperation* (Houndmills, Basingstoke, Hampshire: Palgrave Macmillan).

Fanthorpe, Richard, 2001, "Neither Citizen Nor Subject? 'Lumpen' Agency and the Legacy of Native Administration in Sierra Leone," *African Affairs*, Vol. 100 (July), pp. 363-386.

Farr, James R., 2000, *Artisans in Europe, 1300-1914* (Cambridge: Cambridge University Press).

Faruquee, Rashid, 1994, "Nigeria: Ownership Abandoned," in *Adjustment in Africa: Lessons from Country Case Studies* (Washington: The World Bank), edited by Ishrat Husain and Rashid Faruquee, pp. 238-285.

Fehr, Ernst and Urs Fischbacher, 2002, "Why Social Preferences Matter—The Impact of Non-Selfish Motives on Competition, Cooperation and Incentives," *Economic Journal*, Vol. 112 (March), pp. C1-C33.

Fernandez, Raquel and Dani Rodrik, 1991, "Resistance to Reform: Status Quo Bias in the Presence of Individual-Specific Uncertainty," *American Economic Review*, Vol. 81 (December), pp. 1146-1155.

Forrest, Tom, 1994, *The Advance of African Capital: The Growth of Nigerian Private Investment* (Charlottesville: University Press of Virginia).

Frank, A. G., 1969a, "The Development of Underdevelopment," in Frank, *Latin America: Underdevelopment or Revolution* (New York: Monthly Review Press), pp. 3-17.

——, 1969b, *Capitalism and Underdevelopment in Latin America* (New York: Monthly Review Press).

Frank, Robert H., 1987, "If *Homo Economicus* Could Choose His Own Utility Function, Would He Want One With a Conscience?" *American Economic Review*, Vol. 77 (September), pp 593- 604.

Frey, B S., and Eichenberger R., 1999, *The New Democratic Federalism for Europe: Functional, Overlapping and Competing Jurisdictions.* (Cheltenham, UK, and Northampton, MA., USA: Edward Elgar).

Fudenberg, Drew, 1992, "Explaining Cooperation and Commitment in Repeated Games," Jean-Jacques Laffont (ed) *Advances in Economic Theory,* Sixth World Congress Vol. 1 (Cambridge: Cambridge University Press), pp.89-131.

Fukuyama, Francis, 1995, *Trust: The Social Virtues and the Creation of Prosperity* (New York: The Free Press).

Gardner, John W., 1990, *On Leadership* (New York: The Free Press).

Geertz, Clifford, 1978, "The Bazaar Economy: Information and Search in Peasant Marketing," *American Economic Review, Papers and Proceedings*, Vol. 68 (May), pp, 28-32.

Glazer, Nathan and Daniel P. Moynihan (eds.), 1975, *Ethnicity, Theory and Practice* (Cambridge, Massachusetts: Harvard University Press).

Goff, Brian L., Robert E. McCormick, and Robert D. Tollison, 2002, "Racial Integration as an Innovation: Empirical Evidence from Sports Leagues," *American Economic Review*, Vol. 92 (March), pp. 16-26.

Goldsbrough, David, Kevin Barnes, Isabelle Mateos y Lago, and Tsidi Tsikata, 2002, "Prolonged Use of IMF Resources: How Much of a Problem Is It?" *Finance & Development*, Vol. 39 (December), pp. 34-37.

Goldsmith, Arthur A., 2000, "Sizing Up the African State," *Journal of Modern African Studies*, Vol. 38 (March), pp. 1-20.

Greif, Avner, 1989, "Reputation and Coalitions in Medieval Trade: Evidence on the Maghribi Traders," *Journal of Economic History*, Vol. 49, pp. 857-82.

Greif, Avner, Paul Milgrom, and Barry R. Weingast, 1994, "Coordination, Commitment, and Enforcement: The Case of the Merchant Guild," *Journal of Political Economy*, Vol.102 (August), pp. 745-776.

Gunning, Jan Willem, 2001, "Rethinking Aid," *Annual World Bank Conference on Development Economics 2000* (Washington: World Bank), pp. 125-144.

Gyimah-Boadi, E. and Nicolas van de Walle, 1996, "The Politics of Economic Renewal in Africa, in *Agenda for Africa's Economic Renewal* (Washington: Overseas Development Council), pp. 211-39.

Haggard, Stephan and Robert R. Kaufman, 1999, "The Political Economy of Democratic Transitions," in Anderson (1999), pp. 72-96.

Hameso, Seyoum H., 1997, *Ethnicity in Africa, A Positive Approach* (Lincoln, Nebraska: iUniversity Press).

Hampshire, Stuart, 2000, *Justice is Conflict* (Princeton: Princeton University Press).

Haque, Nadeem Ul, Nelson Mark, and Donald J. Mathiesen, 2000, "Rating Africa: The Economic and Political Content of Risk Indicators," in *Investment and Risk in Africa*, edited by Paul Collier and Catherine Pattillo (Houndsmills, Basingstoke, Hampshire: Macmillan), pp. 33-70.

Hassan, Ahmed Issack, 2001, "Constitution of Kenya Review Commission Discussion Paper on the Review Process," *www.kenyaconstitution.org/docs/02d001.htm*

Hayek, Friedrich A., 1973, *Law, Legislation, and Liberty*, 3 Vols. (Chicago: University of Chicago Press).

Hazlewood, Arthur, 1979, "The End of the East African Community: What Are the Lessons for Regional Integration Schemes?" *Journal of Common Market Studies* (London), Vol. 18 (September), pp. 40-58.

Hechter, Michael, 1987, *Principles of Group Solidarity* (Berkeley and Los Angeles: University of California Press).

Helleiner, Gerald K., 1994, "From Adjustment to Development in Sub-Saharan Africa: Consensus and Continuing Conflict," in *From Adjustment to Development in Africa: Conflict, Controversy, Convergence, Consensus?* edited by Giovanni Andrea Cornia and Gerald K. Helleiner (New York: St. Martin's Press), pp. 3-24.

Hentz, James J., 2005, "South Africa and the Political Economy of Regional Cooperation in Southern Africa," *Journal of Modern African Studies*, Vol. 43 (March), pp. 21-51.

Himbara, David, 1994, "Domestic Capitalists and the State in Kenya," in Berman and Leys (1994), pp. 69-93.

Hirshleifer, Jack, 1977, "Economics from a Biological Viewpoint," *Journal of Law and Economics*, Vol. 20 (April), pp. 1-52.

——, 1982, "Evolutionary Models in Economics and Law: Cooperation versus Conflict Strategies," *Research in Law & Economics*, Vol. 4, pp. 1-60.

Hodgson, Geoffrey M., 1993, *Economics and Evolution: Bringing Life Back into Economics* (Ann Arbor: University of Michigan Press).

Huber, Evelyne, Dietrich Rueschemeyer, and John D. Stephens, 1993, "The Impact of Economic Development on Democracy," *Journal of Economic Perspectives*, Vol. 7 (Summer), pp. 71-85.

Hymer, S., 1972, "The Multinational Corporation and the Law of Uneven Development," in J. N. Bhagwati (editor), *Economics and World Order* (New York: Free Press), pp. 113-140.

Ikelegbe, Augustine, 2001, "The Perverse Manifestation of Civil Society: Evidence from Nigeria," *Journal of Modern African Studies*, Vol. 39 (March), pp.1-24.

IMF Independent Evaluation Office (IMFIEO), 2002, *Evaluation of Prolonged Use of IMF Resources* (Washington: IMF).

Isichei, Elizabeth (1997) *A History of African Societies to 1870* (Cambridge: Cambridge University Press).

Ivanova, Anna, Wolfgang Mayer, Alex Mourmouras, and George Anayiotos, 2003, "What Determines the Implementation of IMF-Supported Programs?" IMF Working Paper WP/03/08 (Washington: IMF).

Jalloh, Alusine, 1999, *African Entrepreneurship: Muslim Fula Merchants in Sierra Leone* (Athens, Ohio: Ohio University Center for International Studies).

Jeon, Yoong-Deok, 1992, "The Determinants of Korean Foreign Direct Investment in Manufacturing Industries," *Weltwirtschaftliches Archiv*, Vol. 128, pp. 527-41.

Jerman, Helena, 1998, "Dynamics of Ethnicity—A Case Study From the Western Bagamoyo District in Tanzania," in Salih and Markakis, pp. 156-179.

Johnson, John H. and Sulaiman S. Wasty, 1993, "Borrower Ownership of Adjustment Programs and the Political Economy of Reform," World Bank Discussion Paper 199 (May).

Johnson, Omotunde E. G., 1972, "Economic Analysis, the Legal Framework, and Land Tenure Systems," *Journal of Law and Economics*, Vol. 15 (April), pp. 259-76.

——, 1974, "Contract Costs and the Liability Structure for Stranger-Tenant Damages in Sierra Leone's Customary Land Law: An Economic Analysis," *African Studies Review*, Vol. 17 (December), pp. 549-559.

——, 1975a, "An Economic Analysis of Corrupt Government, with Special Application to Less Developed Countries," *Kyklos*, Vol. 28 (Fasc.1), pp. 47-61.

——, 1975b, "Direct Credit Controls in a Development Context: The Case of African Countries," in *Government Credit Allocation: Where Do We Go from Here?* (San Francisco, Institute of Contemporary Studies), pp. 151-180.

——, 1976, "Economic Aspects of the Structure of Land Rights," in J. Levi, et al, *African Agriculture: Economic Action and Reaction in Sierra Leone* (Farnham Royal, Bucks, England: Commonwealth Agricultural Bureaux), pp. 203-236.

——, 1977a, "Use of Fund Resources and Stand-By Arrangements," *Finance & Development*, Vol. 14 (March), pp. 19-21.

——, 1977b, "Economic Dependency Theory: An Interpretation," *Nigerian Journal of Economic and Social Studies*, Vol. 19 (July), pp. 63-80.

——, 1986, "Political Leadership and the Economic Development Process," *Nigerian Journal of Economic and Social Studies*, Vol. 28 (July), pp. 213-228.

——, 1991, "Economic Integration in Africa: Enhancing Prospects for Success," *Journal of Modern African Studies*, Vol. 29 (March), pp. 1-26.

——, 1994, "Managing Adjustment Costs, Political Authority, and the Implementation of Adjustment Programs, with Special Reference to African Countries," *World Development*, Vol. 22 (March), pp. 399-411.

——, 1995, "Regional Integration in Sub-Saharan Africa," *The Journal of European Integration*, Vol. 18, pp. 201-34.

——, 2004, "How Will Good Economic Policy Environments Emerge in Africa?" *Journal of Policy Reform* 7, 151-164.

——, 2005a, "Country Ownership of Reform Programmes and the Implications for Conditionality," 35 (New York and Geneva: United Nations Conference on Trade and Development), January.

——, 2005b, "Addressing Ethnicity in Sub-Saharan Africa: Institutions and Agency," *Constitutional Political Economy, Vol.* 16, pp. 49-69.

—— and Jean-Claude Nascimento, 1993, "On Monetary and Financial Factors in Development," *The Courier* (Brussels) No. 139 (May–June), pp. 63–67.

—— and Joanne Salop, 1980, "Distributional Aspects of Stabilization Programs in Developing Countries," *International Monetary Fund Staff Papers*, Vol. 27, pp. 1-23.

Joseph, Richard, 1999, "Democratization in Africa after 1989: Comparative and Theoretical Perspectives," in Anderson, pp. 237-260.

Kagwanja, P. M., 2003, "Facing Mount Kenya or Facing Mecca? The Mungiki, Ethnic Violence and the Politics of the Moi Succession in Kenya, 1987-2002," *African Affairs*, Vol.102, pp. 25-49.

Kahler, Miles, 1992, "External Influence, Conditionality, and the Politics of Adjustment," in *The Politics of Economic Adjustment*, edited by Stephan Haggard and Robert R. Kaufman (Princeton: Princeton University Press), pp. 89-136.

Kahneman, D., J. Knetsch, and R. Thaler, 1991, "The Endowment Effect, Loss Aversion, and the Status Quo Bias," *Journal of Economic Perspectives*, Vol. 5 (Winter), pp. 193-206.

Kakoza, Joseph, 1972, "Common External Tariff and Development in the East African Community," *Finance and Development*, Vol. 9 (March), pp. 22–29.

Kallon, Kelfala M., 1990, *The Economics of Sierra Leonean Entrepreneurship* (Lanham, Maryland: University Press of America).

——, 2004, *Political Economy of Corruption in Sierra Leone* (Lewiston, Queenston, Lampeter: The Edwin Mellen Press).

Kenya, 2000, *The Constitution of Kenya Review Act*.

Khan, Mohsin S. and Sunil Sharma, 2001, "IMF Conditionality and Country Ownership of Programs," IMF Working Paper No. WP/01/142 (IMF: Washington).

——, 2002, "Reconciling Conditionality and Country Ownership," *Finance & Development*, Vol. 39 (June), pp. 28-31.

Killick, Tony, 1997, "Principals, Agents and the Failings of Conditionality," *Journal of International Development*, Vol.9 (June), pp. 483-495.

——, with Ramani Gunatilaka and Ana Marr, 1998, *Aid and the Political Economy of Political Change* (London and New York: Routledge).

Klein, Daniel B., 1997, *Reputation: Studies in the Voluntary Elicitation of Good Conduct*, Ann Arbor, University of Michigan Press.

Knack, Stephen, 2003, "Groups, Growth and Trust: Cross-Country Evidence on the Olson and Putnam Hypotheses," *Public Choice*, 117, 341-355.

Knack, Stephen and Philip Keefer, 1997, "Does Social Capital have an Economic Payoff? A Cross-Country Investigation," *Quarterly Journal of Economics*, Vol. 112 (November), pp. 1251-1288.

Kopytoff, Igor, 1987, "The Internal African Frontier: The Making of African Political Culture," in *The African Frontier: The Reproduction of Traditional African Societies*, edited by Igor Kopytoff (Bloomington and Indianapolis: Indiana University Press), pp. 3-84.

Kreps, David M., Paul Milgrom, John Roberts, and Robert Wilson, 1982, "Rational Cooperation in the Finitely Repeated Prisoners' Dilemma," *Journal of Economic Theory*, Vol. 27 (August), pp.245-252.

Krueger, Anne O., 1974, "The Political Economy of the Rent-Seeking Society," *American Economic Review*, Vol. 69 (June), pp. 291-303.

Krugman, P., 1990, "Policy Problems of Monetary Union," in P. De Grauwe and L. Papademos, eds., *The European Monetary System in the 1990s* (Harlow: Longman), pp. 48–64.

Lall, Sanjaya and Francess Stewart, 1996, "Trade and Industrial Policy in Africa," in *Agenda for Africa's Economic Renewal* (Washington: Overseas Development Council), pp. 179-209.

Lancaster, C., 1999, "Aid Effectiveness in Africa: the Unfinished Agenda," *Journal of African Economics*, Vol.8 (No. 4), pp. 487-503.

La Porta, R., Lopez-de-Silanes, F., Shleifer, A., and Vishny, R., 1999, "The Quality of Government," *Journal of Law, Economics, & Organization*, Vol.15 (No. 1), pp. 222-279.

Lavergne, Réal (editor), 1997, *Regional Integration and Cooperation in West Africa: A Multidimensional Perspective* (Trenton: Africa World Press, Inc.).

Lee Kuan Yew, 2000, *From Third World to First—the Singapore Story: 1965-2000* (N.Y: HarperCollins Publishers).

Lemarchand, René, 1998, "Genocide in the Great Lakes: Which Genocide? Whose Genocide?"*African Studies Review*, Vol. 41 (April), pp.3-16.

Lewis, David, 1969, *Convention: A Philosophical Study* (Oxford: Basil Blackwell, 1969).

Leys, Colin, 1965, "What is the Problem About Corruption?" *Journal of Modern African Countries*, Vol. 3, pp. 215-230.

Lijphart, Arend, 1977, *Democracy in Plural Societies: A Comparative Exploration* (New Haven and London: Yale University Press).

Lin, Nan, 2001, "Building a Network Theory of Social Capital," in *Social Capital: Theory and Research* edited by Nan Lin, Karen Cook, and Ronald S. Burt (New York: Aldine de Gruyter), pp. 3-29.

Lindenberg, S., 2002, "Solidarity, its Microfoundations and Macrodependence: A Framing Approach," in *Conventions and Structures in Economic Organization: Markets, Networks and Hierarchies*, edited by Olivier Favereau and Emmanuel Lazega (Northampton, MA: Elgar), pp. 282-328.

Lucas, Robert E. Jr., 1967, "Adjustment Costs and the Theory of Supply," *Journal of Political Economy*, Vol. 75, pp. 321-334.

Lui, F. T., 1985, "An Equilibrium Queuing Model of Bribery," *Journal of Political Economy* Vol. 93 (August), pp.760-781.

Lukács, E., 1987, "Stepping Stones and Stumbling Stones on the Path Towards Economic Integration: The Not Very Special Case of West Africa," Institute of Development Studies (Brighton, Sussex), Discussion Paper No. 235 (September).

Macauley, Stewart, 1963, "Non-Contractual Relations in Business: A Preliminary Study," *American Sociological Review*, Vol. 28, pp. 53-67.

Macbean, A., 1966, *Export Instability and Economic Development* (London: Allen & Unwin).

Macharia, Kinuthia, 1997, *Social and Political Dynamics of the Informal Economy in African Countries* (Lanham, NY, Oxford: University Press of America, Inc).

Magnusson, Bruce A., 2005, "Democratic Legitimacy in Benin: Institutions and Identity in a Regional Context," in Leonardo A. Villalón and Peter VonDoepp, (eds.) *The Fate of Africa's Democratic Experiments: Elites and Institutions* (Bloomington and Indianapolis: Indiana University Press).

Mahant, Edelgard, and Xavier De Vanssay, 1994, "The Origins of Customs Unions and Free Trade Areas," *Journal of European Integration* (Saskatoon, Saskatchewan), Vol. 17 (Winter/Spring), pp. 181–210.

Mamdani, Mahmood, 1996, *Citizen and Subject: Contemporary Africa and the Legacy of Late Colonialism* (Princeton: Princeton University Press).

Mansbridge, Jane J., 1990, *Beyond Self-Interest* (Chicago: University of Chicago Press).

Masanjala, Winford H., 2002, "Can the Grameen Bank be Replicated in Africa? Evidence from Malawi", *Canadian Journal of Development Studies*, Vol. 23 (No. 1), pp. 87-103.

Mauro, Paolo, 1995, "Corruption and Growth," *Quarterly Journal of Economics*, Vol.110 (August), pp.681-712.

McGinnis, M. D., 1999, editor, *Polycentric Governance and Development: Readings from the Workshop in Political Theory and Policy Analysis* (Ann: University of Michigan Press).

McGuire, Martin C. and Mancur Olson, Jr., 1996, "The Economics of Autocracy and Majority Rule: The Invisible Hand and the Use of Force," *Journal of Economic Literature*, Vol. 34 (March), pp. 72-96.

McMullan, M., 1961, "A Theory of Corruption," *Sociological Review* (New Series), Vol. 9, pp.181-201.

Mecagni, Mauro, 1999, "The Causes of Program Interruption," *Economic Adjustment and Reform in Low-Income Countries*, Studies by the Staff of the International Monetary Fund, edited by Hugh Bredenkamp and Susan Schadler (Washington: IMF), pp. 215-252.

Melton, James Van Horn, 2001, *The Rise of the Public in Enlightenment Europe* (Cambridge: Cambridge University Press).

Mengisteab, Kidane, 1997, "New Approaches to State Building in Africa: The Case of Ethiopia Ethnic-Based Federalism," *African Studies Review*, Vol. 40 (December), pp. 111-132.

Miller, Garry J., 1992, *Managerial Dilemmas: The Political Economy of Hierarchy* (Cambridge: Cambridge University Press).

Mistry, Percy S, 2000, "Africa's Record of Regional Co-operation and Integration," *African Affairs*, Vol. 99 (October), pp. 553-73.

Misztal, Barbara A., 1996, *Trust in Modern Societies* (Cambridge: Polity Press).

Mkandawire, Thandika and Charles C. Soludo, 1999, *Our Continent, Our Future: African Perspectives on Structural Adjustment* (Trenton: Africa World Press, Inc.).

Mookherjee, D. and Png, I. P. L., 1995, "Corruptible Law Enforcers: How Should They Be Compensated?" *Economic Journal*, Vol. 105 (January), pp. 145-159.

Moore, Barrington, 1966, *Social Origins of Dictatorship and Democracy: Lord and Peasant in the Making of the Modern World* (Boston: Beacon Press).

Moore, Michael O. 1993, "Determinants of German Manufacturing Direct Investment: 1980-1988," *Weltwirschaftliches Archiv*, Vol.129, pp. 120-38.

Morishima, Michio, 1982, *Why Has Japan 'Succeeded'?* Cambridge: Cambridge University Press.

Mueller, Dennis C., 1996, *Constitutional Democracy* (Oxford: Oxford University Press).

——, 2001, "On Writing a Constitution," in *Rules & Reason*, edited by Ram Mudambi, Pietro Navarra, and Guiseppe Sobbrio (Cambridge: Cambridge University Press), pp. 9-32.

Mugaju, Justus and J. Oloka-Onyango (editors), 2000, *No-Party Democracy in Uganda: Myths and Reality* (Kampala: Fountain Publishers Ltd.).

Museveni, Yoweri K., 2000, *What is Africa's Problem?* (Minneapolis: University of Minnesota Press).

Mutebile, Emmanuel T., 1999, "Better Public Sector Resource Management: Capacity Building and Good Governance," in Laura Wallace (editor), *Africa: Adjusting to the Challenges of Globalization* (Washington: International Monetary Fund), pp. 107-113.

Myrdal, Gunnar, 1953, The Political Element in the Development of Economic Theory (London: Routledge & Kegan Paul).

——, 1957, *Economic Theory and Underdeveloped Regions* (New York: Harper and Row).

——, 1970, "The Soft State in Underdeveloped Countries," in Paul S. Streeten, editor, *Unfashionable Economics* (New York: Weindenfeld and Nicolson).

Ndikumana, Léonce, 1998, "Institutional Failure and Ethnic Conflicts in Burundi," *African Studies Review*, Vol. 41 (April), pp. 29-47.

Neher, Clark D. and Ross Marlay, 1995, *Democracy and Development in Southeast Asia, the Winds of Change* (Boulder: Westview Press).

Nelson, Richard R., 1995, "Recent Evolutionary Theorizing About Economic Change," *Journal of Economic Literature*, Vol. 33 (March), pp. 48-90.

Nkrumah, Kwame, 1970, *Africa Must Unite* (New York: International Publishers).

Nomvete, Bax, 1991/92, "Economic Integration: Why It Doesn't Work," *Southern African Economist* (Zimbabwe), Vol. 4 (December /January), pp. 51–55.

North, Douglass C., 1990, *Institutions, Institutional Change and Economic Performance* (Cambridge: Cambridge University Press).

North, Douglas C. and Barry R. Weingast, 1989, "The Evolution of Institutions Governing Public Choice in 17th Century England," *Journal of Economic History*, Vol.49 (December), pp. 803-32.

——, 1996, "Constitutions and Commitment: the Evolution of Institutions Governing Public Choice in Seventeenth-Century England," in Alston, Lee J., Thráinn Eggertsson, and Douglas C. North, *Empirical Studies in Institutional Change* (Cambridge University Press), pp. 134-165.

Nurkse, Ragnar, 1953, *Problems of Capital Formation in Underdeveloped Countries* (Oxford: Oxford University Press).

Nyerere, Julius K, 1968, *Ujamaa: Essays in Socialism* (Oxford: Oxford University Press).

Obeng, P. V., 1996, "Stakeholder Participation in the Design of a Structural Adjustment Program: Case Study of Ghana," *Participation in Practice: The Experience of the World Bank and Other Stakeholders*, edited by Jennifer Rietbergen-McCracken, World Bank Discussion Paper No. 333, pp. 63-67.

Ohemeng, Frank Louis Kwaku, 2005, "Getting the State Right: Think Tanks and the Dissemination of New Public Management Ideas in Ghana," *Journal of Modern African Studies*, Vol. 43, pp. 443-465.

Okeahalam, C. C. and I. Bah, 1998, "Perceived Corruption and Investment in Sub-Saharan Africa," *South African Journal of Economics*, Vol. 66 (September), pp. 364-386.

Oliver, Robert T., 1989, *Leadership in Asia: Persuasive Communication in the Making of Nations, 1850-1950* (Newark: University of Delaware Press).

Olson, Jr., Mancur, 1997, "The New Institutional Economics: The Collective Choice Approach to Economic Development," in Christopher Clague (editor) *Institutions and Economic Development: Growth and Governance in Less-Developed and Post-Socialist Countries* (Baltimore: Johns Hopkins University Press), pp.37-64.

Organization of African Unity (OAU), 1991, *Treaty Establishing the African Economic Community.*

Ostrom, Elinor and Roy Gardner, 1993, "Coping With Asymmetries in the Commons: Self-Governing Irrigation Systems Can Work," *Journal of Economic Perspectives*, Vol.7 (Fall), pp. 93-112.

Ostrom, Elinor, James Walker, and Roy Gardner, 1992, "Covenants With and Without a Sword: Self-Governance is Possible," *American Political Science Review*, Vol. 86 (June), pp. 404-417.

Paldam, M., 2002, "The Cross-Section Pattern of Corruption: Economics, Culture and the Seesaw Dynamics" *European Journal of Political Economy,* Vol. 18 (No. 2), pp. 215-240.

Parsons, Talcott, 1975, "Some Theoretical Considerations on the Nature and Trends of Change of Ethnicity," in Glazer and Moynihan, pp. 53-83.

Pearce, David G., 1992, "Repeated Games: Cooperation and Rationality," in Jean-Jacques Laffont (ed.) *Advances in Economic Theory,* Sixth World Congress Vol. 1 (Cambridge: Cambridge University Press), pp.132-174.

Pindyck, Robert S., 1982, "Adjustment Costs, Uncertainty, and the Behavior of the Firm," *American Economic Review*, Vol. 92, pp. 415-27.

Polinsky, A. M. and Shavell, S., 2001, Corruption and Optimal Law Enforcement. *Journal of Public Economics*, Vol. 81 (No.1), pp. 1-24.

Poluha, Eva, 1998, "Ethnicity and Democracy—A Viable Alliance?" in Salih and Markakis (1998), pp. 30-41.

Prebisch, R., 1962, "The Economic Development of Latin America and its Principal Problems," *Economic Bulletin for Latin America* (U.N.), Vol. 7 (February), pp.1-22.

Prunier, Gérard, 1995, *The Rwanda Crisis: History of a Genocide* (New York: Columbia University Press).

Przeworski, Adam, 1988, "Democracy as a Contingent Outcome of Conflicts," in *Constitutionalism and Democracy*, edited by Jon Elster and Rune Slagstad (Cambridge: Cambridge University Press), pp. 59-80.

Radzicki, Michael J. and John D. Sterman, 1994, "Evolutionary Economics and System Dynamics," in Richard W. England (ed) *Evolutionary Concepts in Contemporary Economics* (Ann Arbor, MI: University of Michigan Press).

Rodrik, Dani, 1996, "Why Is There Multilateral Lending," *Annual World Bank Conference on Development Economics 1995* (Washington: World Bank), pp. 167-193.

Rosenberg, Christoph B., 1995, "Fiscal Policy Coordination in the WAEMU After the Devaluation," IMF Working Paper 95/25, February.

Rosenberg, Nathan and L. E. Birdzell, 1986, *How the West Grew Rich* (New York: Basic Books).

Rothchild, Donald, 1997, *Managing Ethnic Conflict in Africa: Pressures and Incentives for Cooperation* (Washington: Brookings Institution Press).

Rowley, C. K., 2000, "Political Culture and Economic Performance in Sub-Saharan Africa" *European Journal of Political Economy,* Vol. 16 (No. 1), pp. 133-158.

Rueschemeyer, Dietrich and Peter B. Evans, 1985, "The State and Economic Transformation: Toward an Analysis of the Conditions Underlying Effective Intervention," in Evans et al, pp. 44-77.

Rueschemeyer, Dietrich, Evelyne Huber Stephens, and John D. Stephens, 1992, *Capitalist Development & Democracy* (Chicago: University of Chicago Press).

Rustow, Dankwart A., 1970, "Transitions to Democracy: Toward a Dynamic Model," *Comparative Politics*, Vol. 2, (April) pp. 337-63.

Ruzindana, Augistine, 1997, "The Importance of Leadership in Fighting Corruption in Uganda," in Kimberly Ann Elliott, editor, *Corruption and the Global Economy* (Washington: Institute for International Economy), pp. 133-145.

Sachs, Jeffrey D. and Andrew M. Warner, 1997, "Sources of Slow Growth in African Economies," *Journal of African Economies*, Vol. 6 (November), pp. 335-76.

Salih, M. A. Mohamed and John Markakis, editors, 1998, *Ethnicity and the State in Eastern Africa* (Uppsala: Nordiska Afrikainstitutet).

Schatzberg, Michael G., 2001, *Political Legitimacy in Middle Africa* (Bloomington: Indiana University Press).

Schelling, Thomas C., 1960, *The Strategy of Conflict* (Cambridge, Massachusetts: Harvard University Press).

Schotter, Andrew, 1981, *The Economic Theory of Social Institutions* (New York: Cambridge University Press).

——, 1986, "The Evolution of Rules," in Richard N. Langlois (ed) *Economics as a Process: Essays in the New Institutional Economics*, Cambridge: Cambridge University Press, pp.117-133.

Schuster, Peter and Karl Sigmund, 1983, "Replicator Dynamics," *Journal of Theoretical Biology*, Vol. 100, pp. 533-538.

Seabright, Paul, 1993, "Managing Local Commons: Theoretical Issues in Incentive Design," *Journal of Economic Perspectives*, Vol. 7 (Fall), pp. 113-34.

Selten, R., 1975, "Reexamination of the Perfectness Concept for Equilibrium Points in Extensive Games," *International Journal of Game Theory*, Vol. 4, pp. 25-55.

Semboja, Joseph and Ole Therkildsen (editors), 1995, *Service Provision Under Stress in East Africa* (Portsmouth, New Hampshire: Heinemann).

Sen, Amartya, 2000, "Merit and Justice," in *Meritocracy and Economic Inequality*, edited by Kenneth Arrow, Samuel Bowles, and Steven Durlauf (Princeton: Princeton University Press), pp 5-16.

Sender, John, 1999, "Africa's Economic Performance: Limitations of the Current Consensus," *Journal of Economic Perspectives* (Vol. 13), No.3 (Summer), pp. 89-114

Sethi, Rajiv and E. Somanathan, 1996, "The Evolution of Social Norms in Common Property Resource Use," *American Economic Review*, Vol. 86 (September), pp. 766-788.

Shivakumar, S. J., 2003, "The Place of Indigenous Institutions in Constitutional Order," *Constitutional Political Economy*, 14 (1): 3-21.

Sierra Leone, 2004, *The Local Government Act*.

Singer, H. W., 1950, "The Distribution of Gains between Investing and Borrowing Countries," *American Economic Review*, Vol. 40 (May), pp. 472-92

Skocpol, Theda, 1985, "Bringing the State Back In: Strategies in Current Research," in Evans, et al, pp. 3-43.

Skyrms, Brian, 1996, *Evolution of the Social Contract* (Cambridge: Cambridge University Press).

Sobel, Joel, 2002, "Can We Trust Social Capital?" *Journal of Economic Literature*, Vol. 40 (March), pp.139-154.

Southern African Economist, 1994, "SADC—Facing New Challenges" (Zimbabwe), No. 7 (March), pp. 14–15.

Stewart, Frances, 1994, "Are Short-term Policies Consistent with Long-Term Development Needs in Africa," in *From Adjustment to Development in Africa: Conflict, Controversy, Convergence, Consensus?* Edited by Giovanni Andrea Cornia and Gerald K. Helleiner (New York: St. Martin's Press), pp. 98-128.

——, 1995, *Adjustment and Poverty* (London: Routledge).

Sugden, Robert, 1986, *The Economics of Rights, Co-operation & Welfare* (Oxford: Basil Blackwell Ltd).

——, 1989, "Spontaneous Order," *Journal of Economic Perspectives*, Vol. 3 (Fall), pp.85- 97.

Szeftel, M., 2000, "Between Governance & Underdevelopment: Accumulation & Africa's Catastrophic Corruption" *Review of African Political Economy*, Vol. 27 (June), pp. 287-306.

Taylor, Peter D. and Leo B. Jonker, 1978, "Evolutionary Stable Strategies and Game Dynamics," *Mathematical Biosciences*, Vol. 40, pp. 145-156.

Thomas, Barbara P., 1985, *Politics, Participation, and Poverty: Development through Self-Help in Kenya* (Boulder: Westview Press).

Tilly, Charles, 1985, "War Making and State Making as Organized Crime," in Evans, Rueschemeyer, and Skocpol, pp.169-191.

——, 1990, *Coercion, Capital, and European States, AD 990-1992* (Oxford: Blackwell Publishers Ltd.).

——, 1997a, "Democracy is a Lake," in *Roads from Past to Future* (Lanham, Maryland: Rowman & Littlefield Publishers, Inc.), pp. 193-215.

——, 1997b, "Parliamentarization of Popular Contention in Great Britain, 1758-1834," in *Roads from Past to Future* (Lanham, Maryland: Rowman & Littlefield Publishers, Inc.), pp. 217-244.

——, 1998, "Where Do Rights Come From?" in Theda Skocpol (editor) *Democracy, Revolution, and History* (Ithaca: Cornell University Press), pp. 25-72.

Tollison, Robert D., 1982, "Rent Seeking: A Survey," *Kyklos*, Vol. 35, pp.575-602.

Tordoff, William, 1984, *Government and Politics in Africa*, (Bloomington: Indiana University Press).

Trakman, Leon E., 1983, *The Law Merchant: The Evolution of Commercial Law*, (Littleton, Colorado: Fred B. Rothman & Co).

Treaty for the Establishment of the Economic Community of Central African States, 1984, *International Legal Materials*, Vol. 23 (Washington, D.C.: American Society of International Law), pp. 945–1008.

Treaty for the Establishment of the Preferential Trade Area for Eastern and Southern African States, 1982, *International Legal Materials*, Vol. 21 (Washington, D.C.: American Society of International Law), pp. 479–541.

Treaty of the Economic Community of West African States, *International Legal Materials*, Vol. 14 (Washington, D.C.: American Society of International Law, 1975), pp. 1200–1209 (excludes the Protocols).

Treisman, D., 2000, "The Causes of Corruption: A Cross-National Study," *Journal of Public Economics,* Vol. 76 (No.3): 399-457.

Tsikata, Yvonne M., 2003, "Owning Economic Reforms: A Comparative Study of Ghana and Tanzania,"in *Reforming Africa's Institutions: Ownership, Incentives, and Capabilities*, edited by Steve Kayizzi-Mugerwa (Tokyo: United Nations University Press), pp. 30-53.

Tullock, Gordon, 1993, *Rent Seeking* (Brookfield, Vermont: Edward Elgar Publishing Limited).

Ullmann-Margalit, Edna, 1977, *The Emergence of Norms* (Oxford: Oxford University Press).

Van de Walle, Nicolas, 2001, *African Economies and the Politics of Permanent Crisis, 1979-1999* (Cambridge: Cambridge University Press).

Van Roy, Edward, 1971, "On the Theory of Corruption," *Economic Development and Cultural Change*, Vol. 19, (Oct.), pp. 86-110.

Villalón, Leonardo A. and Peter VonDoepp (2005), *The Fate of Africa's Democratic Experiments: Elites and Institutions* (Bloomington and Indianapolis: Indiana University Press).

Vronen, Jack J., 1995, *Economic Evolution: An Enquiry into the Foundations of New Institutional Economics* (New York: Routledge).

Wallerstein, Immanuel, 1961, *Africa: The Politics of Independence* (New York: Vintage Books).

——, 1964, "Voluntary Associations," in *Political Parties and National Integration in Tropical Africa*, edited by James S. Coleman & Carl G. Rosberg, Jr. (Berkeley and Los Angeles: University of California Press), pp. 318-339.

Waterbury, John, 1999, "Fortuitous Byproducts," in Anderson (1999), pp. 261-83.

West Africa, 1995, "Getting to Know ECOWAS" (London), No. 4032 (16–22 January), p. 61.

Wheeler, David and Ashoka Mody, 1992, "International Investment Location Decisions: the Case of U.S. Firms," *Journal of International Economics*, Vol. 33, pp. 57-76.

World Bank, 1998, *Assessing Aid: What Works, What Doesn't and Why* (Oxford University Press for the World Bank).

Yamagashi, Toshio, Karen Cook, and Motoki Watabe, 1998, "Uncertainty, trust, and Commitment Formation in the United States and Japan," *American Journal of Sociology*, Vol. 104 (July), pp. 165-194.

Young, H. Peyton, 1993a, "The Evolution of Conventions," *Econometrica*, Vol. 61 (January), pp. 57-84.

——, 1993b, "An Evolutionary Model of Bargaining," *Journal of Economic Theory*, Vol. 59 (February), pp. 145-168.

——, 1996, "The Economics of Convention," *Journal of Economic Perspectives*, Vol.10 (Spring), pp. 105-122.

Zartman, I. William, 1991, "Conflict Reduction: Prevention, Management, and Resolution," in *Conflict Resolution in Africa*, edited by Francis M. Deng and I William Zartman (Washington: The Brookings Institution), pp. 299-319.

——, 1997, *Governance as Conflict Management: Politics and Violence in West Africa* (Washington: Brookings Institution Press).

Zolberg, Aristide R., 1966, *Creating Political Order: The Party-States of West Africa* (Chicago: Rand McNally & Company).

Author Index

(A)

Achebe, Chinua, 163
Addis, Adeno, 122
Ade Ajaye, Jacob F., 115
Adejugbe, M.O.A., 219
Agarwal, Jamuna, 204
Agyemang, Augustus Asante, 227
Ahmed, Masood, 21, 80
Aiyede, E. R., 123
Ake, Claude, 31, 123, 178, 180
Alchian, Armen, 38, 44
Alejandro, Carlos F. Diaz, 193
Alesina, Alberto, 29, 39, 73, 86, 93
Aly, Ahmad A. H. M., 210
Anayiotos, George, 72
Anderson, Lisa, 177
Andreoni, J., 42
Aoki, Masahiko, 35
Arijo, Ademola, 219
Arndt, Heinz W., 169, 172
Arnold, Guy, 216, 219
Arrighi, G., 192
Arthur, Brian W., 44
Aryeetey, Ernest, 210
Awasom, N. F., 17
Axelrod, Robert, 43, 47, 48
Ayittey, George B. N., 113, 115 163

(B)

Bah, I., 204
Balogh, Thomas, 189
Baran, Paul A., 190
Bardhan, Pranab, 107
Barr, Abigail, 53
Barrell, Ray, 204
Barro, Robert J., 135, 176
Barry, Kevin, 90
Belderbos, René, 204
Benson, Bruce L., 50
Bethlehem, Douglas W., 54
Bhagwati, Jagdish N., 151
Binmore, Ken, 47
Bird, Graham, 84, 86
Birdzell, L. E., 39, 50
Boahen, Adu, 115
Bourdieu, Pierre, 40
Brennan, G., 107
Brown, M. Leann, 219
Burns, James MacGregor, 167
Burnside, Craig, 29

(C)

Callaghy, Thomas M., 239
Campos, Jose Edgardo, 64, 76
Cho, Lee-Jay, 64
Claessens, S., 87
Cohen, Mark A., 47
Coleman, James S., 39
Collier, Paul, 29, 55, 80, 85, 86, 88, 94, 124, 128, 163
Collier, Ruth Berins, 178
Cook, Karen, 38, 39

(D)

Dabee, Rajen, 205
Dahl, Robert A., 175
Davidson, Sinclair, 204
Dawes, Robyn M., 42
De Grauwe, Paul, 226
De Vanssay, Xavier, 227
Decalo, Samuel, 124
Deng, Francis M., 103
Diamond, L., 123
Dixit, Avinash, 205
Djah, Kouacou, 223
Dollar, David, 29, 73, 86, 93
Doornbos, Martin, 101
Dunbar, Robin, 39

(E)

Easterly, William, 29, 124, 204

Eichenberger, 107
Eken, Sena, 212, 219
Eller, Jack David, 103, 104
Elster, Jon, 42, 47
England, Richard W., 44, 165
Evans, Peter B., 36
Evenett, Simon J., 199

(F)

Fanthorpe, Richard, 180
Farr, James R., 50
Faruquee, Rashid, 74
Fehr, Ernest, 123
Fernandez, Raquel, 136
Fischbacher, Urs, 123
Forrest, Tom, 205
Frank, A. G., 189
Frank, Robert H., 42
Frey, B. S., 107
Fudenberg, Drew, 42
Fukuyama, Francis, 40, 41

(G)

Gardner, John W., 167, 171-173
Gardner, Roy, 47
Garg, Ashish, 55
Geertz, Clifford, 43
Ghatttas, 80
Glazer, Nathan, 42, 103
Goff, Brian L., 123
Goldsbrough, David, 90
Goldsmith, Arthur A., 84
Greenaway, David, 205
Greif, Avner, 47, 50
Guillaumont, Patrick, (see Paul Collier)
Guillaumont, Sylviane, (see Paul Collier)
Gunning, Jan Willem, 29, 94, 163
Gyimah-Boadi, E., 163

(H)

Haggard, Stephan, 177
Hameso, Seyoum H., 101
Hamlin, A., 107
Haque, Nadeem Ul, 204
Hassan, Ahmed Issack, 110
Hayek, Friederich A., 45, 46
Hazlewood, Arthur, 212, 219
Hechter, Michael, 104
Helleiner, Gerald K., 84
Hentz, James J., 228
Himbara, David, 205
Hirshleifer, Jack, 44
Hodgson, Geoffrey M., 44
Huber, Evelyne, 177, 199
Hymer, S., 192
Hyung-Ki kim, 35

(I)

Ikelegbe, Augustine, 31, 123
Isichei, Elizabeth, 51
Ivanova, Anna, 72

(J)

Jalloh, Alusine, 54
Jerman, Helena, 101
Johnson, John H., 69, 71, 74, 218
Johnson, Omotunde E. G., 15, 27, 38, 51, 56, 60, 68, 73, 80, 83, 103, 118, 129, 139-141, 152, 166, 188, 204, 210, 212, 219, 220, 222, 227, 229,
Jonker, Leo B., 44
Joseph, Richard, 177

(K)

Kagwanja, P. M., 108
Kahler, Miles, 87, 88
Kahneman, D., 46
Kakoza, Joseph, 220
Kallon, Kelfala M., 53, 157
Kaufman, Robert R., 177
Keefer, Philip, 53
Khan, Mohsin S., 89, 90, 92, 93
Killick, Tony, 29, 69, 71, 85, 87-89
Kim, Chung-yum, 35, 63, 65
Kimaro, Sadiliel, 103
Klein, Daniel B., 50
Knack, Stephen, 40, 53

Knetsch, J., 46
Kopytoff, Igor, 118
Kreps, David M., 41
Krueger, Anne O., 151
Krugman, P., 226

(L)

La Ferrara, Eliana, 39
La Porta, R., 128
Lago, Isabelle Mateos y, 90
Lall, Sanjaya, 206
Lancaster, C., 29
Lane, Timothy, 80
Lavergne, Réal, 210
Lee Kuan Yew, 61, 62, 64, 65
Lemarchand, René, 103, 104
Lewis, David, 46
Leys, Colin, 129
Lijphart, Arend, 105
Lin, Nan, 40
Lindenberg, S., 104
Lopez-de-Silanes, 128
Lucas, Robert E. Jr., 205
Lui, F. T., 135
Lukács, E., 219
Lyons, Terrence, 103

(M)

Macauley, Stewart, 39
Macbean, A., 194
Macharia, Kinuthia, 53
Magnusson, Bruce A., 124
Mahant, Edelgard, 227
Mamdani, Mahmood, 181
Mansbridge, Jane J., 41
Markakis, John, 101
Masahjiro Okuno-Fujiwara, 35
Masanjala, Winford H., 51
Mathiesen, Donald J., 204
Mauro, Paolo, 129
Mayer, Wolfgang, 72
McCormick, Robert E., 123
McGinnis, M. D., 18
McGuire, Marten C., 128
McMullan, M., 127, 129
Mecagni, Mauro, 72, 98
Melton, James Van Horn, 28
Mengisteab, Kidane, 112
Milgrom, Paul, 42, 47
Miller, Gary J., 42, 44
Mistry, Percy S., 210, 225
Misztal, Barbara, 38
Mkandawire, Thandika, 20, 84, 205
Mody, Ashoka, 204
Mookherjee, D., 135
Moore, Barrington, 165
Moore, Michael O., 204
Morishima, Michio, 63, 64
Motoki, Watabe, 38, 39
Mourmouras, Alex, 72
Moynihan, Daniel P., 42, 103
Mueller, Dennis C., 18
Mugaju, Justus, 178
Museveni, Yoweri K., 156, 163, 178
Mutebile, Emmanuel T., 99
Myrdal, Gunnar, 129, 189

(N)

Ndikumana, Léonce, 19-21, 103
Neher, Clark D., 175
Nelson, Richard R., 44
Nkrumah, Kwame, 19-21
Nomvete, Bax, 219
North, Douglass C., 38, 63, 165
Nurkse, Ragnar, 190
Nyerere, Julius K., 20, 21, 193

(O)

Obeng, P. V., 76
Ohemeng, Frank Louis Kwaku, 30
Okeahalam, C. C., 204
Okuno-Fujiwara, Masakjiro, 35
Oliver, Robert T., 170
Oloka-Onyango, J., 178
Olson, Mancur, Jr., 128
Orbell, John M., 42
Ostrom, Elinor, 47

(P)

Pain, Nigel, 204
Paldam, M., 128
Parsons, Talcott, 103
Pearce, David G., 42
Pindyck, Robert S., 205
Png, I. P. L., 135
Polinsky, A. M., 135
Poluha, Eva, 112
Prebisch,R., 189, 194
Prunier, Gérard, 103
Przeworski, Adam, 177

(R)

Radzicki, Michael J., 44
Ravenhill, John, 239
Roberts, John, 42
Rodrik, Dani, 87, 88, 136
Rosenberg, Christoph B., 39, 50, 223
Rosenberg, Nathan
Ross, Levine, 29, 124, 204
Ross, Marlay, 175
Rothchild, Donald, 103, 105
Rowley, C. K., 127
Rueschemeyer, Dietrich, 36, 177
Rustow, Dankwart A., 177
Ruzindana, Augistine, 157

(S)

Sachs, Jeffrey D., 15
Samuelson, Larry, 47
Schatzberg, Michael G., 165
Schelling, Thomas C., 46
Schotter, Andrew, 46
Schulze-Ghattas, Marianne, 21, 80
Schuster, Peter, 44
Seabright, Paul, 44
Selten, R., 45
Semboja, Joseph, 52, 57
Sen, Amartya, 117
Sender, John, 84
Sethi, Rajiv, 47, 48
Sharma, Sunil, 89, 90, 92, 93
Shavell, S., 135
Shivakumar, S. J., 18
Shleifer, A., 128
Sigmund, Karl, 44
Singer, H. W., 189
Skocpol, Theda, 37
Skyrms, Brian, 45, 46
Sleuwaegen, Leo, 204
Sobel, Joel, 40
Soludo, Charles C., 20, 8a4, 105
Somanathan, E., 47, 48
Stephens, John D., 177
Sterman, John D., 44
Stewart, Frances, 78, 84, 206
Sugden, Robert, 45, 46
Svensson, Jakob, 73, 86
Szeftel, M., 127

(T)

Taylor, Peter D., 44
Thaler, Richard H., 42, 46
Therkildsen, Ole, 52, 57
Thomas, Barbara P., 58
Tidy, Michael, 115
Tilly, Charles, 23, 24, 34, 35, 175
Tollison, Robert D., 123, 151
Tordoff, William, 229
Trakman, Leon E., 50
Treisman, D., 128
Tsikata, Yvonne M., 71, 76
Tullock, Gordon, 151

(U)

Ullmann-Margalit, Edna, 47

(V)

van de Kragt. Alphons J. C., 42
van de Walle, Nicholas, 163
Van Roy, Edward, 129
Villalón, Leonardo A., 178
Vishny, R., 120
VonDoepp, Peter, 124
Vronen, Jack J., 43, 44

(W)

Walker, James, 47
Wallerstein, Immanuel, 19, 22, 40, 57
Warner, Andrew M., 15
Wasty, Sulaiman S., 69, 71, 74
Waterbury, John, 177
Wheeler, David, 204
Wilson, Robert, 42

(Y)

Yamagashi, Toshio, 38, 39
Young, H. Peyton, 47, 116

(Z)

Zartman, I. William, 103, 116
Zolberg, Aristide R., 103, 178

Subject Index

(A)

Acheampong, 132
African Development Bank, 1
African Economic Community (AEC), 215, 220
African socialism, 20
African Union, 210, 215, 220, 228
Afrifa, 132
Ahidjo, 17
Akuffo, 132
Algeria, 215
Altruists, 122, 123, 240
Angola, 103, 210, 211, 212, 217
Anti-corruption norm, 131, 133-137, 139, 162
Arab Maghreb Union (AMU), 215
Arusha, 212
Ashanti, 114
Authoritarian order (see Order authoritarian), 5, 33, 34, 39, 60, 61, 65, 66, 122, 130, 133, 175, 178, 241

(B)

Balewa, Abubakar Tafewa , 21
Benin, 124, 178, 210, 211, 213
Botswana, 25, 163, 202, 212
Burkina Faso, 210, 211, 213
Burundi, 103, 103, 210, 211, 214, 217

(C)

Cameroon, 17, 210, 212
Cape Verde, 210, 213, 217
Central African Customs and Economic Union (CACEU), 212
Central African Economic and Monetary Community (CAEMC), 212, 215, 218, 220
Central African Republic, 178, 202, 210, 212
Chad, 210, 212
Chiluba, 178
Citizenship rights, 180
Civil society, 4-7, 10, 16, 20, 21, 25, 27-29, 31, 33, 34, 37, 55, 56, 58-60, 69, 70, 74, 102, 103, 109, 111, 121-124, 131, 135, 156, 158, 159, 174, 181, 207, 230, 233, 240
Commodity terms of trade, 187, 194, 195
Common Fund for Commodities (CFC), 199
Community of Eastern and Southern Africa (COMESA), 211, 213-220, 227, 232
Comoros, 211
Conakry, 211
Conditionality, 6, 67, 68, 72, 80-90, 92-95, 97, 98, 186, 201, 203
Confucianism, 63
Congo, 105, 110-113, 116, 125, 146, 154, 178, 210, 212
Constitution of Kenya Review Act, 111
Constitution, political, 3-12, 15, 17-19-22, 24, 27-29, 31, 143, 241
Conventions, 39, 46, 47, 49, 199
Cooperation deficit, 12, 33, 236, 237
Coping behavior, 25, 51
Corruption revenue,3-5, 7, 8, 10, 26, 108, 138-140, 143-149, 151, 153, 160, 173, 181, 182, 241, 243
Corruption, 16, 21, 27, 29, 37, 52-56, 127-137, 154-159, 161-163, 169, 172, 173, 181, 182, 186, 194, 202, 205, 206, 207, 236, 238, 241, 243
Côte d'Ivoire, 21, 210, 211, 213
Country ownership, 2, 3, 10, 12, 29, 67, 69, 70, 75, 78, 91, 92, 98, 185, 186, 236, 243

(D)

Dahomey, 114
Deliberation councils, 64, 76

Democracy, 177
Democratic Republic of Congo, 103, 202, 210, 211, 212, 217
Dependency theory, 10, 187-191
Developmental state, 20, 21, 36, 163, 233, 243
Distributive justice, 7, 17, 112, 116-119, 126
Djibouti, 211, 214

(E)
East African Community (EAC), 212, 215, 216, 219, 220, 222, 223, 229
East Asian Miracle, 3
Economic Commission for Africa, 210, 220
Economic Community of the Central African States (ECCAS), 210, 212, 213, 215, 217, 218, 220, 224, 227
Economic Community of West African States (ECOWAS), 210, 213, 215, 217-220, 227, 228
Egypt, 211, 214
Enlightenment, 29
Equatorial Guinea, 210, 212, 218
Eritrea, 211
Ethiopia, 17, 107, 112, 119, 202, 211, 214
Ethnic consciousness, 6, 101, 102, 180
Ethnicity, 3, 5-7, 10, 16, 27, 29, 30, 37, 52, 53, 55, 56, 58, 101-104, 107-110, 112, 121, 122, 124, 125, 130, 131, 134, 138, 139, 161, 165, 173, 178, 190, 181
European Union, 1

(F)
Federalism, 105, 107
Focal point(s), 6, 46, 47, 59, 60, 63, 66, 78, 102, 103, 108, 112, 114-116, 119-121, 241
Foreign direct investment (FDI), 11, 81, 87, 187, 203, 206, 209, 230

(G)
Gabon, 202, 210, 212
Gambia, The, 202, 210, 213, 214, 217, 218
Ghana, 19, 21, 30, 76, 78, 132, 183, 205, 210, 213, 214, 218
Ghana, Economic Recovery Program, 78
Ghana, Program of Action to Mitigate the Social Costs of Adjustment (PAMSCAD), 78
Grand coalition, 105, 106
Group solidarity, 43, 53, 57, 103, 104, 138, 183
Guinea, 178, 202, 210, 211, 213, 214, 217, 217
Guinea-Bissau, 21, 178, 202, 210, 217

(H)
Houphouët-Boigny, Felix, 20, 21
Hutu(s), 105

(I)
Institutions, the role of, 37, 236
International Cocoa Organization, 199
International Coffee Organization, 199
International Monetary Fund (IMF), 1, 2, 67, 72, 74, 77, 80, 81, 86, 89, 90, 92, 93, 95, 97, 98, 152, 179, 185, 188, 193, 242

(J)
Japan, 61-64, 66
Joint ventures, 11, 202, 204

(K)
Kaunda, Kenneth , 21
Keita, Modibo, 21
Kenya. 21, 52, 108, 110, 111, 115, 202, 205, 211, 212, 214, 222, 229

Kenyatta, Jomo, 21
Korea, 61, 63, 66
Kufuor, John, 183

(L)

Lagos Plan of Action, 210
Land tenure, 118, 121
Leadership (civil society, political, transforming), 3, 5-10, 12, 16, 19, 20, 21, 27-29, 31, 33, 37, 55, 56, 58-61, 63, 65, 66, 69, 95, 103, 122, 123, 131, 132, 136, 137, 139-142, 156, 160, 162-176, 178, 181, 182, 186, 194, 228, 236, 239-243
Legitimacy/Legitimation, 6, 8, 18, 19, 28, 59, 60, 64, 66, 68, 72-76, 79, 92, 96, 102, 108, 155, 157, 131, 165, 176, 233, 236
Lesotho, 202, 212
Liberia, 17, 202, 210, 211, 213, 214, 218
Libreville, 210
Libya, 211, 215
Lissouba, Pasca, 1541
Loyalty, 7, 9, 12, 19, 63, 64, 130, 131, 133, 138, 140, 144-146, 155, 162, 165, 173, 180, 181, 236, 238
Luxembourg, 202

(M)

Madagascar, 178, 211, 212, 214
Malawi, 178, 211, 212, 214, 217
Mali, 21, 178, 210, 211, 213
Mano River Union (MRU), 211, 215, 217
Mauritania, 215
Mauritius, 25, 163, 185, 196, 205, 211, 212, 214, 217
Meiji Revolution, 63
Ministry of Health and Social Welfare, Korea, 65
Moral ethnicity, 108
Morocco, 215
Mozambique, 103, 178, 212
Multiculturalism, 110, 119, 120
Multinational corporation, 6, 21, 88, 191, 242
Muluzi, 178
Museveni, Yoweri, 156, 163, 178
Mutual respect, 5, 7, 56, 122
Mutual veto, 105, 106

(N)

Namibia, 212
National Wages Council of Singapore, 64
Niger, 178, 210, 211, 213
Nigeria, 21, 31, 74, 103, 106, 107, 120, 157, 202, 205, 210, 213-215, 217, 218
Nkrumah, Kwame, 19-21
Norm of cooperation, 42, 43
Norms, 7, 9, 37, 39, 46-49, 108, 116, 131, 133, 134, 139, 148, 162, 164, 173, 182, 241
Nyerere, Julius, 20, 21, 193

(O)

Obasanjo, Olusegun, 157
Obote, Milton, 21
Office of Labor, Korea, 65
Order (authoritarian, spontaneous), 25, 28, 45, 59, 228
Organization of African Unity (OAU), 22, 210, 215
Organization of Petroleum Exporting Countries (OPEC), 199
OXY— An American oil company, 154

(P)

Park Chung Hee, 65
Parliament, 5, 6, 10, 24, 28, 34, 72, 110, 111, 139, 164, 179, 181
Parliamentarization, 24
Petty bourgeoisie, 127
Pluralistic solidarity, 7, 120, 122
Polycentric governance, 18
Poor policy environment equilibrium trap, 25

Preferential Trading Area for Eastern and Southern Africa (PTA), 210, 211
Principal-agency, 105
Proportionality, 105, 106

(R)

Rawlings, Jerry, 132
Reduction of dependence, 193
Regional Economic Communities (RECs), 213
Rent seeking, 151
Rwanda, 103, 105, 210, 211, 214, 217

(S)

Sao Tome and Principe, 210
Segmental autonomy, 105, 107, 108
Selective intervention, 64, 84, 151, 154, 201, 222, 223
Selectivity, 6, 67, 68, 80, 88-91, 94, 95, 244
Self-interest, 5, 6, 12, 33, 37, 38, 41, 46, 48, 49, 55, 56, 59-61, 65, 66-68, 122, 123, 133, 162, 166, 174, 183, 200, 235, 237-241
Self-interested, 41, 48, 122, 129-241
Senegal, 21, 210, 211, 213
Senghor, Léopold, 21
Seychelles, 211
Sierra Leone, 53, 54, 108, 118, 153, 157, 202, 210, 211, 213, 214, 218
Singapore, 61, 62, 64, 66, 202
Social Capital, 4, 22, 29, 40, 41, 56
Societal civility, 7, 22, 29, 112, 241
Society, 4, 5, 9, 17, 18, 20, 24, 27, 30, 31, 33, 35-38, 47, 56-60, 64-66, 106, 112, 116, 117, 199, 122, 123, 125, 129-131, 135-137, 139-147, 149, 150, 153, 155-157, 160, 162, 165, 166, 169-172, 174, 181, 182,231
South Africa, 103, 105, 211, 212, 216, 227
South Africa, 163, 185
Southern African Customs Union (SACU), 212, 217
Southern African Development Community (SADC), 211, 212, 215-220, 227
Southern African Development Coordination Council (SADCC), 211, 216
Spontaneous order (see Order-spontaneous), 5, 7, 33, 41, 46, 49-52, 55, 56, 59, 60, 65, 66, 122-124, 133, 135,-137, 161, 202, 241
Stabex, 199
Stable equilibrium determination process, 4, 7, 9, 12, 17-19, 24, 28, 102, 103, 112, 114, 115, 119-121, 140, 162, 237, 241, 242
State, role of the, 20, 34, 35174, 182
Structural Adjustment Program(s), 76
Sudan, 103, 202, 211, 214
Swaziland, 202, 211, 212, 216
Sysmin, 199

(T)

Taiwan, 61
Tanzania, 21, 52, 76, 193, 212, 216, 222, 229
Think Tanks, 30, 186, 244
Tit-for-tat strategy, 43, 45
Togo, 210, 211, 213
Trust (generalized, mutual), 5, 7, 13, 27, 38-40, 43, 44, 51-57, 59, 60, 65, 66, 207, 236, 237, 243
Trust, 5, 7, 13, 109, 122, 125, 134, 163, 236-238, 243
Tunia
Tutsi(s), 105

(U)

Uganda, 21, 52, 99, 103, 156, 211, 212, 229
Union Douanière et Economique de l'Afrique Centrale (UDEAC), 212, 215

United Nations Development Program (UNDP) , 1, 30

(V)

Voluntary associations, voluntary associational life, 21, 29, 40, 56, 239, 241

(W)

West African Economic and Monetary Union (WAEMU), 211, 215, 217, 220
West African Monetary Union (WAMU), 211
Windhoek, 211
World Bank, 1, 29, 69, 71, 73, 81, 86, 87, 92, 95, 179, 185, 188, 193, 242
World Trade Organization (WTO), 97, 199-201

(Z)

Zambia, 21, 178, 211, 212, 214, 217
Zimbabwe, 53, 103, 211, 212, 214, 217
Zulu Kingdom, 114